GREEK IN JEWISH PALESTINE

STUDIES IN THE LIFE AND MANNERS OF JEWISH PALESTINE
IN THE II–IV CENTURIES C. E.

by

SAUL LIEBERMAN

Professor of Palestinian Literature and Institutions,
The Jewish Theological Seminary of America

NEW YORK
THE JEWISH THEOLOGICAL SEMINARY OF AMERICA
5702–1942

PRINTED IN THE UNITED STATES OF AMERICA
PRESS OF THE JEWISH PUBLICATION SOCIETY
PHILADELPHIA, PENNA.

TO

THE MASTER OF HALACHA AND HAGGADA

PROFESSOR LOUIS GINZBERG

CONTENTS

	PAGE
Preface	vii
Introduction	1
The Greek of the Rabbis	15
The Greek of the Synagogue	29
Gentiles and Semi-proselytes	68
Pleasures and Fears	91
Oaths and Vows	115
Greek and Latin Proverbs in Rabbinic Literature	144
Misunderstood Expressions and Words	161
Appendix (X and Θ)	185
Additions and Corrections	192
Key to Abbreviations	194
Indices	196

PREFACE

This book is the fourth link in a series of small publications which the author felt impelled to prepare at the expense of his regular work and studies. In the first, תלמודה של קיסרין, "The Talmud of Caesarea," the object is to prove that the tractate Nezikin (Baba Kamma, Baba Mezia and Baba Bathra) constitutes the oldest portion of the Palestinian Talmud and that it was redacted in Caesarea Maritima. Hence it should be studied in the light of the conditions which prevailed in the Hellenistic city of that time.

In the second, שקיעין, an attempt is made to show that valuable Jewish matter is imbedded in mediaeval Christian and Karaite polemistic writings, which frequently offers considerable aid towards the understanding of Rabbinic texts. Fragments of Midrashim otherwise unknown to us have been unexpectedly preserved in such works.

The third, מדרשי תימן (A lecture on the Yemenite Midrashim), seeks to demonstrate that many apocryphal Midrashim which were banned by the official Synagogue have survived in the literature of the Yemenite Jews. These uneducated people naively and indiscriminately copied sundry Hebrew scraps which occasionally represent uncensored traditions previously altogether unknown or available only in the works of the Church Fathers.

In the present book the author tries to develop the subject of the relation between the Jewish and non-Jewish cultural spheres in Palestine. This undertaking, I feel, is justified and desirable in view of the opinion to which my very learned colleagues, the Talmudists, persistently adhere, namely, that the Rabbis were very little influenced by the outside Hellenistic world.

The book also emphasizes that a new method of research is required in the investigation of Talmudic literature. Halachic

discussions are avoided as far as possible (Whenever, in matters
of Halacha or Haggada, the phrase "see my remarks ad loc."
occurs, it refers to הירושלמי כפשוטו — a commentary on the
Palestinian Talmud — vol. I, תוספת ראשונים — a commentary on
the Tosephta — vol. I–IV, and Debarim Rabba, ed. Lieberman)
in order not to overburden the English readers with questions
which are familiar only to the Talmudists. The Talmudic and
Midrashic material under discussion is generally confined to the
II–IV centuries. Unless otherwise specified all the dates mentioned in this work are C.E.

While one of the principal aims of the book is the explanation and the elucidation of Rabbinic texts in the frame of the
cultural conditions of the Mediterranean world, light is incidentally shed upon many a Greek and Latin text. See, for instance,
below p. 32, n. 21; p. 33 n. 51 (supplemented on p. 144, n. 2);
p. 41–43; p. 42, n. 69; pp. 46, 94, 96, 128, 152–153, 186, n. 10
and elsewhere. All suggestions made by scholars of classic
literature will be highly appreciated by the author who hopes
to avail himself of their erudition.

Prof. Abraham S. Halkin of Brooklyn College spent many
days with me in reading through the whole manuscript. I am
indebted to him not only for the revision of the English style
but also for many suggestions in connection with the presenta-
tion of the subject-matter. I frequently relied on his good
taste and lucid judgment.

Part of the proofs was read by Dr. Judith Lieberman to
whom I wish to acknowledge my gratitude.

Professor Louis Finkelstein, President of the Jewish Theological Seminary, made my work possible by providing for me all
the necessary accomodations. Having left my entire library in
Jerusalem, it was through the kind efforts of Prof. Alexander
Marx that I experienced no difficulty in procuring the indispensable books. The authorities and the staff of the Library of
the Union Theological Seminary were most obliging in supplying
me with the necessary books. To all of them I extend my
sincerest thanks.

Finally, I have to mention my great obligation to my friend, Mr. Harry Fischel of New York, founder of the Harry Fischel Institute for Talmud Studies in Jerusalem, where I have served as dean for the last six years. Many manuscripts and photostats of mss. were accessible to me only thanks to the generosity of Mr. Fischel.

New York, N. Y., December 1941.

GREEK IN JEWISH PALESTINE

INTRODUCTION

"There were a thousand young men in my father's house, five hundred of whom studied the Law, while the other five hundred studied Greek wisdom," said Rabban Simeon (the son of Rabban Gamaliel the Patriarch[1]). This is first-hand evidence that an academy of Greek wisdom existed in Jewish Palestine under the auspices of the Patriarch. It was established in the beginning of the second century for the purpose of facilitating the relations between the House of the Patriarch and the Roman government.[2] The Rabbinic sources have not provided us with a clear statement of what they called "Greek Wisdom." Did it include all the Hellenistic sciences and arts of that time or only the superficial oriental knowledge of certain branches of Greek literature which were prerequisite to acceptance into Roman high-official society?

Although we are unable to answer this question we can assert that the very existence of an officially recognized "Academy of Greek Wisdom" in Jewish Palestine is of great importance. The members and teachers of the academy were in a position to make valuable information from Greek sources available to the Rabbis. Good literary style was probably one of the main subjects studied in this academy, and we can expect that certain Rabbis were well equipped to speak and write literary Greek.

It seems that the foundation of this academy marked a turning point in Jewish literary history. The Jewish leaders felt that not only is "Greek Wisdom" indispensable for proper relations with the Roman government but that Greek philosophy is a useful instrument in religious discussions, especially with the Gentile Christians who became more and more influential. Yet it is obvious that Greek philosophy was the appanage of only very few outstanding Rabbis. The great majority, like the

[1] See below p. 20.
[2] See below p. 20 n. 33.

1

majority of the average middle-class men, possessed only a
slight second-hand knowledge of "Greek Wisdom."

The Greek language was known to the Jewish masses; certain
formulas of oriental Graeco-Roman law were popular among
them in the original language; the current motifs of Hellenistic
literature may have infiltrated into them, but real Greek culture
was probably scarce in Jewish Palestine.

In proof of the assertion that Greek was familiar to the
Jewish masses in the synagogue we shall try to show that
Biblical events were elucidated by the Rabbis in the light of
Greek sources[3] and that the preachers used Greek translations
of the Bible in their sermons.[4]

On the other hand, Eusebius informs us[5] that Procopius was
(around 286) a Reader and *Interpreter from Greek into Aramaic*[6]
in the church of Scythopolis.[7] In the Hellenized town of Scythopolis it was necessary to render a Greek passage in Aramaic
before the people could understand it! But Zahn[8] is quite right
in his remark that whereas the Biblical lessons, the liturgy and
the sermons in the church of Scythopolis were in Greek, there
was need of an Aramaic translator for the benefit of the peasants
who attended the church. Probably even the peasants knew the
limited practical everyday vocabulary of Greek,[9] but explanations by an interpreter (תורגמן) in the mother-tongue of the
masses were quite welcome. For a similar reason the Jewish
preachers adopted the same method (in the opposite direction)
when they preached in the Hellenized towns; they delivered
their sermons in Aramaic, but illustrated and explained certain
passages in Greek for the benefit of the townspeople.

The Greek of the Palestinian Rabbis is mainly the Greek of
the middle-class man of Palestine. We must first of all establish

---

[3] See below p. 39 seq.

[4] See below p. 47 seq.

[5] Mart. Pal., the Syriac version, ed. Cureton, p. 4.

[6] ‎ובטכסא דעדתא בתלת צבון שמש הוא. קדמית קריא הוא הוא, ובטכסא אחרנא לשנא,
‎בית שאן town Palestinian famous the is Scythopolis .יוניא לארמיא מתרגם הוא'...

[7] Comp. also Krauss, Synagogale Altertümer, p. 178, n. 4; Th. Zahn,
Tatianus Diatessaron, 1881, p. 19, n. 1.

[8] Ibid., p. 20.

[9] See below p. 39, n. 53.

the exact meaning conveyed by the Greek words as recorded in Palestinian Rabbinic literature. We have to turn to a definite kind of sources.

Since the last century our knowledge of the ancient world has been immensely enriched by a previously unutilized source of information. Archaeology has helped us to become familiar with various aspects of history in a way which the formal historical documents had never served us. Through the work of the spade we have learned to know part of the material life of the people,— their occupations, their homes, their utensils etc.,— and also their general culture, religious ideas, habits and amusements. Towards the understanding of the latter the uncovered written material has made an especially great contribution. In this written material papyri, as is well known, occupy a very important place. Being the product of the simple folk who wrote neither for publicity nor for fame they form an authentic source, in so far as they go, for the study of the cultural level of the masses.

The results of the investigation by modern scholars in this field are particularly instructive for the understanding of Palestinian Rabbinic literature. The latter embodies many elements similar to those contained in the so-called documentary papyri. The life of the common people is often mirrored in Rabbinic literature with the simplicity of life itself. Facts bearing on the operation of law in ancient Palestinian society as well as legal documents are found there in abundance. The common talk of the man of the people is not infrequently quoted verbatim. It contains a wealth of material concerning the social and economic condition of the people. This evidence is all the more trustworthy since the facts are often recorded incidentally and casually. In all this Rabbinic literature has much in common with the non-literary papyri and the inscriptions.[10]

---

[10] Prof. L. Blau (Papyri und Talmud in gegenseitiger Beleuchtung, Leipzig 1913 and elsewhere) was the first to point out the importance of the papyri for the understanding of the Talmud. The relation between the papyri and Talmudic law has been searchingly studied by the late Prof. Gulak (in his book "Das Urkundwesen in Talmud, Jerusalem 1935 and in a series of brilliant articles).

Moreover, the comparative study of these two kinds of popular monuments very often brings to light the similarity of certain economic and legal conditions in Palestine and Egypt. Many passages in the Palestinian Talmud can be better understood in the light of the evidence furnished by the Egyptian Greek papyri.

So, for instance, we read in TP:[11] [12]אמר ר' מנא אף על גב ד]לית[רבי יוסי רבו[13] גבי עיצומין מודה באילין דיהבון בניהון לאומנותא דאינון הברית חיי מפני עיצומין גבוי. "R. Manna said: although my teacher R. Jose does not order the collection of עיצומין he grants that those who commit their sons for apprenticeship are entitled to עיצומין, because the livelihood of men requires such a measure."

The commentaries ad loc. disagreed as to the interpretation of the word עיצומין. But there can be no doubt that the author of the פני משה is right in explaining this word to mean "forfeiture,"[14] i. e. an agreement containing a forfeiture clause. According to R. Jose, "forfeiture" is collectible in case of an agreement in matters of apprenticeship. The Talmud of the school of Tiberias did not even mention that forfeiture is conditional in this kind of agreement.[15] It took forfeiture for granted in accordance with the probably general practice in Palestine in the IV century.

Now, agreements of apprenticeship to weavers drawn up in Egypt in the years 66[16] and 183[17] contain the clause that in case of the recall of the apprentice by his father within the specified period the latter has to pay one hundred drachmae as compensation to the master and the like sum as penalty to the treasury. If the master fails to instruct the boy fully he is liable to the same penalties. We therefore see that for more

---

[11] Gittin V. 8, 47b.

[12] So in the parallel Baba Bathra X. V, 17c.

[13] Read: רבי.

[14] He correctly referred to Tosephta Baba Mezi'a I. 16, 372₂₀.

[15] The parallel Baba Bathra (in which a tradition of a different school prevailed, see my תלמודה של קיסרין, p. 1 seq.) states clearly: דיהב ברה גו אומנתה ועצמון ביניהון.

[16] Pap. Ox. II, 275.

[17] Ibid. IV, 725.

than a century it was the common practice not only to include
a clause of forfeiture in agreements of apprenticeship but also
to exact the same amount of penalties from the violator of the
agreement. Palestine of the fourth century followed the same
practice as Egypt.

The following presents another parallel between the two
countries. The Talmud speaks of sand[18] or pebble[19] content in
grain, or of barley in wheat,[20] and declares such mixtures not to
be חטים ברורות.[21] The papyri also often qualify pure wheat as
πυρὸς καθαρὸς, ἄδολος, ἄβωλος (or ἄβολος) ἄκριθος, κεκοσκινευ-
μένος,[22] "pure, unadulterated, sandless, barleyless, sifted wheat."

An even more important illustration of the relation between
the two countries may be cited here.

The prodigious fall of currency values during the IV century
which is so clearly reflected in the Egyptian papyri is hardly
alluded to in Palestinian literature. But TP[23] records a strange
question of R. Jonah (fl. around the middle of the IV century)
which is reminiscent of the situation in Egypt. He asked:
נפל כיסו לבור ובו מאה ריבוא והיה יכול להוציא חמישים רבוא להעלותן.
"If a man's purse which contained *one hundred myriads* of
Denars fell into a pit and the owner had to spend *fifty myriads*
to take it out." The tremendous sum of a hundred myriads
(one million!) of Denars contained in one purse and the terrific
expense of half of it required to take out the purse from the pit
indicate the total devaluation of the Denar. It corresponds to
its state in Egypt around 330–335.[24]

The operation, in numerous cases, of similar law in both
countries can be ascertained from the studies of Prof. Gulak.[25]
Thus, there is no doubt that many passages in Rabbinic litera-

---

[18] A Baraitha quoted in TB Baba Bathra 94a.

[19] TP Kilaim II. 1, 27c; Baba Bathra VI. 1, 15b; TB ibid. 93b and
parallel.

[20] TP Terumoth V. 8, 43d; TP Baba Bathra l. c.

[21] TP Kilaim l. c.

[22] See Preisigke s. v. ἄδολος, ἄβολος, ἄβωλος and ἄκριθος.

[23] Maaser Sheni I. 2, 52d.

[24] See the conclusions of Prof. A. Segré, Metrologia pp. 459 and 535 seq.
Comp. also TP ibid. IV. 1, 54d.

[25] See above, p. 3 n. 10.

ture will be best understood in the light of the life in Egypt as reflected in the papyri.

This comparative study will convince the student of the close contact between Jewish Palestine and the Hellenistic world in general. One of the surest means for the study of this contact is provided by the analysis of the Greek vocabulary which is contained in Rabbinic literature. A new edition of a dictionary of loan-words in the Talmud and Midrashim is an urgent need. In the present century the scholarly world has been enriched by critical editions of the Halachic Midrashim[26] and Bereshith Rabba[27] and by the Geniza fragments of the Palestinian Talmud,[28] which make authentic texts available for the lexicographer.

But before undertaking the compilation of such a lexicon a complete change in the method of the investigation is absolutely necessary. Words cannot be treated singly; they can be understood only in a context, within the frame of the surrounding world. Almost every loan-word reflects a certain phase of the contact between Jew and Gentile. The word has to be defined within a given cultural setting.

It goes without saying that as a result of the contact between Aramaic and Greek certain words of the latter became part and parcel of the former. But many Greek words occur in Rabbinic literature only rarely, and give the impression of being borrowed foreign elements. This category has been handled very unfortunately by our dictionaries. Almost every foreign word and phrase have their "raison d'être" in Rabbinic literature. We shall try to demonstrate[29] that all the Greek phrases in Rabbinic literature are quotations.[30]

[26] Mekiltha, ed. Horovitz and ed. Lauterbach, Sifre Num., ed. Horovitz and Sifre Deut., ed. Finkelstein.

[27] Ed. Theodor and Albeck.

[28] Published by Prof. L. Ginzberg in his Yerushalmi Fragments (New York 1909) and Genizah Studies I (ibid. 1928), pp. 390–448; Prof. I. N. Epstein in Tarbiz III pp. 16–26, 124–133, 237–248.

[29] Below p. 39 seq.

[30] The only Greek phrase we were not able to decipher is in Midrash Shir Hashirim Rabba (II.15): קינינין מכללה וריארטיה עתידין מן בלטווראדא דיחתו So ed. pr. The reading of the later editions has וייטורד זה שטיהר אחריהם בים (So ed. pr. The reading of the later editions has

The single loan-words should subsequently be arranged according to subject-matter. Prof. I. Loew, the great master in Jewish philology, was the first to prepare such an index to Krauss' LW.[31] A list of the foreign words arranged according to subject-matter will help us not only better to understand the exact meaning of the word but also to appreciate why the Rabbis employed that word. It will bring to light the influence of the outside world on certain branches of Jewish life.

We read, for instance, in Wayyikra Rabba:[32] קופרמסאות נתנו ביניהם שאינו כופר בהם והם אינם כופרים בו. "They (i. e. the Lord and the Jewish nation) made promises to each other that He would never disown them, nor they Him." Instead of קופרמסאות R. Samuel Jama in his אגור[33] reads: אורקמסיות. This reading is too original to be a mere scribal error; it seems to be a genuine reading. Schorr[34] and Krauss[35] explained it to mean ὀρκωμοσία ("an oath"), but Loew[36] decides that this is a false identification. And indeed the use of a Greek word in place of the common שבועה, and the plural form of the word, argue against this identification.

In reality the word does not mean ὀρκωμοσία (ἡ) but ὀρκω-μόσια (τά), swearing to a treaty.[37] The whole context in our Midrash suggests an agreement accompanied by oaths and sacrifices.[38] The plural suffix of the word is now perfectly explained. The choice of the Greek word is now understandable; the Rabbis employed a legal term. The word has to be listed (in the subject-index) among the international terms of law.

no basis). The interpretation of the dictionaries cannot be considered seriously. We have here either a corrupted quotation from a hunter's manual or a mutilated citation from a Greek commentary on Is. XLIII.17. In the latter case we have to read the first word קסנינון, ἐξαγαγών, the Greek translation of המוציא.

[31] P. 623 seq.
[32] VI. 5.
[33] Jubelschrift . . . Graetz, p. 34.
[34] החלוץ XIII, p. 116.
[35] LW 510–511.
[36] Ibid., p. 671.
[37] See Liddell and Scott s. v. ὀρκωμόσια II.
[38] Hesych. s. v. defines: ὀρκωμόσια· θύματα ἐφ' ὧν ὅρκοι γίνονται.

Again, both Hadrian[39] and Diocletian[40] are reported to have
said: קיליוון אנא. The dictionaries explain it to mean κελεύων,
but the combination of the participle with the pronoun is out
of place here. The real form is [ἐ]κέλευον,[41] "I have ordered."
This inflected form of the verb suggests that our word properly
belongs in the terminology of the royal decrees.

Again we read in Debarim Rabba:[42] אמן הזה יש בו שלש אספליאות
שבועה וקבלה ואמנה. Krauss[43] explains אספליאות to mean ἀσφάλεια,
"Sicherheit, Versicherung." But the plural form and the fact
that the word occurs only once in Rabbinic literature does not
support this explanation.

The word represented by אספליאות is ἀσφάλειαι, a law-term
(Lat. cautiones), bond, warranty. The translation of the Midrashic passage is: "Amen contains three kinds of pledges: oath,
consent and confirmation." This word should be included (in the
subject-index) among the law-terms. The same is true of the
word χαρίζομαι[44] which is not even recorded in Krauss' lexicon.[45]

The like can be said about דולוס, δόλος. This word occurs
frequently in Rabbinic literature.[45a] But in all the Rabbinic
sources it has not the general meaning of deceit or treachery or
cunning, but (unlike Samaritan and Arabic) only of admixture,
of adulteration of pure objects. It served as a technical com-
mercial term[46] for adulteration of merchandise-ware, and its
place in the subject-index is accordingly under "commerce".

Another example is found in Moses' request of Pharaoh:
מבקש אני ממך להעשות על ארגון שלך[47]. It means: "I request thee to

[39] VayR XXV.5 and parallel.
[40] BR LXIII.8, 690₂ (See ibid. 688₈ and the variants).
[41] See Preisigke s. v. κελεύω.
[42] VII. 1.
[43] LW 89 (bottom).
[44] See below p. 44.
[45] Comp., however, LW I, p. 276–277.
[45a] See Loew in Krauss' LW p. 190 and the material adduced in my
Tosefeth Rishonim II, p. 93, n. 22.
[46] Comp. Preisigke s. v. ἄδολος and Deissmann, Bible Studies, p. 256.
[47] Tanhuma Cod. Oxf., as recorded by Buber Tanhuma וארא, p. 22, n.
151. Comp. also Prof. Louis Ginzberg, Genizah Studies I, p. 113, bottom.

appoint me ἐπὶ τῶν ἔργων σου. Moses wished to become the
ἐπιστάτης τῶν δημοσίων ἔργων,[48] the superintendent of the
public works. The word ארגון which is not found anywhere else
in Rabbinic literature[49] is taken from the official terminology
and belongs to the particular rubric in the subject-index.

There are many more instances of this kind which the student
may discover for himself when he reexamines Loew's Sachregister.[50]

The list of the Greek words which, according to Krauss, are
found in Rabbinic literature only[50a] requires a thorough re-
examination. Some of them are wrongly identified; others are
now found in the newly discovered material of the papyri and
inscriptions. For instance, אנדרטין (and its inflected forms) is
probably not ἀνδριάντη[51] but ἀνδριάντιν = ἀνδριάντιον,[52] a form
which occurs more than once in Greek inscriptions.[53]

Likewise, אנקלסיא is not a new form, ἐγκλησία,[54] but the
Aramaic plural of ἔγκλησις (=ἔγκλημα), a word met with in
the papyri and elsewhere.[55]

However, the word פרוטוגמיא, πρωτογάμια, which occurs frequently in Palestinian Rabbinic literature,[56] and is found in an
episcopal decree (V c.?): appellatur protogamia,[57] sheds some
light on the obscure contents of the latter.

The following instance is highly instructive. The Mishna[58]
and Tosephta[59] mention קרטיסים (קרטיסים, קרטיסין), κράτησις, as

[48] See Liddell and Scott s. v. ἐπιστάτης III, 2.
[49] Krauss did not record it at all.
[50] LW, p. 623 seq.
[50a] Ibid. I, p. 198 seq.
[51] Krauss LW, 65; Loew ibid., 656.
[52] See below p. 157, n. 185.
[53] See Liddell and Scott s. v.
[54] Krauss and Loew LW 76 and 561.
[55] See Liddell and Scott s. v.
[56] See LW 484.
[57] Corpus Inscriptionum Latinarum vol. VIII, No. 25045 (Carthage),
referred to by Liddell and Scott.
[58] Aboda Zara I. 3.
[59] Ibid. I. 4, 460₂₇.

a festival of the Gentiles. Krauss and Loew[60] mark this word with an asterisk, as an expression not found anywhere else. The Talmuds[61] explain the word to mean: יום שתפשה בו רומי מלכות, "The day on which Rome seized an empire." TB, more explicitly, states: בימי קלפטרא מלכתא, "In the days of Queen Cleopatra [of Egypt],"[62] namely the day when the Romans conquered Egypt in the time of Cleopatra.

Now, the papyri frequently record[63] the dating τῆς καίσαρος κρατήσεως. Wilcken[64] proved that κράτησις here refers to the date of the capture of Alexandria by Augustus. He quoted the decree of the Roman Senate establishing this day[65] as a festival and as the beginning of an era.[66]

The explanation of the Talmuds is in perfect accordance with the historic facts and magnificently corroborates Wilcken's conclusions.[67]

On the other hand Krauss listed passages under קרטיסים where this word has an entirely different meaning. He refers to Pesiktha deR. Kahana:[68] למלך שהיה משיא את בתו וקבע קרטיסין, בני רומי לא יחתון לסוריא ובני סוריא לא יסקון לרומי, וכיון שהשיא את בתו התיר קרטיסין. "Like a king who was going to give away his daughter in marriage and issued a κράτησις that the Romans must not go down to Syria and the Syrians must not go up to Rome, but after he married his daughter he cancelled the

---

[60] LW pp. 568 and 667.

[61] TP ibid. I. 2, 39c and TB 8b.

[62] Comp. TP and Tosephta l. c. Comp. also TP ibid. (in the name of R. Johanan): מלכות מצרים ומלכות רומי ... תתפוס המלכות המלכות תחילה.

[63] See Fayum Towns and their Papyri by Grenfell, Hunt and Hogarth, London 1900, No. 89 and the comments ibid., p. 223 (referred to by Liddell and Scott).

[64] Ostraka I, p. 788 (referred to by Grenfell etc., l. c.). Comp. also Brüll, Jahrbücher I, 162; Krauss, Byzantinische Zeitschrift II, 536 seq.; H. Lewy, Philologus LII, 733; Krauss LW I, 203; H. Blaufuss, Römische Feste etc. I, p. 12.

[65] The first of August, 30 B.C.E.

[66] Dio LI. 19.6: τήν τε ἡμέραν ἐν ᾗ ἡ Ἀλεξανδρεία ἑάλω, ἀγαθήν τε εἶναι καὶ ἐς τὰ ἔπειτα ἔτη ἀρχὴν τῆς ἀπαριθμήσεως αὐτῶν νομίζεσθαι.

[67] See Ostraka l. c., p. 788, n. 1.

[68] 104b (and parallels), in the name of R. Abba b. Judan (IV c.).

κράτησις."[69] A similar version of this parable is found in Shemoth Rabba[70]; but the passage there is defective. It seems to me that the original wording of the latter is recorded (a fact overlooked by all commentaries) by Rabbi Isaac Arama[71] from an unknown Midrash: משל למלך שגזר על מלכותו, בני רומי לא ירדו לסוריא ובני סוריא לא יעלו לרומי. לימים בקש המלך לישא אשה מסוריא עמד וביטל הגזירה ואמר מכאן ואילך ירדו בני רומי לסוריא ויעלו בני סוריא לרומי ואני אתחיל. "Like a king who issued a decree that the Romans must not go down to Syria and the Syrians must not go up to Rome. Some time later the king wished to marry a woman from Syria. He thereupon cancelled the decree and said: 'Henceforth the Romans may go down to Syria and the Syrians may go up to Rome, and I shall be the first to do it'." This version is much more logical and understandable. According-ing to it, the prohibition of intermarriage between the Romans and the *peregrini*[72] existed long before it proved a hardship on the king. Furthermore, what he desired was to marry a Syrian woman himself (and not to give his daughter in marriage). It seems to remind us of historical facts. Septimius Severus married a Syrian woman[73]— Julia Domna.[74] Both the Emperor

[69] See also the parallels noted by I. Ziegler, Die Koenigsgleichnisse des Midrash, p. CXXVII, n. 6.

[70] XII. 3 and parallels.

[71] Akedah, Jethro, Gate 44 (beginning).

[72] This is the meaning of "going to Syria" here. Comp. Ziegler ibid., p. 349; J. Marquardt, De l'organisation militaire etc., p. 308, n. 1.

[73] Script. Historiae Augustae, vita Sept. Sev. III. 9. Severus was also responsible for a military reform in matters of *connubium* (Herodian III.8.5). H. M. D. Parker (A History of the Roman World etc., p. 86) goes so far as to assert that according to this reform "the alliance of a legionary with a native woman was recognized as a *iustum conubium* from the time of its contraction etc." Comp. also M. Platnauer, The Life and Reign of Septimius Severus, p. 167 seq. Although I am not able to share this opinion, it is very likely that Severus permitted the Syrian soldiers to take with them their Syrian wives to other provinces, or something similar. The Rabbis associated this reform with the fact that Severus himself formerly married a Syrian woman for whose sake he subsequently granted many privileges to her native country. The fact that Julia Domna was probably a Roman citizen does not, of course, alter the force of the Midrashic homily.

[74] Ziegler ibid., p. 350, surmises that the preacher had Alex. Severus in mind, and he refers to Hist. August., vit. Alex. Sev. 5!

and the Queen were popular among the Palestinian Jews,[75] and
their marriage must have impressed the oriental world. The
Jewish preachers utilized it in their homilies and elucidated by
it verses of the Bible.

As for the word κράτησις in the Pesiktha, there is no doubt
that the meaning is "prohibition."[76] This word is used by
Joannes Jeiunator[77] (end of VI c.) in his sermo de poenitentia:[78]
Τοῖς γὰρ τοιούτοις οὐ δίδοται οἰαδήποτε ἐπιτίμησις ἢ βρώσεως
ἢ κοινωνίας τὸ σύνολον κ ρ ά τ η σ ι ς,   μόνη ἡ παῦσις τῆς
ἱερωσύνης. "Upon those [transgressors] no penalty, nor any
prohibition whatever of food or 'Communion', shall be imposed,
other than the cessation of priesthood." Κράτησις, therefore,
means here "a royal prohibition", as translated by Jastrow
who was correctly guided by the context.

Thus, in both cases (Mishna Aboda Zara and Pesiktha) the
Rabbis did not coin the word but used a good Greek term which
was in vogue in the ancient world.

Finally, we have to point out that greater efforts ought to
be spent on the investigation of the vocalization of foreign
words. Texts coming from different countries sometimes bear
traces of different traditions in spelling or vocalization or
both.

We shall quote one instructive instance. TP[79] mentions:
אנטלר ... ואנטלר. This reading is corroborated by the commentary of R. Hananel,[80] by Aruch,[81] Raaban[82] and many
other authorities.[83] Our dictionaries correctly explain it to mean

_____

[75] See the inscription in their honor in CI, by S. Klein, p. 81, No. 11.
[76] The gloss גזירתא in Midrash Mishle (XXI.22, ed. Buber, p. 90) is the
true translation of קרטסיס. Jastrow in his dictionary followed it.
[77] Referred to by Sophocles, lexicon, p. 689.
[78] Migne PG 88, p. 1932c.
[79] Sanhedrin II. 1, 19d.
[80] On TB ibid., 18a (bottom).
[81] S. v. אנטלר.
[82] 115, ed. Prague 41a.
[83] See Kohut's note, Aruch Compl. I, p. 146. Comp. also Me'iri, Sanhedrin, pp. 59, 60.

ἐντολάριος, a representative, an agent. The word is not found in Greek sources. In Syriac we find[84] אנטלום which is good Greek — ἐντολεύς.

But a ms. fragment of TP found in Egypt[85] reads: א נ ט י ל ר ... וא נ ט י ל ר. This reading is corroborated by other sources of Palestinian and Egyptian origin. We read in a power-of-attorney written in Ramleh (Palestine) in 1015:[86] ושמתיהו אפטרפוס וא נ ט י ל ר ... שמניתיהו אפטרפוס וא נ ט י ל ר. "And I made him a representative and agent . . . for I appointed him a representative and agent." The same spelling is found in Egyptian documents:[87] כתב א נ ט י ל ר ו ת, "Letter of attorney." Now there is no doubt that אנטילר represents not ἐντολάριος but ἐντελλάριος. The Egyptian papyri supply us with exactly the same combination of אפיטרופוס and אנטילר as found in the above Palestinian ἐπιτροπή.[88] We read in a papyrus of the VI c.:[89] ἐπιτρέπομεν και εντείλομέν[90] σοι. "I authorize and commission thee." Again, in a papyrus of the IV century[91] we read:[92] ἐντέλλομαί σοι [καὶ ἐπιτρ]έπω. Thus, ἐπίτροπος καὶ ἐντελλάριος seems to have been a common legal phrase in Egypt and Palestine.

[84] See Loew apud Krauss LW 72.
[85] L. Ginzberg, Yerushalmi Fragments, p. 256₂5, 26.
[86] S. Assaf, מספרות הגאונים א', p. 207₁0, 21.
[87] Mann, The Jews in Egypt, II, p. 356; comp. n. 3 ibid. The ms. reads (according to Assaf ibid., p. 205) אנטילרות and not אנטיל.
[88] The Hebrew reads: שטר אפטרפוס (See Assaf ibid., p. 207, n. 8). We find the same combination of the two terms in the Leges Saeculares (Land, Anecd. Syr. I, p. 38; Bruns and Sachau, p. 10): או אפטרופא או א נ ט ל י ק ו ן נתל לה, "Or to give him a power of attorney or an authorisation." Land, (Latin part, p. 189) remarks that ἐπιτροπή in the sense of "power of attorney" is not found anywhere else. Bruns and Sachau (p. 11) offered a forced translation of this phrase. However, the Egyptian papyri and Jewish documents confirm Land's interpretation. See the pap. Maspero referred to below and Preisigke s. v. ἐπιτροπή.
[89] Jean Maspero, Catalogue du Musée du Caire I, p. 198, No. 67124₆.
[90] Read: ἐντέλλομεν.
[91] Mitteis, Griechische Urkunden der Papyr. zu Leipzig I, 1906, No. 38₆.
[92] According to the restoration of Preisigke.

The respective spelling אנטלר, אנטילר may sometimes help us in establishing the origin of a text.

Sufficient material, I trust, has been adduced here to prove the necessity of a new approach, following the suggestions made above, in the investigation of Talmudic literature and in the preparation of a lexicon of the foreign vocabulary in that literature.

THE GREEK OF THE RABBIS

Whoever turns to Loew's Index of Greek words in Krauss' "Lehnwoerter im Talmud" etc. p. 655 seq. is undoubtedly struck by the overwhelming number of Greek words in Talmudic literature. A careful reading of Loew's "Vorbemerkung" and "Sachregister"[1] will reveal to the student the presence of Greek words in every branch of Jewish life in Palestine, insofar as it is recorded in Rabbinic literature of the first four centuries C. E. A natural question comes to mind: Who of the Jews used those Greek words? Was it the common people, the peasants of the country, the artisans, the petty tradesmen in the markets of the Palestinian towns, or were the learned Rabbis and the higher classes of Jewish society the only ones to employ them? We shall presently find the answer.

But we shall first dwell on the use of Greek by the Rabbis. We have to examine the general acquaintance of the Rabbis with Hellenistic culture, to investigate how well they were versed in the Greek language and literature. We shall let the statements of the Rabbis speak for themselves.

According to Tosephta Sanhedrin[2] the understanding of seventy languages[3] was required of all the members of the Jewish High Court, and at least two members were expected

---

[1] Ibid. p. 619 seq.

[2] VIII.1, 427₈ (TP Shekalim V.1, 48d, TB Sanhedrin 17a).

[3] On this number see L. Ginzberg, Legends V p. 194–195 n. 72–73. Sifre Deut. 311, ed. Finkelstein p. 352 and parallel sources (see Prof. Finkelstein's notes ad loc.) speak of one hundred and forty nations. The Jewish text of the famous Incantation republished by Deissmann (Light, p. 255 seq.) with improved readings and facsimilies mentions (l. 3056): τὰς ἑκατὸν τεσσεράκοντα γλώσσας (the 140 languages), which is in agreement with the Sifre and its parallels. Deissmann's note (p. 262 n. 4) has to be corrected accordingly. In a Mandaic Incantation (Pognon, Inscriptions Mandaïtes p. 77) three hundred and twenty six nations are mentioned.

to possess the ability to speak them. In the Court of Jabneh (II c.) there were four members who spoke them. According to the tradition recorded in the Babylonian Talmud[4] these four learned members were: R. Eliezer, R. Joshua, R. Akiba and Simeon of Teman.[5] They were the distinguished linguists of the Court in Jabneh.

The first of them, one of the leading Tannaim at the beginning of the II century, was the son of a rich landowner. He joined the school of R. Johanan b. Zaccai when he was more than twenty years old. Prior to that he had been entirely ignorant of Jewish learning.[6] It is possible that he acquired his secular learning in his youth, while still at home.

The second, R. Joshua, was famous for his secular wisdom.[7] His association with Hadrian[8] and his visit to Athens[9] indicate that he was well versed in the Greek language and literature. When asked once whether a Jew is allowed to teach his son Greek,[10] he replied: "Let him teach him Greek at a time when it is neither day nor night, for it is written (Joshua I, 8), '*Thou shalt meditate thereon* (i. e. on the Law) *day and night.*'" Thus, Greek education is forbidden inasmuch as it interferes with the study of the Law.[11]

---

[4] Sanhedrin 17b.

[5] Comp. however תשובות גאונים קדמונים, end, יד רמ'ה ad loc. and Ratner to Shekalim p. 30. TP Shekalim V.1, 48d preserves a variant tradition. The ability to speak a foreign language does not imply a fair command of that language, as it seems to be the case with R. Akiba. See below.

[6] Aboth deR. Nathan Version I, VI, Vers. II, XIII, p. 30 and parallels (see Schechter's notes).

[7] See Bacher, Die Agada der Tannaiten I, p. 161 n. 1.

[8] Bacher ibid., p. 176 seq.

[9] See JE VII p. 291b.

[10] TP Pe'a I.1,15c (and parallel) reads: מהו שילמד אדם את בנו יונית, but Tosephta Aboda Zara I.20, 4612₉ (ed. pr. and cod. Vienna) reads: ס פ ר יוני. Midrash Tehilim I.17, ed. Buber p. 16, reads: חכמת יונית. These expressions make it evident that the question was regarding the teaching of not only the spoken language but of Greek literature as well. See also below p. 23, n. 54.

[11] See TP and Midrash Tehilim referred to in the previous note. Comp. however TB Menahoth 99b, Tosaphoth ibid. 64b s. v. ארור and below p. 24. The attitude of the Rabbis towards Greek education varied according to individuals, places and times.

More convincing evidence of their (i. e. R. Eliezer's and R. Joshua's) control of Greek is afforded by the following passage of the Palestinian Talmud:[12] רבן שמעון בן גמליאל אומר ... בדקו ומצאו שאין התורה יכולה להיתרגם כל צורכה אלא יוונית. ב ו ר נ נ י אחד בידה להם א ר מ י ת מתוך יונית. ר' ירמיה בשם ר' חייא בר בא תירגם עקילס הגר התורה לפני ר' אליעזר ולפני ר' יהושע וקילסו אותו ואמרו לו יפיפית מבני אדם.

Before translating the text we shall try to establish the correct reading and meaning of the words. In Midrash Esther[13] we read: ברברי אחד להון לשון רומי כלשון יוני which is to be corrected: ברברי אחד [בידה] להון לשון רומי [מ]לשון יוני. All other readings are later emendations and have no authority whatever. Now the word בידה does not mean "invented" but "selected", "took out". We often find this verb used as a synonym for ברר.[14] Thus, the translation of the above text will be: "Rabban Simeon b. Gamaliel said . . . It was investigated and found that the Tora could not be perfectly translated except in Greek. A watchman[15] (or merely a Roman soldier) 'took out'[16] for them the Latin from the Greek.[17] R. Jeremiah in the name of R. Hiyya b. Abba said: Aquila the Proselyte presented his translation of the Tora before R. Eliezer and R. Joshua and they

[12] Megilla I.11, 71c.

[13] IV, end (to I.22), ed. princeps.

[14] See Menahoth V.1 and the variants of בודה recorded in Mishna ed. Romm, Tosephta Pesahim 15614 and Tosefeth Rishonim ad loc.; BR XXXIV, 3207 and my remarks in שקיעין p. 74. Likewise we read in TB Nedarim 10a: לשון ש ב ד ו להם חכמים, but the parallel passage in TP Nazir I.1, 51a reads: לשונות ש ב י ר ר ו להן ראשונים. See also Lewy, Woerterbuch s. v. בדה.

[15] According to Midrash Esther: a *Barbarian*. This reading, which was overlooked by all scholars, is of far-reaching importance. It is authoritative evidence that an old Latin translation of the Bible was "concocted" from the Greek by a Barbarian, i. e. neither by a Greek nor by a Roman. The Vetus Latina is particularly famous for its barbaric style, as already observed by the earlier Christian churchfathers. See the literature referred to by Blondheim, Les Parlers Judeo-Romans p. CXIX seq.; ibid. p. C.

[16] The verb בידה is used here figuratively: The soldier (or the Barbarian) did not understand Hebrew and he only paraphrased the contents of the Torah in contradistinction to a literal translation. בידה is used here in the same sense like בידה את השאור.

[17] On the subject, see Krauss in Magazin für WdJ XX, 107, Bacher in REJ XXXIII, 109, Blau in JQR NS XIX, 163, Ratner to Megilla p. 23.

praised him, and said to him: *'Thou art fairer than the children of men'* " (Ps. XLV, 3). The word יפיפית in this verse is an unequivocal allusion to יון — יפת,[18] and is in accordance with the saying of Bar Kappara:[19] שיהו. יפת אלקים ליפת וישכן באהלי שם. מדברין בלשונו של יפת באוהלו של שם. בני יפת... ויון " *'May God enlarge Japheth, and may he dwell in the tents of Shem'* (Gen. IX, 27), i. e. let them speak[20] the language of Japheth in the tent of Shem. *The sons of Japheth ... Javan"* (ibid. X. 2).

Hence there can be no doubt whatever that TP speaks of the Greek translation of the Bible by Aquila, who read it before R. Eliezer and R. Joshua, and was highly praised for it. This commendation can be appreciated only if the men who uttered it were qualified to pass judgment on the style and exactness of the translation. And it is obvious that the source in TP regarded them as able critics of Greek style.

Moreover, the conclusion that R. Eliezer and R. Joshua were authorities on Greek language and style will solve a hitherto unexplained difficulty. According to the above tradition Aquila's translation was presented before R. Eliezer and R. Joshua,[21] whereas the inner evidence of the translation[22] demonstrates the influence of the school of R. Akiba.[23] This evidence is corroborated by the tradition of Jerome in his commentary on Is. VIII, 14: "Akibas, quem magistrum Aquilae proseliti

[18] See TB Megilla 9b.

[19] TP Megilla I.11, 71b (BR XXXVI.8, 342 and parallels).

[20] In BR: may the words of the Tora be spoken in the language etc.

[21] See also TB Megilla 3a.

[22] Such as σύν for את etc.

[23] See Swete, Introduction p. 32, JE II 36 and the bibliography ibid. p. 38.

We may add an interesting example. Lev. V.2: או נפש אשר תגע בכל טמא ("Or if any one touch any unclean thing") is translated by Procopius from Aquila (as quoted by Field ad loc. p. 175): qui conspurcaverit se *verbo* aliquo inquinato ("who will defile himself by unclean word"). This translation of דבר with "word" is in full accordance with R. Akiba's opinion. So we read in Tosephta Shebuoth I, 44624: בכל טמא. מה תלמוד לומר דבר. ר' עקיבא אומר לרבות את הנגעים שאין טומאה יורדת בהן אלא בדבר. "[It is written] *'any unclean thing'* (Lev. V.2), what is intimated by דבר (word)? R. Akiba said: It includes plagues, since uncleanliness does not rest upon them unless by word" (of the priest who has to pronounce טמא).

autumant." Although the tradition of Jerome in this passage is rather confused,[24] it is nevertheless unlikely that Jerome was mistaken regarding Aquila, a man in whom the Christian world took such a great interest.

In my opinion, this discrepancy can be explained by assuming that R. Akiba was not versed in the Greek language to such a degree as to judge the translation as a whole. It may be that the original draft, or the first edition of the translation, was confirmed by R. Eliezer and R. Joshua as regards style and exactness, whereas in method and in the translator's corrections in the second edition[25] he was guided by R. Akiba whom he consulted in Hebrew or Aramaic.[26]

Furthermore, attention should be called to the remarkable fact that all the translations of Aquila recorded in Rabbinic literature are in Greek[27] with only two exceptions: 1. ויאמר אחד קדוש לפלמוני המדבר ר' הונא אמר לפלוניה, תרגם עקילס לפנימי דיבר וכו'[28] *"And one saint said unto that certain saint who spoke* (Dan. VIII, 13), R. Huna said: to the certain one. Aquila translated: to the inner one."

From the wording of the Midrash we see that Aquila's rendering of this word was associated here with R. Huna's translation. It is therefore very probable either that R. Huna himself offered this interpretation in the name of Aquila (in opposition to his own view, as is usual in Talmudic literature), or that it was pointed out to him in his school by one of his disciples. And since R. Huna came to Palestine from Babylonia it is quite natural that he did not understand Greek,[29] and Aquila's translation had to be retranslated to him into Hebrew.

2. The second exception is recorded in the Palestinian Talmud.[30] אמר ר' יוסי בשם ר' יוחנן תירגם עקילס הגר לפני ר' עקיבה והיא

---

[24] See Prof. Louis Ginzberg's remark in Jewish Studies in Memory of G. A. Kohut, p. 291.

[25] See Field, Prolegomena p. XXV seq.

[26] On the *floruit* of Aquila see Swete, Intoduction p. 32.

[27] See Krauss, Steinschneider's Festschrift p. 151 seq.

[28] BR XXI.1, p. 1985.

[29] Very likely it is the same R. Huna about whom it is clearly stated in TP Baba Bathra X.1, 17c that he did not understand Greek. See below p. 26.

[30] Kiddushin I.1, 59a.

שפחה נחרפת לאיש בכתושה לפני איש וכו'. "R. Jose in the name of
R. Johanan (III, c.) said: The Proselyte Aquila rendered the
word *betrothed* (Lev. XIX, 20) to R. Akiba as meaning
'pounded'". Here also the Palestinian Talmud recorded not
the Greek translation of Aquila[31] but the Hebrew equivalent.
The reason is probably to be found in the exactness of the
tradition: R. Akiba did not understand Greek sufficiently
well to appreciate the exact Greek equivalent of נחרפת, and
Aquila had to consult R. Akiba on this point in Hebrew.[32]

Considering the authenticity of this last statement we can
realize how trustworthy the previous tradition is that R. Eliezer
and R. Joshua were able to pass judgment on the exactness
and beauty of Aquila's translation, a fact which presupposes a
fair knowledge of Greek literary style.

A definite statement bearing on the attitude of their contemporary, Rabban Gamaliel, towards Greek culture is recorded in Tosephta:[33] התירו להם לבית רבן גמליאל ללמד בניהן יוונית
מפני שהן קרובין למלכות "Permission was given to the House of
Rabban Gamaliel to teach their children Greek[34] owing to their
relation with the (Roman) government."

Even more definite testimony is borne by TB[35] in the name
of R. Simeon — son of Rabban Gamaliel: אלף ילדים היו בבית
אבא חמש מאות למדו תורה וחמש מאות למדו חכמת יונית. "There were a
thousand young men in my father's house, five hundred of
whom studied the Law, while the other five hundred studied
Greek Wisdom." Thus, five hundred young men connected
with the house of the Jewish patriarch devoted their time to
the study of Greek literature.

---

[31] See Prof. L. Ginzberg's remarks in Festschrift Schwarz, p. 355.

[32] A third instance of an Aramaic translation in the name of Aquila is
recorded in Koheleth Rabba XI.3 (=Yalkut Hamakiri to Isa. p. 40). But
the name "Aquila" there is an error as already noted by R. David Luria
ad loc. Furthermore, the interpretation is entirely alien to the spirit of
Aquila's literal translation.

[33] Sota XV, 322₆ (ed. pr. and cod. Vienna). Comp. also TP Shabbath
VI.1, 7d (and parallels), TB Sota 49b (and parallels).

[34] In TB Sota 49b: Greek wisdom.

[35] TB Sota 49b (and parallels).

The son of the latter, R. Juda Hanassi went one step
further, declaring:[35a] בארץ ישראל לשון סורסי למה, או לשון הקדש או
לשון יוונית "Why speak Syriac in Palestine? Talk either Hebrew
or Greek."

It is hard to believe that this attitude towards Greek culture
was limited only to the house of the patriarch. We know how
eagerly the middle class imitates the upper class, and how
readily the lower strata follow the example of the middle groups.
The degree of a person's Hellenistic culture depended on his
social standing. Probably the upper class knew Greek literature,
the middle class was less conversant with it, while the knowledge of the lower class was limited to the vernacular only.

Some of the Rabbis, especially those who lived in the Hellenized centers of Palestine, were skilled in the peculiarities and
nuances of the Greek language. What refined linguistic taste,
for example, is displayed by R. Jonathan of Eleutheropolis
(III c.), the author of the famous sentence about the respective
qualities of the four languages: Greek, Latin, Syriac and
Hebrew![36] According to his view Greek is most suitable for זמר,
which in this instance means song in the larger sense of the
word — poetry.[37] Only a man who knew the Greek literary
style well could express an opinion on the superior suitability of
Greek for the genre of poetry.

A younger contemporary of R. Jonathan of Eleutheropolis,
R. Abbahu, the head of the Rabbinical school in Caesarea and
one of the pillars of the Palestinian Talmud, was a man of
high Hellenistic culture.

He played with Greek words just as he played with Aramaic
ones. We know his habit of indulging in enigmatic speech
(לשון חכמה), based on the double meaning of words.[38] In line
with this characteristic of his we can perhaps explain the difficult
passage in TP Bikkurim III. 3, 65d where it is related that R.

[35a] Ibidem.

[36] TP Megilla I.11, 71b (and parallels). Comp. also Krauss LW I, XIX
seq.

[37] Just as in TB Hagiga 15b: זמר יוני לא פסק מפומיה, "He never ceased
reciting Greek poetry."

[38] TB Erubin 53b. Comp. TP Maasroth II.7, 50a.

Abbahu sent a letter to R. Simeon b. Abba in which he en-
closed gray hairs[39] and wrote: בגין אילין סבתא קום אתהלך לארעא
דישראל, "For the sake of these gray hairs come back to Palestine."
It seems to me that we may treat all the words in this letter
as enigmatic — לשון חכמה. By סבתא R. Abbahu designates
זקנות, which in Hebrew means ordination.[40] The meaning of the
letter is therefore: "For the sake of ordination come back to
Palestine."[41]

Similarly, Bacher in his AdPA[42] points to TP[43] where it is
recorded that R. Abbahu wrote an enigmatic letter playing on
the Greek meaning of the Hebrew words.[44]

R. Abbahu's familiarity with Greek is especially obvious in
the following phonetic play on Greek words:[45] בעון קומי ר' אבהו
מנין שהנוצר לשבעה חי. אמר להון מדידכון אנא ממטי לכון זיטא איפטה
איטה אכטו. "R. Abbahu was asked: Whence do you know that
a child [formed to be] born after seven months of pregnancy
can live? He replied: From your own language I will prove it
to you, ζ (ζῆτα) = ἑπτά, η (ῆτα) = ὀκτώ."

R. Abbahu's words "from your own language" etc. offer
evidence that the inquirers were non-Jews, probably Christians,
with whom R. Abbahu had frequent discussions.[46] Perhaps they
were stimulated by the Haggada stating that all prophets were
born after seven months of pregnancy,[47] and they taunted R.
Abbahu by questioning the survival of those children.

[39] See my Tosefeth Rishonim II, p. 227.

[40] = πρεσβεία. See Aruch Completum III, 315 s. v. זקן; TP Moed
Katan III.1, 81c (end) and TP Bikkurim III.3, 65d. Comp. also Tosephta
Hullin II 50322 (Cod. London and ed. pr.) which reads: שהסיבות הללו, but
in the parallel TB Aboda Zara 16b we read: שכמותך זקן ז.

[41] For the explanation of the rest of the letter see my comments in Klein's
article in MGWJ vol. LXXVII (1933) p. 364.

[42] II, 95, n. 1.

[43] Megilla III.2, 74a.

[44] Bacher, however, failed to mention that the right interpretation of the
Greek names is already available in Schoenhak's המשביר s. v. אבדוקוס, and
that it is already called לשון חכמה in the Aruch s. v. אבדוקוס.

[45] BR XIV.2, 1272 and parallels indicated by Theodor ad loc.

[46] See Bacher AdPA II p. 96 seq., ibid 115 seq.

[47] Midrash Haggadol on Exod. II.2, p. 13: שכל הנביאים לא נולדו אלא לשבעה
חדשים.

Theodor in his notes to BR ibid. as well as all our dictionaries misunderstood and misinterpreted R. Abbahu's reply, although they correctly realized that it is based on the respective numerical value of the letters ζ and η. The best explanation of R. Abbahu's reply was given by L. Cohn in the name of O. Crusius:[48] "ζ=7, η=8" has to be deciphered as: ζῆ τὰ ἑπτὰ [μᾶλλον] ἢ τὰ ὀκτώ, i. e. "Infants of seven months are more likely to survive than those of eight." R. Abbahu manipulates with Greek as he does with Aramaic and Hebrew.

Nor was his method of לשון חכמה foreign to the Greeks.[49] Alcaeus of Mitylene in an epigram on the two letters φ' he saw on a tombstone said:[50] ἆρα γυναικὶ τᾷ χϑονὶ κευϑομένᾳ Χιλιὰς ἦν ὄνομα ... ἤ ... Φιδίς; "Was the name of the woman hidden in the soil Chilias[51] ... or ... Phidis"?[52] And Alcaeus praises highly the man who cleverly chiselled this puzzle on the stone.[53]

The Rabbis, on the other hand, condemned word-plays in secular matters. An anonymous Haggadist in Koheleth Rabba I. 8 said: כל הדברים יגעים וגו' דברי הבטלה מיגעין את האדם וכו' "All things toil to weariness (Eccl. I. 8) etc., idle talk wearies a man" etc. In illustration a number of this kind of play on words (לשון חכמה) is quoted.[54] But it seems that R. Abbahu resorted to this "idle talk" when he did not want to be understood by everybody, or when circumstances required it. He was the cultured man of his time and of his place.

Not only did he himself study Greek, he also gave his daughters a Greek education. He taught in the name of R. Johanan:[55] מותר לאדם ללמד את בתו יוונית מפני שהוא תכשיט לה. "A

[48] MGWJ XLIV (1900) p. 569.

[49] Comp. Irenaeus, Adv. Haeres. II.24.1.

[50] Greek Anth. VII.429.

[51] The numerical value of φ' is 500, twice φ' =1000 =χιλιάς.

[52] φ δίς, twice φ. Comp. however Liddell and Scott, lexicon (1939), p. 1920 s. v. φεῖ.

[53] Comp. also ibid. X.43 quoted by M. Sachs, Beitraege I, 110, and see A. Bruell, Fremdsprachliche Redensarten p. 16, n. 2, Krauss LW I, p. 154.

[54] Comp. also Rashi's opinion on Greek wisdom in his commentary to TB Baba Kamma 83a s. v. חכמת יונית and Menahoth 64b s. v. חכמת יונית.

[55] TP Pe'a I.1, 15c and parallels.

man is permitted to teach his daughter Greek for it serves her
as an ornament". Greek literature only (and not vulgar Greek)
could serve as an ornament to young ladies of social standing
such as the daughters of R. Abbahu. Nor did R. Abbahu content himself with teaching this principle in theory; he behaved
according to his teaching as we shall see presently.

But we must not disregard the violent protest of R. Abbahu's
colleague and friend — R. Simeon b. Abba. He questioned R.
Abbahu's tradition in this respect, and doubted if R. Johanan
had ever uttered such an opinion. He ironically remarked:
בגין דו בעה מלפה בנתיה, הוא תלי ליה בר' יוחנן "Because he wants to
teach his daughters (Greek) he ascribes it to R. Johanan!⁵⁶

R. Hiyya b. Abba, the contemporary and relative⁵⁷ of R.
Simeon b. Abba, taught in the name of R. Johanan in the
same spirit. He explained⁵⁸ that the prohibition of Greek education aimed at the informers (מפני המסורות). If this be the reason,
there is, of course, no difference between teaching Greek to
boys or to girls. Jastrow in his dictionary⁵⁹ remarks: "Studying
of Greek was forbidden on account of the informers, whose
familiarity with Greek tempted them to treason."

This is a wrong conception; we need not go so far. The
real reason was that people who knew Greek well could occasionally undermine the existence of the Jewish courts. If the
person involved was dissatisfied with the decision of the court
he could appeal to the Roman Government. As a matter of
fact R. Hiyya b. Abba himself was the victim of such a case.
A woman named Tamar complained of the decision of his court
to the proconsul in Caesarea.⁶⁰

Both R. Hiyya b. Abba and R. Simeon b. Abba behaved
according to their teaching. There is no trace in their numerous

---

⁵⁶ In accordance with this view we find in the late Midrash, Pirke deRabbi
ed. Grünhut p. 58 (see my booklet שקיעין p. 17 and p. 98 on the time of this
Midrash): אמר ר' יוחנן ... ולא ילמד אדם את בתו יונית ואסור לו שילמד יונית. "R.
Johanan said ... and a man should not teach his daughter Greek, and he
himself is forbidden to study Greek."
⁵⁷ Probably a brother.
⁵⁸ TP ibidem.
⁵⁹ P. 805, s. v. מסור.
⁶⁰ TP Megilla III.3, 74a.

sayings of any knowledge of Greek. Both of them were extremely honest, righteous and pious. Both of them seem to have
had a similar fate.

R. Hiyya was supported by a rich family of landowners in
Tiberias[61] named סילני[62], but the pious R. Hiyya had to leave
Palestine in order to make a living[63] and to avert the unfounded
suspicion that he was too favorably inclined towards his sup-
porters, the rich landowners.[64]

R. Simeon b. Abba too was famous for his poverty,[65] and it
was reported[66] that a landowner named אילופוסה offered him
tithes, but the pious R. Simeon hesitated to accept them, doubting
the trustworthiness of the man in respect of tithes and Teruma.
He consulted R. Johanan, and the latter told him: אילופוסה
אחינו נאמן הוא "Our brother אילופוסה is trustworthy."

Since both R. Simeon b. Abba and R. Johanan lived in
Tiberias, and R. Johanan knew well the character of the landowner, we can assume with certainty that the landowner lived
in the same place. It is very noteworthy that in this case
probably not only R. Simeon b. Abba had to leave Palestine,[67]
but the family of his supporter as well.

A Greek inscription on a tomb in Italy[68] reads:[69] Ἀλύπις
Τιβερ[ι]εὺς καὶ υἱοὶ αὐτοῦ Ἰοῦστος καὶ Ἀλύπις Ἑβρέοι . . .
"Alypis from Tiberias and his sons Justus and Alypis,
Hebrews" . . . I think we shall not err if we identify this name
with אילופוסה from Tiberias.

Thus, we obtain a picture of the three pillars among R.
Johanan's disciples: righteous, pious and intelligent men. But

[61] TP Shebiith III.1, 34c. See also Theodor's notes to BR 692₃.

[62] In a bilingual inscription on a Jewish tomb in Italy (Frey CIJ, I, 630)
we read: "filius Silani" in the Latin and בן סילנו in the Hebrew. According
to Lenormant the inscription is not earlier than the XI or the XII c., but
Frey remarks that the use of Latin argues against such late date.

[63] TP Hagiga I.7, 76d and parallel.

[64] TP Shebiith III.1, 34c, Maaser Sheni V.5, 56b.

[65] TP Bikkurim III.3, 65d, Baba Mezia II.3, 8c.

[66] TP Terumoth I.1, 40c.

[67] TP Moed Katan III.1, 81c, Bukkurim III.3, 65d.

[68] Date not identified.

[69] Frey, CIJ, 502 (p. 367).

one of them (R. Abbahu) is in addition a man of the world, a man well versed in secular culture, who lived in a Hellenized town (Caesarea), whereas the two others (R. Hiyya and R. Simeon b. Abba) are opposed to Greek culture, and are themselves ignorant of Greek.

However we must bear in mind that the latter were both of Babylonian origin and were brought up in Babylonia.[70] The Babylonian scholars who immigrated to Palestine did not ordinarily acquire this foreign language. TP Gittin[71] assumes as a matter of course that the great Babylonian scholar, Rab (III c.), who immigrated to Palestine did not know how to read Greek.

Another noteworthy episode regarding a Babylonian scholar in Palestine is recorded in the Palestinian Talmud:[72] שטר נפק ר' חונה לר' שמי אוגרוי (אוגדוי) read: מחיק, קונטא לא מחיק. אמר ר' חונה לר' שמי. פוק חמי עד ההן קונטא משמש. נפק ומר. עם טרייא קונטא. מי נפק. אמר הדא מיבעי מיתגרה תלת[ין] אפסדת עשר[ין].

Rabbi Z. M. Pineles[73] correctly explained[74] that we have before us a case of a document written in Greek where the number πεντήκοντα (fifty) was altered to ὀγδοήκοντα (eighty). The correct translation of the text will accordingly be: "A document passed from R. Huna[75] to R. Shammai, in which "ὀγδοη" was blurred and "κοντα" was clear. R. Huna said to R. Shammai: Go and see what is the lowest number in Greek that "κοντα" is combined with.[76] He went out and said: It is

---

[70] TP Maasroth, end, 52a, Shabbath VI, 8a, bottom.

[71] IX.9, 50c, bottom.   [72] Baba Bathra X.1, 17c.

[73] דרכה של תורה p. 134.

[74] The commentaries ad loc. misunderstood the text. The honor of the correct emendation and explanation of the text belongs to this brilliant Galician scholar.

[75] IV c., of Babylonian origin, and who did not know Greek.

[76] It was the usual practice of the Rabbis to consult the linguists when they came across a foreign term which they did not understand. So TP Baba Bathra VIII.8, 16c records that R. Joshua b. Levi consulted all linguists about the meaning of the word דיאתימון (διεθέμην), "I have bequeathed"— a common formula in wills — and nobody knew the meaning of it. It seems that the linguists misunderstood him, taking the word as a substantive; a lawyer would have probably answered the question. See A. Gulak in Tarbiz I fasc. 4, p. 144 and Tosefeth Rishonim II, p. 148.

τριάκοντα (thirty). When the litigants left R. Huna remarked: That party wanted to gain thirty (by the erasure) and lost twenty."[77]

A similar case is found in a Greek document written in Persia:[78] δραχμὰς τριάκοντα, τειμὴν ἀμπέλου . . . but in the "outer" duplicate:[79]

δραχμὰς τρία-(altered to τεσσαρᵃ) κοντα τειμὴν ἀμπέλου . . . Exactly the same kind of alteration as recorded in the Palestinian Talmud. The editor of the Greek parchment remarks:[80] "This is too obvious to be fraudulent." But the fact remains a fact. Human nature does not change.

Between these two opposite poles of native Palestinian scholars, on the one hand, who lived in Hellenized towns and were at home in Greek culture, and Babylonian immigrants, on the other hand, who were entirely ignorant of it, we have to place the average Rabbi who lived in the provincial towns and villages. His level of secular culture was probably only somewhat superior to that of the middle class inhabitant of the country. A closer inquiry into the cultural state of such scholars and of the middle class among the masses will be most welcomed.

The previously discussed instances of the house of the patriarch and the house of the head of the academy in Caesarea prove that these were inherent factors favoring the spread of Greek culture among the Jewish masses. The middle class[81] had before it a good example to imitate, they followed in the steps of their superiors. On the other hand, the lower class, whose vocabulary of both Aramaic and Greek was poor and vulgar,

[77] For the decision of the court was that the document is valid only for "thirty", the lowest number with which "κοντα" is combined.

[78] In 88 B. C. E. Published by E. H. Minns in The Journal of Hellenic Studies XXXV (1915) p. 28, l. 10.

[79] Ibid. p. 29, l. 10.

[80] Ibid. p. 49.

[81] The exact definition of this middle class in Palestine, its importance as a powerful factor in the Synagogue, its general condition in the III and the IV centuries, still awaits study. See meanwhile A. Buechler, The Economic Conditions of Judaea after the Destruction of the Second Temple p. 29 seq.

began slowly to develop a kind of Aramaic Greek Jargon.[82]
Even Semitic words bearing on practical life sometimes assumed
a Greek form. In TP[83] we find חליטר and נחתומר;[84] the common
folk added the Greek suffix –άριος[85] to the Semitic חליטא and
נחתום, and such words found their way into the language of the
Rabbis, when they spoke of everyday matters.

[82] See the excellent article of Prof. M. Schwabe in ידיעות החברה העברית
לחקירת א״י vol. V, p. 86.
[83] Halla II.6, 58c and elsewhere.
[84] Baba Bathra II.3, 13b.
[85] The usual suffix for professionals. Comp. also Schwabe ibid. II, p. 57.

THE GREEK OF THE SYNAGOGUE

Cleomedes the Mathematician and Astronomer in attacking the Greek style of Epicurus remarks:[1] Ἐπεὶ γε πρὸς τοῖς ἄλλοις καὶ τὰ κατὰ τὴν ἑρμηνείαν αὐτῷ ποικίλως διεφθορότα ἐστί, σαρκὸς εὐσταθῆ καταστήματα λέγοντι καὶ τὰ περὶ ταύτης πιστὰ ἐλπίσματα καὶ λίπασμα ὀφθαλμῶν τὸ δάκρυον ὀνομάζοντι καὶ ἱερὰ ἀνακραυγάσματα καὶ γαργαλισμοὺς σώματος καὶ ληκήματα καὶ ἄλλας τοιαύτας κακὰς ἄτας· ὧν τὰ μὲν ἐκ χαμαιτυπείων ἄν τις εἶναι φήσειε, τὰ δὲ ὅμοια τοῖς λεγομένοις ἐν τοῖς Δημητρίοις ὑπὸ τῶν θεσμοφοριαζουσῶν γυναικῶν, τὰ δὲ ἀπὸ μέσης τῆς προσευχῆς καὶ τῶν ἐπ' αὐλαῖς προσαιτούντων, Ἰουδαϊκά τινα καὶ παρακεχαραγμένα καὶ κατὰ πολὺ τῶν ἑρπετῶν ταπεινότερα.

According to this testimony such expressions as "σαρκὸς εὐσταθῆ καταστήματα" or "πιστὰ ἐλπίσματα" etc. were current "among the harlots, among the women who celebrated the Ceres' festivals, within the synagogue and among beggars — Jewish expressions much lower than reptiles."

It is to be deeply regretted that we know neither the exact date nor the place of Cleomedes.[2] But for our purpose it is important to note that the Jews in the Diaspora were not accused of speaking bad Greek like foreigners, but were blamed for employing vulgar — but good — Greek like the "θεσμοφοριάζουσαι",[3] for talking the common Greek spoken by the lowest classes of society.[4]

Cleomedes' remark does not, of course, refer to the Greek of the Bible read in the synagogues of the Diaspora, nor to the

---

[1] De motu circulari corporum caelestium II.1, 91, ed. Ziegler p. 166.

[2] Ziegler, De Vita et scriptis Cleomedis p. 14, places his *floruit* at the III c. in Rome.

[3] The Greek of the Thesmophoriazusae is well known from Aristophanes' comedy bearing this name.

[4] See Durham, Donald, The Vocabulary of Menander p. 27.

Greek of the regular prayers which were translated by learned
men, but to the speech of the minor preachers, to the religious
discussions that occasionally took place within the walls of the
synagogues and, finally, to the common talk of the people
gathered in the houses of worship.

But since we are concerned here only with the Greek of
the Palestinian Synagogue we have to consider how far that
language penetrated into the Synagogue and into Jewish religious
life. It is stated in the famous passage in the Palestinian Talmud that in the Hellenized town of Caesarea there were Jews
who read[5] the Shema in Greek.[6] Of the Jewish inscriptions
found in the coastal town of Jaffa (mostly in the cemetery)
sixty are in Greek and only six are in Hebrew and Aramaic.[7]
The Greek accompanied the dead to their eternal resting place.
In the midland towns of Palestine as well a great many Greek
inscriptions have been discovered in the synagogues and the
cemeteries.[8]

The very poverty and vulgarity of the language of these
inscriptions show that it was spoken by the people and not
written by learned men only. We shall presently see that the
learned and cultured Jews of Palestine spoke a good Greek as
the educated Jew in England speaks a literary English.

And alhough it is quite certain that the regular prayers in
the midland synagogues of Palestine were offered in Hebrew
and Aramaic, striking evidence, it seems to me, is available
that even there the people sometimes said their special prayers
in Greek.

In addition to the regular services in the Synagogue, prayers
were offered in the streets on special occasions such as droughts;
during these the scholars sometimes turned to the pious man
among the common folk to intervene before God on their
behalf. Already the Mishna contains the order of the street-

---

[5] In the IV c.

[6] Sota VII.1, 21b. Comp. also לקט מדרשים ed. Wertheimer p. 3.

[7] Prof. M. Schwabe in his Introduction to the ספר הישוב, Vol. I, part I,
p. 41.

[8] Schwabe ibid. p. 39 seq.

service in times of droughts.[9] The common people often played a leading part in these prayers. It is related in the Palestinian Talmud[10] that the prayer of an ass-driver brought down rain. But the story related[11] about a man named Pantokakus is particularly instructive.

This story which is recorded incidentally and is told with the simplicity of life itself sheds a bright light on the everyday-life, on the pious man of the people who nevertheless belonged to the dregs of Jewish society. The story runs as follows:[12]

אתחמי לר' אבהו פנדקקא[13] יצלי ומטרא נחית. שלח ר' אבהו ואיתיתיה.
א' ליה, מה אומנך. א' ליה, ה' עבירן ההוא גברא עבד בכל יום, משפר תייטרון,
ומוגר זנייתה, ומיעל מניהון לבני, ומטפח ומרקד קומיהון, ומקיש בבוליא[14]
קומיהון. א' ליה, ומה טיבו עבדת. א' ליה, חד זמן ההוא גברא משפר תייטרון
ואתת חדא איתתא[15] וקמת לה חורי עמודא בכיה. אמרית לה, מה עסקיך.
אמרה, בעלה דההיא אנתתה חבישונה, בעיא מחמי מה מעבד ומפניניה, וזבנית
פרוסי ופרוסי[16] ערסי, ויהבית לה טימיתון, ואמרית לה, הא לך פניי בעליך,
ולא תחטיי. א' ליה כדי את מצלייה ומתענייה.

"It appeared to R. Abbahu[17] that παντόκακος[18] ought to pray so that rain would come down. R. Abbahu had him

---

[9] Taanith II 1–2. Comp. also Tosephta ibid. I p. 215 l. 18–26 and the Talmuds ad loc.

[10] Taanith I.4, 64a. Comp. also Vayyikra Rabba XXXIV.14 (end).

[11] TP ibid.

[12] The text of the modern editions of the TP is very corrupted. The best text is preserved in the fragments published by Prof. Louis Ginzberg in Genizah Studies I p. 403. I record in the notes the better readings of the ed. pr.

[13] Ed. pr.: פנטקקה.

[14] Ibid.: בבבוליא.

[15] Ibid.: איתא.

[16] Ibid.: ערסי ופרוס.

[17] In Caesarea, see above p. 21 seq.

[18] See Krauss LW, 465. Loew's choice in this connection is wrong. Although TP mentions five sins here, five is a round number in Rabbinic literature. It is similarly reported in TB Baba Bathra 16b that Esau committed five sins in one day. A man who commits five sins in one day is a thorough sinner and deserves his surname παντόκακος. On five as a round number see the Hebrew periodical ציון ed. Jost vol. I (1840) p. 40 seq. and Rabbinica by G. Kittel (Leipzig 1920) p. 39 seq. The material from Talmudic sources recorded in both articles is very far from exhaustive. On five virtues, see Kittel ibid. p. 43. On πέντε=πάντα, see ibid. p. 45.

brought to him and asked him: 'What is your occupation'?
Pantokakus said (referring to himself): 'This man commits
five sins every day: he adorns[19] the theatre, engages the hetaerae,[20] brings their clothes to the bath-house, claps hands and
dances before them, and clashes the cymbals[21] before them'.
[R. Abbahu] said to him: 'What good deed did you perform'?
He said (again referring to himself): 'This man was once adorn-
ing the theatre when a woman came in and stood behind the
column (of the theatre) crying. I asked her: What is your
business' (what do you want)? She said (about herself): 'They
imprisoned the husband of this woman and she wants to see
what she can do to release him' (implying that she wants to
be engaged to work in the theatre). I sold my bed and the
curtain of my bed[22] and I gave to her the money I received for
it and told her: 'Here you have the money, release (or: here
is the release of) your husband and do not sin'. R. Abbahu
said to him: 'You are entitled to offer the prayer and to be
answered (by God).' "

We have here an excellent picture of a man who was of the
dregs of Jewish society in Caesarea. The one man adorns the

---

[19] Σκηνογραφεῖ?

[20] I. e. musicians and dancers.

[21] All our dictionaries misunderstood the origin of this word. בבוליייא
means βαβούλια — cymbals. The modern Greek lexicons do not record
this word, but Hesychius in his lexicon s. v. Κύμβαλον records: "Κύμβαλον...
βαβούλιον εἶδος ὀργανοῦ μουσικοῦ." It is very noteworthy that this term
which is not found anywhere else except in the lexicon of an Alexandrian
is preserved in the Palestinian Talmud in a quotation from the vocabulary
of the theatre in Caesarea.

The reading of the ed. pr. ומקיש בבבולייא seems to be preferable and corresponds to the Mishna (Tamid VII.3): והקיש בן ארזא בצלצל, but the reading
of the Geniza Ms. ומקיש בבוליא is also acceptable, corresponding to: καὶ
κρούει τὰ βαβούλια.

[22] According to the reading of ed. pr. But the story preceeding ours,
which is related in TP ibid. implies rather that Pantokakus sold his profes-
sional tools. May be that ערסי is only a different spelling for ארסי, just as
אריס (tenant) and עריס are interchangeable (See Jastrow s. v. עריס II). Then
ערס=ארוס, drum (See Sota IX, 14, Kelim XV, 6 and commentaries ibid.
Comp. also Krauss, Talmudische Archaeologie III p. 281 n. 112). The
translation should therefore be: I sold my drum and the items belonging
(πρός) to my drum.

theatre, engages the hetaerae, takes care of their clothes and teaches them to dance and to play.[23] We probably have before us a mime[24] or a pantomimist of a small theatre in Caesarea. Both types were called ὀρχηστής in ancient times.[25]

The ὀρχηστής was profoundly despised by the Jews. Already the Septuagint translated אחד הרקים[26]— one of the worthless[27] — with: εἰς τῶν ὀρχουμένων. The Septuagint did not read הרקדים,[28] but paraphrased the ריק with "dancer." This is corroborated by the comment of a Palestinian scholar of the end of the III c.:[29] מהו הרקים. א״ר בא בר כהנא הריקים שבריקי' זו ארכסטס. "What does הריקים mean? R. Abba b. Kahana said: The lowest of the low, namely an ὀρχηστής (a dancer).

Thus our theatre man, our Pantokakus who was one of the lowest of the low, sold his last belongings in order to save an innocent married woman from sin.

A similar anecdote is told[30] of a poor ass-driver who sold his beast in order to prevent a woman from sin; he likewise prayed for rain and was answered. These people of the lowest classes of Jewish society said their prayers in the streets of Palestine. They prayed for bread for the poor, they prayed for rain; they prayed in their plain and simple style, and they were answered.

It seems to me that we are able to recover a fragment of such a "street-prayer" in a halachic passage of the Palestinian Talmud:[31] חזקיה אמר אהן דמשתבע על תרין דאינון תרין לוקה משום שבועת שוא. ר' מנחם בשם ריש לקיש אהן דחמי מיטרא נחית ואמ' קורי פלי בריכסון לוקה משום שבועת שוא. "Hezekia said: He who swears that

---

[23] The function of this man was misunderstood and misinterpreted by Krauss, Talmudische Archaeologie III p. 118.

[24] See Krauss ibid. 117 and 293 n. 290 on the mime of Caesarea in the III and IV centuries.

[25] See Daremberg et Saglio, Dictionnaire des Antiquités etc. IV, p. 316a n. 1; ibid. III p. 1899b.

[26] II Sam. VI, 20.

[27] Comp. ῥακά in Matt. V, 22 and the "Kommentar" ad loc.

[28] See The Intern. Crit. Com. ad loc., p. 297.

[29] TP Sanhedrin II.4, 20b and parallels.

[30] TP Taanith I.4, 64a, immediately before the story of Pantokakus.

[31] Shebuoth III.10, 34d and parallels.

two are two is liable to be flogged for the sin of taking a vain
oath. R. Menahem in the name of Resh Lakish (III C.) said:
He who sees that it is beginning to rain and says קורי פלי בריכסון
is to be flogged for the sin of taking a vain oath."

Hezekia's statement is clear; one swore that two are two.[32]
But the second oath, the oath of a man in the market[33] swearing that it is raining, is difficult to understand. Some of our
lexicons explain that the man swore and said קורי פלי בריכסון,
κῦρι[33a] πολὺ ἔβρεξεν, "God, how much it rained"![34] Some explain this phrase as: κῦρι[33a] πολὺ βρέξον, "By God, bring
much rain!"[35]

These explanations are far from satisfactory. If Resh Lakish
wanted to quote a theoretical illustration, why did he choose an
oath in Greek? We can only assume that the illustration was
drawn from life as a well known practice.

Our commentaries, however, misunderstood here the meaning of שבועת שוא. An oath involving an evident fact is not an
oath, it is a vain mention of His name. Even in post-Biblical
times an oath and a vain mention of His name were synonymous.
Ben Sira (XXIII.10) says: ὁ ὀμνύων καὶ ὀνομάζων διὰ
παντὸς, ἀπὸ ἁμαρτίας οὐ μὴ καθαρισθῇ, "He that sweareth
and continually nameth (the Holy one) is not cleansed from
sin." Ὀμνύειν and ὀνομάζειν are synonymous here.

The same is true of Rabbinic literature. In Tosephta[36] we
read: כל הזוכר ומזכיר עבודה זרה, "He who knows how to mention

---

[32] Or as proved in my note to ערוגת הבושם ed. Urbach p. 183 that the
correct reading in TP is: תנין דאינין תנין which we have to vocalize תֵּינִין (=תאנין).
The man swore that figs are figs, a self-evident fact. We are reminded of
the Greek proverb: τὰ σῦκα σῦκα ... λέγει, "He calls figs figs" (See Liddell
and Scott s. v. σκάφη). In Pesiktha Rabbathi XXII, ed. Friedmann 113a it
is stated: חזקיה אמר אפילו אמר על הזית שהיא זית ועל התאינה שהיא תאינה
הרי זו שבועת שוא. ר' חני ור' מנחם בשם ר' שמעון בן לקיש זה שהוא עובר בשוק
וראה את הגשמים יורדים ואמר כלי (פלי: read) קרי אברוכסים הרי זו שבועת שוא.

[33] See Pesiktha Rabbathi quoted in the previous note.

[33a] =κύριε. See J. Psichari, Bibliothèque de l'école des hautes études
vol. 92 (Paris 1892) p. 227 seq. and p. 235 seq.

[34] See Lewy Woerterbuch I, 266 s. v. בריקסון and Loew in Krauss' LW
II, p. 166.

[35] See Kohut Aruch Completum II p. 194 s. v. and Krauss LW ibid.

[36] Aboda Zara III, 46412.

the name of an idol." The Mekiltha[37] explains that in this case "to mention" means to take a vow in (or to swear by) his name. מזכיר is thus synonymous with נודר or נשבע.

Moreover, TB[38] states clearly in the name of this very Resh Lakish: כל המברך ברכה שאינה צריכה עובר משום לא תשא, "He who pronounces a benediction when it is not required transgresses the commandment: *'Do not invoke the name of the Lord'* " (Exod. XX. 7) etc.

This Jewish tradition was probably the source of Theodoretus (V c.) in his Quaest. in Exod. ad loc.,[39] who wrote: τινὲς δὲ τὸ ὀμωμοκότα ψεύσασθαι. Ἐγὼ δὲ οἶμαι, τὸν θεῖον παρακελεύεσθαι νόμον, δίχα διδασκαλίας, ἢ προσευχῆς, ἢ ἀναγκαίας τινὸς χρείας, τὴν θείαν μὴ προφέρειν προσηγορίαν. "Some say that the verse (Ex. XX.7) relates to him who pronounces a false oath, but I think that the Divine Law enjoins us not to mention His name except in teaching, praying and in cases of urgent need." This is in perfect accordance with the statement of Resh Lakish. Rabbi M. Maimonides codified this statement[40] כל המברך ברכה שאינה צריכה הרי זה נושא שם שמים לשוא והרי הוא כנשבע לשוא "He who pronounces a benediction when it is not required is mentioning the name of the Lord in vain and is regarded as one who swears in vain."

Thus, Resh Lakish in full consistency with his own opinion could teach that he who mentioned God's name in useless prayer is liable to be flogged for a vain oath.

Therefore it seems quite clear that "κῦρι πολὺ βρέξον" (Lord, let much rain fall) is neither more nor less than the first verse of a prayer for rain (תפלת הגשמים), an opinion already uttered by N. Brüll.[41] This prayer for rain was offered by the

---

[37] Mishpatim XX, ed. Horovitz p. 331.

[38] Berakoth 33a (bottom).

[39] Migne, PG LXXX, 268d.

[40] In הלכות ברכות I, 15.

[41] Jahrbücher I, 130. Brüll quoted only the Greek phrase without paying any attention to the context of the Talmud which mentions שבועת שוא, a vain oath. All Jewish scholars (Kohut, Loew, Jastrow, especially Fürst in his Glossarium s. v. אבריכסין) rejected the opinion of Brüll as being incom-

common people in the streets and in the markets[42] of Tiberias[43] in their plain and simple phraseology. J. Grimm[44] quotes a prayer for rain in Neo-Greek:

> θεέ μου, θεέ μου, βρέξε μιὰν βροχήν,
> μιὰν βροχήν, μιὰν σιγανήν

> "My God, my God send one rain,
> One rain, a gentle rain."

Grimm did not give his source; the Μεγάλη Ἑλληνικὴ Ἐγκυκλοπαιδεία[45] quotes a similar prayer:

> ρῖξε, θεέ μου, μιὰ καλὴ βροχὴ νὰ γίνουν τὰ σπαρτά.
> "Send, my God, one good rain that the crops may grow."

These simple prayers are strikingly similar to the Jewish prayer. The supplication was probably short and unadorned, perhaps not more than something like this: κῦρι πολὺ βρέξον, βρέξον ἐπὶ τοὺς ἀγροὺς τοῦ λαοῦ σου. The Roman Emperor, M. Aurelius Antoninus recorded[46] a similar people's prayer for rain: Εὐχὴ Ἀθηναίων· ὗσον, ὗσον, ὦ φίλε Ζεῦ, κατὰ τῆς ἀρούρας τῆς Ἀθηναίων καὶ τῶν πεδίων. "A prayer of the Athenians: Rain, rain, o dear Zeus, down upon the tilth of the Athenians and the plains."

The Roman Emperor, admiring this simple prayer, remarked: ἤτοι οὐ δεῖ εὔχεσθαι, ἢ οὕτως, ἁπλῶς καὶ ἐλευθέρως. "Either we ought not to pray at all, or we ought to pray in this way — simply and freely." The learned Rabbis likewise were appreciative of the simple prayers of the people, but Resh Lakish had nevertheless to warn the ignorant man not to pray

---

patible with the context. But considering all the material adduced above there is no doubt that the excellent scholarly instinct of Brüll did not mislead him.

[42] In Pesiktha Rabbathi quoted above: זה שהוא עובר בשוק.
[43] The dwelling place of Resh Lakish.
[44] Kleinere Schriften II, Berlin 1865 p. 448, referred to by Brüll ibidem.
[45] Vol. VII, p. 804 s. v. βροχή.
[46] Medit. V. 7, quoted by Grimm and Brüll.

for rain after it began to fall (a sure means that the prayer will be answered), or he will be flogged like a perjurer.[47]

Thus, we have prayers in Greek not only in the sea-port synagogues, but also in the streets and markets of the midland towns.

And if the Greek of the common people in the market was poor and vulgar, that of the learned Rabbis was far superior and of higher taste.

The Rabbis elucidated the verses of the Bible not only by means of quoting from Jewish sources but sometimes also from Greek law and literature as well as proverbs. R. Eleazar (b. Pedath, Tiberias, III c.) in drawing a parallel between the behavior of the Lord of the world and that of an earthly king, began his explanation with a Greek proverb. He said:[48] פְּרָא בָּסִילְיוֹס אוֹנוֹמוֹס אוּנְרָפּוֹס[49] בְּנוֹהַג שֶׁבָּעוֹלָם מֶלֶךְ בָּשָׂר וָדָם גוֹזֵר גְּזֵירָה רוֹצֶה

[47] The vain mention of His name was especially abused by ignorant women. TB Nedarim 7b records the story of a woman who mentioned His name in vain and was banned by R. Huna (in Babylonia, III c.).

More instructive is the story related in TB Kethubot 85a: הַהִיא אִיתְּתָא דְאִיחַיְּיבָא שְׁבוּעָה בֵּי דִינָא דְרָבָא. אָמְרָה לֵיהּ בַּת רַב חִסְדָּא יָדַעְנָא בָּהּ דַּחֲשׁוּדָה אַשְׁבוּעָה אַפְּכָהּ רָבָא לִשְׁבוּעָה אַשְׁכְּנַגְדָּהּ. "A woman was required to take an oath at the court of Raba (Babyl. IV c.), but when R. Hisda's daughter (Raba's wife) said to him: 'I know that she is suspected of [taking false] oaths,' Raba transferred the oath to her opponent." The Talmud does not state what prompted Raba's wife to suspect the woman of swearing falsely, but according to an old Geonic tradition (Halakoth Gedoloth שבועה ה', ed. Warsaw 115c, bottom, ed. Hildesheimer p. 482) she heard the woman uttering the Lord's name in vain (דהות מפקא שם שמים לבטלה. See also the Geonic sources in אוצר הגאונים Kethuboth ad loc. p. 262 and אוצר הפירושים ibid. p. 50). It is true that Tosaphoth to Shebuoth 46b s. v. אבל interpreted this phrase to mean that she pronounced false oaths, but the simple meaning of the context argues against this forced interpretation (Comp. also Ritba Kethuboth ad loc.).

The woman behaved in the typical manner of the market-monger, and it is no wonder that Raba's wife suspected her of being likely to take a false oath. Resh Lakish would probably order such a woman to be flogged.

[48] TP Rosh Hashana I.3, 57a. I quote the Greek words according to the reading and vocalization contained in the Geniza mss. of the Yerushalmi Fragments ed. Ginzberg p. 145₁₉.

[49] In Yer. Fr. ibid. p. 152¹⁴: בָּסִילְיָאוֹס אוֹ נוֹמוֹס אַגְרָפּוֹס (!)פדיה בן 'אלע א"ר. The Aruch s. v. בסיליוס (and parallels) quotes from VayR. (XXXV.3): בסיליאוס נומוס אנרפוס. This is not found in our editions of VayR., but is pre-

מקיימה רצה[50] אחרים מקיימים אותה אבל הקב״ה אינו כן אלא גוזר גזירה
ומקיימה תחילה וכו'.

"Παρὰ βασιλέως ὁ νόμος ἄγραφος — on the king the law
is not binding[51]—. Ordinarily a human king issues a decree and
if he chooses he obeys it, otherwise others obey it, but when
the Holy One blessed be He issues a decree He is the first to
obey it."

Thus, R. Eleazar quoted in the synagogue (or in the academy)
a Greek proverb in the Greek language and did not translate
it, assuming that everybody understood it.[51a]

We seize this occasion to take exception to the fatal mistake made by great scholars who maintained that the Jewish
preachers used Greek words in order to boast before the public;
that in reality the audience did not understand it, but were
impressed by it; that the preacher resorted to Greek expressions
when there were adequate Hebrew or Aramaic ones available.
So, for example, the great contemporary philologist, Prof.

served in the mss. So cod. Brit. Mus.: ר' לעזר א' בסיליוס נומוס אינגרפוס; cod.
Vat.: א״ר אלעזר בר'(!); cod. Oxf.: א' ר' אלעזר בכל יום(!) נומוס אנגריפוס בסליאוס
נימוס אנגרפוס. R. Samuel Jama (Jubelschrift ... Graetz p. 25) quotes from TP:
מצאתי פי' ידי רב ניסים ז״ל מנהג המלך תורתו. He adds: פרא יוסלי אוס אונימוס אנגריפוס
אינה כתובה.

[50] So Geniza ms. Ed. pr.: רצו.

[51] This proverb was quite popular in the Orient. H. Lewy (Philologus
LII, 1893, p. 568) pointed to Porphyrio, a contemporary of R. Eleazar, who
quotes (in Horat. ad Sat. II. 3, 188): Μωρῷ καὶ βασιλεῖ νόμος
ἄγραφος, "On the fool and on the king the law is not binding" (Comp.
ed. A. Holder, 1894, p. 302 and the editor's notes). This quotation more
closely approximates the reading of the Midrashim |which have νόμος without
the article ὁ. It also finally establishes the correct vocalization of אונגרפוס.
See Prof. Ginzberg's note in Krauss' תוספות הערוך השלם, p. ח'כ. In Shemoth
Rabba (XXX.9), where R. Eleazar's statement is reported in the name of
Tannaim (I/II c.), who included it in their sermon in Rome, the Greek
proverb is missing. For further elucidations see below p. 144, n. 2.

[51a] A Greek proverb was also cited by R. Aha (Pesiktha deR. Kahana
191b and parallels): תהא מן הרואין ולא מן הנראין, תהא מטב ברטי ולא מ קנוניא
(See Aruch s. v. טבריטי and Buber's note ad loc. n. 36). "Be among the
onlookers and not among those on view! Be among the spectators (θεωρητής.
See Krauss and Loew LW 256 s. v. טבריר) and not among the gladiators!"
(on κυνηγός as bestiarius, θηριομάχης, see Liddell and Scott s. v. κυναγός,
end).

I. Loew[52] contends. According to him, the Jewish preachers employed Greek words in order to draw the attention of the audience, to parade their knowledge before the hearers. He further maintains that the use of many Greek words betrays the bad taste of both the preachers and the hearers. On this occasion I am compelled to disagree with the opinion of our distinguished scholar. To maintain this view means to do an injustice both to the Rabbis and to the historical truth.

The Greek language took hold of all classes among all the nations in the Mediterranean world.[53] The Jews were no exception in this respect. We have already seen how deeply Greek penetrated into all the classes of Jewish society in Palestine. The Rabbis spoke to the people in their language, and if in the midst of their Aramaic speeches they often inserted Greek words[54] and expressions they had very good reasons for it.

Our Talmudic dictionaries overlooked the very important fact that the Rabbis took whole sentences from Greek proverbs current among the people, from Greek legal documents, literature and similar sources. Many Greek expressions can be understood only when taken as quotations. I shall cite a few striking instances.

וינגע ה' את פרעה נגעים גדולים ואת ביתו וגו' אמר ר' ברכיה על דטלמסן למנע בסמה דמטרונ'.[55] "'*And God plagued Pharaoh and his house with great plagues*' (Gen. XII.17). Rabbi Berechia (IV c.) said: Because he durst touch the body of the matron." If we write the Greek words in Greek script and the Aramaic in square we shall read: על ד־ ἐτόλμησεν למנע ב־ σῶμα ד־ ματρῶνα. At first sight it resembles a real jargon; it seems to support Loew's theory that the preacher sought to show off before the public by displaying his knowledge of Greek; otherwise why did he not state in plain Aramaic: על דאתחצף למנע בגופה דמטרונה.

But the suggestion of desire to impress the audience does not solve the problem. R. Berechia was one of the most famous

---

[52] "Vorbemerkung" in Krauss' LW, p. 620 seq.

[53] See the very instructive note by J. H. Moulton, Prolegomena, p. 6, n. 1.

[54] Words which did not become part of the Aramaic.

[55] TP Kethuboth VII (end), 31d.

scholars and preachers in Palestine, and his statement that God plagued Pharaoh because "he dared touch the body of the matron" must have explained the matter to his audience. We shall be able to understand it only if we consider his statement as a quotation from a source well known at that time.

We must first establish the correct reading of R. Berechia's sentence. In BR[56] we read: על דטולמיסן למקרב ל מ ס נ ה דמטרונא. Here we have למקרב למסנה (to come near the shoe) instead of למגע בסמה (to touch the body) of the TP. Whereas the reading למסנה seems to be based on a different tradition (see below), there is probably no difference of tradition in the variant למקרב and למגע; the Septuagint translates both נגע (to touch) and קרב (to come near) ἄπτεσϑαι, and we have every reason to suppose that the original Greek phrase contained this verb.

As for the syntactical structure of the sentence we may reconstruct it as: ἐτόλμησε τοῦ ματρώνης σώματος ἄψασϑαι.[57] R. Berechia was reluctant to apply to our matriarch Sara the Greek verb ἄπτεσϑαι which has a definite meaning when used in connection with a woman, and he tried to avoid it by replacing this word with the Aramaic למגע or למקרב. The introduction of the Aramaic word into the Greek sentence is now perfectly understandable.

It remains only to trace the real meaning of the phrase. Fortunately we can be helped by the context of the Midrash itself. We see there that the Rabbis wanted to understand the supreme justice of Pharaoh's punishment; since Pharaoh had only bad intentions which he did not succeed in putting into action, why was he so severely punished? It seems to me that one misunderstood word sheds light on the whole question. In BR[58] we read: על ידי שמשכה פרעה לילה אחד לקה הוא וביתו בנגעים "Because Pharaoh seized her (Sara) for one night he and his house were smitten with plagues." The word משכה is a legal term here — to seize by virtue of the law. This meaning is

---

[56] XL.2, 3892 and parallel.

[57] After the sentence of Socrates about Critobulus (Xenophon, Memor. I.3.10): ἐτόλμησε τὸν Ἀλκιβιάδου υἱὸν φιλῆσαι, "He dared kiss Alcibiades' son."

[58] Ibid. 3887 and 11561. See also Bemidbar Rabba III, 1.

rendered doubtless by the reading of a Geniza fragment[59] "שמשכנה". The verb משכן[60] is often used in Rabbinic literature as a legal term for seizure by decision of court.[61]

The Rabbis were lawyers; their mind followed the logic of the law, and they wanted to clarify the legal aspect of Pharaoh's action. They most probably knew the procedure of the Egyptian officials in their time, and they certainly possessed first hand information on life in Alexandria.[62]

They tried to picture the whole Sara-Pharaoh affair in the way of the Egypt of their own times. So, according to the picture portrayed by the Midrash,[63] Abraham had his wife in a closed carriage when he entered Egypt. The customhouse officials ordered him to open the carriage, but he refused to declare its contents saying that he was prepared to pay the highest duty as if the carriage were full of precious stones. The officials however forced him to open the carriage,[64] and then they seized her[65] and brought her before Pharaoh.

Now the question arose what offence did Pharaoh commit by temporarily seizing our matriarch Sara. This was the problem that our preacher, R. Berechia, wished to solve. He declared: "Pharaoh dared touch (=seize) the body of a matron," ἐτόλμησε

[59] Mann, The Bible as read etc. p. קצ״ב.

[60] Mann misunderstood the word משכן and he referred to his note 680 on page רכ״ב where he associates it with the text ibid. which reads: אף פרעה ואבימלך שנזדקפו לשרה. But our משכן has nothing to do with this passage. The meaning is that Pharao and Abimelech took occasion to trump up charges against Sara. In Midrash Haggadol Genes., ed. Schechter p. 401 we find: אברהם נסתקפו על אשתו וכו׳, "They trumped up charges against Abraham's wife" etc. And נזדקפו is only a variant for נסתקפו. We find this spelling of the word in Midrash Tannaim ed. Hoffmann p. 139: ושם לה עלילות דברים. התחיל מזדקף לה. "And [if] he lay shameful things to her charge (Deut. XXII.14), he began to trump up charges against her." See also Prof. L. Ginzberg's note in MGWJ vol. 78, p. 30–31.

[61] See Mishna Kethuboth XIII.8, Arakin V. 6 and elsewhere.

[62] See the abundant material recorded in S. Rapoport's ערך מלין s. v. אלכסנדריה.

[63] BR ibid. 385, Tanhuma, ed. Buber I p. 66.

[64] According to Tanhuma the officials opened the carriage against his will.

[65] Confiscated her as a beautiful slave who was about to be smuggled in.

μaτρώνηs σώματοs ἄψασθαι. This looks like the quotation of
a law which was well known at the time. Fortunately we are
able to prove it.

The Roman writer Valerius Maximus (I c.) describes[66] the
legal status of the Roman matron. He maintains[67]: *in ius
vocanti matronam corpus eius attingere non permiserunt.*
"They did not permit to touch (=seize) the body of a matron summoned to court." R. Berechia's quotation, word for word! But
R. Berechia seems to have quoted the Greek text[68] of the law.[69]

Valerius Maximus, however, did not state the punishment
for the transgression of the law. From R. Berechia's sentence
we may infer that corporal punishment was inflicted on the
transgressor. For the main point of R. Berechia's statement
was: וינגע ה' את פרעה. [לקה בגופו][70] על דטולמיסן למגע בסמה דמטרונה
"*And God plagued Pharaoh* (Gen. XII.17): [corporal punishment
was inflicted on him] since he dared touch (=seize) the body of
a matron."[71]

Now, about two hundred and fifty years later a law of
Justinian was published to the effect that a woman cannot be
imprisoned for either private or fiscal debts. The officials who
dare transgress the law will be severely punished.[72] He also
ordered the punishment of the creditors who dare seize the
children of the debtors. He says:[73] καὶ σωματικαῖς ποιναῖς
αὐτὸν καθυποβάλλεσθαι . . . ἐπειδὴ πρόσωπον ἐλεύθερον ὑπὲρ
χρέους ἐτόλμησε κατασχεῖν . . . "And corporal punishment

[66] Factorum dictorumque memorabilium II.1.

[67] Ibid., London 1823, p. 234.

[68] On the sources of Valerius Maximus see C. Bosch, Die Quellen des
Valerius Maximus p. 13 seq., p. 109 seq.

[69] Moreover, not only has part of the Greek text of this law been preserved in the Palestinian Talmud, but it is highly noteworthy that the school
of the Rabbis in Tiberias supports the tradition of the majority of codices of
Valerius Maximus' work, which read "corpus ejus," against the codices
which omit it (see the various readings ad loc.).

[70] See Shabbath 97a. Comp. also Midrash Tehilim XCII, ed. Buber p. 410.

[71] R. Levi, the teacher of R. Berachia, interpreted (BR ibid. 389₆) the
verse to mean that an angel whipped Pharaoh for his attempt to touch Sara.

[72] Novell. 134. 9.

[73] Ibid. 134.7.

shall be inflicted upon him ... since he dared seize a free person for debts[74]. . ."

R. Berechia did not preach in Greek, he only quoted part of the law in its original. But the hearers who knew Greek and were aware of the language of the law certainly appreciated R. Berechia's admirable interpretation; they caught the play of words associated with the Biblical verse and the law; they could have imagined they were listening to R. Berechia as he said in Greek: Καὶ ἥπτετο[75] ὁ κύριος τοῦ Φαραώ . . . ἀφαῖς[75] μεγάλαις (Gen. XII.17) — σωματικαῖς ποιναῖς καθυπεβλήθη, ἐπειδὴ ἐτόλμησε τοῦ ματρώνης σώματος ἅψασθαι.[76]

Thus, we now see that R. Berechia's remark is neither part of a Greek Jargon nor an attempt to show off, but an excellent application of a well known law to a Biblical narrative.

---

[74] Justinian probably made use of the contents and language of an older law which he reenacted. This older law presumably imposed corporal punishment for the illegal seizure of free persons.

[75] So Aquila.

[76] This likewise confirms the principle consistently maintained by me (Bibliographical Quaterly ספר קרית vol. XIV p. 324 seq. and Introduction to Tosefeth Rishonim IV p. 13) that we have no right to correct old Jewish texts on the authority of parallel sources. In different texts we often have different traditions. When Theodor in his commentary to BR (p. 390 n. 3, end) maintains that the reading of TP בסמה (the body) is a mere error for במסנא (the shoe), the law as recorded by Valerius Maximus entirely disproves his contention. The question, however, is whether the reading of BR למסנה is to be regarded as a mere error for לסמה. It is my conviction that we have no right to correct BR on the authority of TP. The reading of BR is confirmed by all codd. ad loc. and p. 5537. This reading was already before Tanhuma, since it reads: בא פרעה לשלוף מנעלה היה מכהו בידו, בא ליגע בבנדיה היה מכה אותו, "When Pharaoh was about to take off her shoe the angel scourged him, when he was about to touch her dress the angel flogged him." Perhaps this sentence is based upon the sermon of a preacher who enlarged R. Berechia's quotation by citing the other part of the law (Valer. Maxim. ibid.) that you are not permitted to touch the body of a matron, so that her "stolé" should remain unprofaned by the touch of a strange hand (ut inviolata manus alienae tactu stola relinqueretur). Yet Pharaoh did dare touch the body of a matron and violated her "stolé" (The Septuagint translates the word סאון — Is. IX.4 — στολή. But I do not believe that the Jews ever identified "stolé" as both shoe and dress), a crime that deserves corporal punishment.

The Rabbis' fondness of the use of legal terms will help us to elucidate one more difficult passage. TP Nedarim[77] accepts the rule that if a man takes a vow that his friend must dine with him, hereby intending to honor the invited, he is not bound by the vow if the guest cannot accept the invitation. Thereupon R. Hela (IV c., beg.) remarks: כן אורחא דבר נשא מימור לחבריה כורוסתי בייה. Jastrow in his dictionary s. v. בייא corrects the word כורוסתי to read: כריזסתי[78] and translates: "That is the way one says to his neighbor χαρίζεσθαι βίᾳ, to do a favor perforce." He transcribed the Greek words correctly, but he entirely misunderstood their real meaning in connection with the subject in the Talmud. R. Hela alluded to the very common legal formula in deeds of gift[79]: ὁμολογῶ χαρίζεσθαί σοι ... "I acknowledge that I have given you". ... The learned Rabbi remarked: "Is it the way of a man to say to his friend (to state in a deed of gift): 'I gave you perforce'?"[80] People do not behave this way when they make a present. A gift is offered with the good will of both parties; the one is desirous of giving, the other of accepting.

We therefore presume that it never occurred to the donor to enforce the acceptance of his present (in our case the invitation to a meal), and he is not bound by the vow if the guest is not able to accept the invitation.

With the aid of our method of considering the Greek expressions of the Rabbis as quotations from Greek sources we shall be able better to understand the hints and the allusions of the Rabbinic preachers.

In Shir Hashirim Rabba[81] we read: רדי ושבי על אפר ... אמר ר' חוניא כך אמרה ירושלים לבת בבל פני פילאי קקום כאמי. מחי את סבורה בעצמך שאת בתולה, זקנה את וכו'. This reading of the Greek words in the modern editions has no basis whatever. Ed. Venice[82]

---

[77] III.3, 38a.

[78] There is no need to alter so much; it is sufficient to alter only one letter, a ו into a ז (a very common mistake in mss.) and to read כורזסתי instead of כורוסתי.

[79] See Presigke s. v. χαρίζομαι.

[80] ὁμολογῶ χαρίζεσθαί σοι βίᾳ.

[81] III.4, ed. Romm 20a.

[82] 1545.

reads: 'פני פיליאי קקיס כאמי מחי את סבורה וכו. Ed. Pesaro: פני
פיליאי קקיס כאמי מאי את סבורה וכו'. But Ed. Constantinople (1520)
and Cod. Vat. read: 'פני פיליאי ק ק י ס כ א ט י מאי[83] את סבורה וכו'.
Cod. Oxf.[84] reads: 'פני פלאיי ק ק י ס ב א ט י מה את סבירא וכו'.
Yalkut Hamakiri[85] reads: 'סני פלייאי ק ק י ם כ א ט י מה וכו'.

Thus, there can be no doubt that the correct reading[86] of
the Greek phrase is [87]פני פיליאי קקיסכאטי. If we transcribe it
into Greek script without any alterations or corrections we
shall read: παγὶ παλαιὰ κακέσχατε! "You old extremely
bad trap"!

Now παγίς as an equivalent for harlot is already used by
Amphis Comicus[88] and probably by Menander[89] as well. But of
greater bearing on our subject is the passage of Lucian of
Samosata[90] about the harlot who was surnamed Trap (ἣν
Παγίδα ἐπικαλοῦσιν), and who pretended that she is not
yet twenty two: Σὺ δὲ ποτέροις πιστεύσειας ἄν, τοῖς ἐκείνης
ὅρκοις ἢ τοῖς σεαυτοῦ ὀφθαλμοῖς; ἐπίσκεψαι γὰρ ἀκριβῶς
ὑποβλέψας ποτὲ τοὺς κροτάφους αὐτῆς, ἔνθα μόνον τὰς
αὐτῆς τρίχας ἔχει· τὰ δὲ ἄλλα φενάκη βαθεῖα . . . περὶ
γὰρ τῶν ἐτῶν κἂν ὁ πάππος διηγήσεταί σοι, εἴ γε ζῇ ἔτι.
"Which are you going to believe, her oaths, or your own eyes?
Just look carefully at her temples some day; only there has she
her own hair, all the rest is a thick wig . . . As to her age, your
grandfather will tell you if he is still alive."

Here we have a true picture of a real Trap (παγίς); she
pretends that she is young when she is already all gray, she
deceives the man by artificial means. And what better name

---

[83] Cod. Vat.: מה.
[84] I am indebted to Prof. M. Kaplan who kindly supplied me with the
readings of the codd. Vat. and Oxford.
[85] Is. p. 164.
[86] As read in cod. Vat. and ed. Constantinople, supported by the reading
of cod. Oxford and Yalkut Hamakiri.
[87] In one word.
[88] As quoted in Athen., Deipnosoph. XIII, 567f. See also Kock in his
edition of the Comicorum Atticorum Fragmenta II, p. 243.
[89] Fabula incertae LXVII.
[90] Dial. meretr. XI (309).

could the oppressed Jew apply to the Roman empire than: Old extremely bad Trap! The power of Rome is only a fiction, she is already old, she lost her charms many years ago. The nations have only to look more carefully at her to see that she is weak and helpless.

Now the translation of the passage will be as follows: " *'Come down, and sit in the dust'* (Isa. XLVII.1). R. Hunia (IV c.) said: thus said Jerusalem to the daughter of Babylon[91]: 'You old extremely bad Trap, sit on the ground, do you imagine that you are a young virgin? You are really an old hag' " etc. The Rabbis utilized a popular motif current in Greek literature of the old Trap who pretends that she is ever young.[82]

The same epithet for Rome is found in the Apocal. of John XVII.1, where she is styled πόρνη μεγάλη (the great harlot); John also calls Rome — Babylon[93] and speaks of her with the same contempt. But we must admit that the expression of the Rabbis παγὶς παλαιά is much stronger than πόρνη μεγάλη.

The use of the word κακέσχατος by the Rabbis is very noteworthy from the linguistic point of view. The Greek lexicons have recorded the word only from a work ascribed to Menander Comicus:[94] Ὕπνος δὲ πεῖναν τὴν κακέσχατον δαμᾷ, "Sleep overcomes the worst hunger." One of its editors remarks[95] that no lexicon has recorded the word from any other source.[96] Here again[97] the Rabbinic school of Tiberias confirms the existence of this word.

[91] Rome. See below.

[92] The explanation of the dictionaries is against the reading of the genuine text, and cannot be taken in consideration, whereas our explanation is fully consonant with both the text and the subject.

[93] As many other authors did, see the Intern. Crit. Comm. ad loc., p. 62. Comp. also Brüll in Jeschurun, ed. Kobak, VII (1871), p. 4, n. 3.

[94] γνῶμαι μονόστιχοι 498.

[95] Brunck, ἠϑικὴ ποίησις, Lipsiae 1817, p. 326.

[96] In the latest edition of the Greek-English lexicon by Liddell and Scott this vocable has been eliminated.

[97] See above p. 32, n. 21 and p. 42, n. 69.

A "superlative" like κακέσχατος[98] is indeed in perfect harmony with the spirit of the comics, the oriental wisdom literature and the κοινή[99] which is naturally what the Greek of the Rabbis represents.

If the Rabbis, then, cited Greek secular sources we can expect them all the more to have quoted Greek translations of the Bible, whether oral or written.

The Septuagint which the Christians treated as a sacred text may have subsequently been condemned and banned by the Rabbis of Palestine,[100] and it is not to be wondered at that we do not find direct quotations from it in Rabbinic literature. Aquila, on the other hand, whom the Rabbis mention by name was too literal in his translation, and could not always be adapted to the needs of the interpreters and preachers. But there were other Greek translations of the Bible[101] current in Palestine[102] whose versions may have found their way into Rabbinic literature. A careful examination of certain passages in the Midrash will confirm this conjecture.

Midrash VayR XXX.6 interprets the difficult verse in Ezek. XXIII.42, but the passage in the printed editions is very corrupt, and the commentaries ad loc., as well as the dictionaries, are quite misleading. We shall, therefore, quote it from Cod. Oxford (No. 147): ר' יהודה בר' סימון[103] אמ' אחרי. אמר להם כשהייתם בארצכם הייתם נעשים הימוניות הימוניות לע"ז הה"ד וקול המון שליו בה ואל אנשיה מרוב אדם מובאים סבאים. מובאים, קטיסון. סבאים רווין. ויתנו צמידין על ידיהן. ר' יהודה בר' סימון אמ' קדשים (היך

[98] See Stephanus, Thesaurus etc. s. v. ἔσχατος.

[99] Comp. Durham, Donald, the Vocabulary of Menander considered in its relation to the koine p. 22 seq., ibid. p. 35.

[100] See Swete, Introduction, p. 29–30 and 41.

[101] See Max L. Margolis, the Story of Bible Translations (Philadelphia 1917) p. 40 seq.

[102] If it is the Quinta which Origen found in Palestine (See Swete ibid. p. 54 and 56), and if, as we have good reason to believe, it was actually current in that country it provides us with characteristic material for the evaluation of one of such translations.

[103] סימון is inserted above the line.

כד"א והצמידים על ידיה[104]. ואמ' לבלה ניאופים, מהו לבלה, תרגם עקילס
(בלשון יון[104] פליאה פורניא[105] וכו'.

Before undertaking a translation of the Midrash it is necessary to establish the correct reading and meaning of some
single words of this passage which explains the difficult verse in
Ezek. XXIII.42.

הימוניות. This word is the Greek ὁμόνοια, concord, harmony,
union. Our dictionaries take it to be a Midrashic play on the
Hebrew המון. But it seems very probable to me that the word
ὁμόνοια is taken from an authentic Greek translation of the
verse. The translators were very fond of rendering the Semitic
words by their Greek homophones,[106] and ὁμόνοια is an excellent homophone of המון. The Septuagint translates the verse:
"καὶ φωνὴν ἁρμονίας ἀνεκρούοντο," ἁρμονία being similar to
ὁμόνοια both in sound and meaning.

קטיסון. Codd. Brit. Mus. and Vat., Yalkut[107] and R. Samuel
Jama[108] read קטיסין. The reading of the ed. pr. קאנוסין[109] cannot
be taken into consideration against all this evidence. קטיסי is
not a Hebrew word, nor an Aramaic one; it looks like Greek.
If we transcribe it[110] into Greek script the result is κάθισαν
(=ἐκάθισαν),[111] "They seated [at the table]," a free translation
of מובאים.

---

[104] This is a gloss of a copyist which has no support whatever.

[105] The א was changed by the copyist to a ס.

[106] See Thackeray, A Grammar of the Old Testament in Greek I (Cambridge 1909) p. 37 seq. and the literature referred to by Blondheim, Les
Parlers Judeo-Romans p. CVIII, n. 4.

[107] Ezek., sect. 362 and Dan. sect. 1061.

[108] In Jubelschrift . . . Graetz, p. 42.

[109] The printer, probably, had קאטסין before him, but mistook the ט for
נו, a very common mistake in Hebrew mss.

[110] The copyists probably considered the word as an Aramaic plural and
copied קטיסין.

[111] In Rabbinic literature the Hebrew letter ט generally represents the
Greek τ, and we should accordingly write κάτισαν, the Jonic spelling for
κάθισαν (See A. Thumb, Die griechische Sprache im Zeitalter des Hellenismus, Strassburg 1901, p. 222 seq. on the abundance of the Jonic elements in
the κοινή), but since the Septuagint and other Jewish Greek sources always
spell this word with ϑ, we may presume that the ט here represents this letter.
(See L. Cohn in MGWJ vol. 44, 1900, p. 564, bottom).

רווין. This is the reading of Codd. Oxford and Vat. R. Samuel Jama[112] has דוריין, a mere corruption from רווין—drunkards.[113] Our reading רווין, drunkards, corresponds to cod. Alex. of the Septuagint (οἰνωμένους) and to Aquila's translation (μεϑυόντων). This Midrash is the only old Rabbinic source which explains סבאים to mean drunkards.

קדשים. The reading of Cod. Oxf. which cites Gen. XXIV.47 is undoubtedly an addition (which is found neither in the editions nor in Codd. Vat. and London) by a copyist who explained קדשים to mean bracelets. קדשין, however, are not bracelets but ear-rings or nose-rings.[114] Moreover, since R. Juda bar Simon was already mentioned at the beginning of the passage as the authority for the entire interpretation of the verse in Ezek., why did the Midrash reintroduce his name before the interpretation of צמידין? This indicates that for this word R. Juda offered his own "homiletic" explanation, unlike all the other interpretations of the word which were simple translations, probably quoted from authoritative versions.

It seems to me, therefore, that קדשין here means "male prostitutes."[114a] R. Juda interpreted צמידין to mean "joiners" like the verse ויצמד ישראל לבעל פעור (Num. XXV.3). Our suggestion is supported by another Midrash in which the same Rabbi employed this word. In Esther Rabba[115] we read: מעולל ... ר' יהודה בר סימון אמר ק ד ש י ן בהון. "R. Juda bar Simon said מעולל (Is. III.12) means [that their masters] prostituted them."

Thus, R. Juda explained the verse in Ezek. in terms of a voluptuous revelry with male and female prostitutes. The translation of the passage is therefore: "R. Juda bar Simon[115a]

---

[112] Jubelschrift . . . Graetz, p. 42.

[113] The dictionaries and commentaries knew only the reading of the printed editions דחיין, and tried vainly to explain it.

[114] See TP Shabbath VI, 8b; Onkelos and ps. Jonathan to Num. XXXI. 50; Paaneah Raza on Gen. XXIV.47 (ed. Amst., 13b, top). Comp. also פירוש מהרז'ו ad loc.

[114a] Comp. מתנות כהונה ad loc. which is very vague.

[115] III.2, ed. Romm 6c.

[115a] Fl. in the beginning of the IV c.

rendered it differently. He[116] told them, when you were in your
own land you used to form unanimous processions for idolatry,
as it is said (Ezek. XXIII.42): '*And the voice of a harmonious
multitude being at ease was therein.*' מובאים. (brought) means
'they[117] seated [at the table].' סבאים means 'drunkards'. '*They
put* צמידין *near their hands,*' this, R. Juda bar Simon said, refers
to the 'male prostitutes'. The verse continues: לבלה ניאופים,
what does לבלה mean? Aquila translated it: παλαιὰ πόρνη
(old harlot)" etc. Accordingly, R. Juda's conception of the
meaning of this verse is as follows: "And the voice of a harmonious multitude being at ease was therein; and with men of
the common sort they (i. e. the harlots) seated drunkards
[who came] from the wilderness. Near themselves they placed
"male prostitutes" with beautiful crowns upon their heads"
etc.

The Rabbi explained the verse in the light of the revelry of
his time; he utilized Greek translations of single words together
with his larger interpretation of the verse.

In Midrash Shemoth Rabba XV.6 we read: ברה כחמה במלכות
יון. סנדריאוס אם אוליאוס (חמה שמה)[118] והשמש גבור נקרא שנאמר ישיש
כגבור לרוץ אורח וכו'. It is obvious that the phrase אם סנדריאוס
אוליאוס is Greek, and the use of it could be justified only if the
Greek sentence is quoted in support of the assertion that the
sun is called a hero (והשמש גבור נקרא). Kohut's[119] statement that
the Greek phrase is a quotation from a recognized translation is
therefore correct. But his (and Krauss') interpretation that
סנדריאוס presents σϑεναρός — mighty — is hardly acceptable.
It presupposes excessive mutilation of the word סנדריאוס.[120] The
Septuagint translates the verse[121] יפה כלבנה ברה כחמה: ὡς καλὴ

---

[116] I. e. Nebuchadnezzar.

[117] I. e. the harlots placed drunkards at the table, [who came] from the
wilderness.

[118] The bracketed words are a gloss to אוליאוס.

[119] Aruch Completum I, p. צ"א s. v. אליאוס.

[120] It should be incidentally noted that Kohut and Krauss take the word
as a masculine adjective, although the corresponding verse (and the translation) speaks of a woman!

[121] Song of Sol. VI.10.

σελήνη, ἐκλεκτὴ ὡς ὁ ἥλιος, "Beautiful as the moon, selected
as the sun," rendering ברה as ברורה — selected.[122]

In my opinion the Greek translation quoted by the Rabbis
read: καλὴ ὡς σελήνη, ἀνδρεία ὡς ὁ ἥλιος.[123] The Hebrew
letters in the Midrash have to be only slightly corrected:
אנדרי אוס[124] או[125] איליאוס, ἀνδρεία ὡς ὁ ἥλιος, "Brave as the sun."

As for ἀνδρεία as the translation of ברה two possibilities
offer themselves: 1. that the original translator took ברה in the
figurative meaning of virtuous, and the Rabbis explained the
Greek translation as "brave"; 2. that בר had the meaning of
strong. So TP Sanhedrin[126] בָּרְרוּ לָהֶם בְּרָרוֹ[127] שֶׁל בַּרְזֶל, "They
selected the strength of iron." The parallel source[128] states
clearly: נִתַּן לְדִבְרֵי תוֹרָה כֹּחַ שֶׁל בַּרְזֶל, "The strength of iron was
given to the words of the Law."

Similarly, Yalkut[129] quotes from Yelamdenu: מי יוכל לראות
פני אחד מהם כדו בברזל. But Aruch s. v. בדה quotes בדידין

<hr>

[122] The word ברור "selected" is a usual attribute in Rabbinic literature.
So Sifre II sec. 21, ed. Finkelstein p. 33: מן הברורים שבכם, מן המסולתים שבכם.
Likewise in a Midrash-fragment (Mann The Bible as read, etc., p. ס׳נ) we
read: אדם ברור שכמותך. The so called "Covenant of Damascus" (ed. Schechter
p. 104) records: אנשים ברורים (See Prof. L. Ginzberg's note in his book "Eine
unbekannte jüdische Secte p. 67), and ps. Jonathan to Deut. I.23 has the
expression: גוברין ברירין. Comp. also BR XXIII.2, 223₂ (and variants ibid.)
and פיוטי יניי ed. Zulay p. 21.

[123] The Hebrew אשת חיל is rendered by the Septuagint γυνὴ ἀνδρεία.
See Prov. XII.4 and elsewhere. Tobit (VI.12, Sinaitic text) reads: τὸ
κοράσιον ... ἀνδρεῖον καὶ καλὸν λίαν, "The maid is brave (or skilful) and very
beautiful," which proves that καλὴ καὶ ἀνδρεία was a conventional phrase
in praise of women.

[124] Yalkut Hamakiri, Joel p. 38, reads: סאנדריאוס. A copyist who was
accustomed to the group of letters סנדרי (in words like סנדרין, אלכסנדר,
אלכסנדריאה) perhaps altered אנדרי into סנדרי and combined the two words
אנדרי אוס into one word. Yet, I hesitate to correct the text against the evidence
of the editions, Cod. Oxf. and Makiri. Perhaps סנדרי represents ζανδρεία,
very brave. See Liddell and Scott s. v. ζα-.

[125] Instead of אם.

[126] X.1, 28a. I quote from the Yerushalmi Fragments ed. Ginzberg 262₃₀.

[127] Midrash Koheleth Rabba (towards the end) ed. Pesaro reads: ובירדו
שֶׁל בַּרְזֶל, but the later editions (ed. Rom 31a) have: וכדורות(!) שֶׁל בַּרְזֶל.

[128] Bemidbar Rabba XIV.4, ed. Rom 58d.

[129] I, sec. 743 (only in ed. Salonica 241c).

בברזל, which seems to me to be an erroneous reading (in Yelamdenu) for ברייין כברזל. The translation of the passage in
Yelamdenu will accordingly be: "Who can see the face of one
of them[130]? They are as strong as iron."[131]

The passage of the Midrash Shemoth Rabba will therefore
be translated: " 'Strong as the sun' (Song of Sol. VI.10) refers
to the Greek kingdom; brave as the sun, for the sun is called a
hero, as it is said (Ps. XIX.6): 'He rejoiceth as a strong man to
run his course'."

Again, we read in Yelamdenu:[132] ברך נבות אלהים ומלך. ברך
בלספימיסון, שנא' ובוצע ברך נאץ ה'. " 'Naboth did bless[133] God and
the King' (I Kings XXI.13), ברך [means here] did blaspheme,
as it is said (Ps. X.3): 'And when the covetous[134] blesseth he
blasphemeth God'." The inflected form[135] betrays a quotation.[136]
Most probably we have here a quotation from a Greek translation of the Bible, which rendered the word ברך: ἐβλασφήμησε.
It is very noteworthy that the Septuagint translates this verb[137]

---

[130] I. e. who can face them in battle, see II Kings XIV.8, 11. Similarly,
we read in Pesiktha deR. Kahana 130a: לנבור ... שהוא יוצא ומראה להם
פנים, מיד הן בורחין, "Like a hero ... who when he faces them in battle he
causes their immediate flight." Buber (Eka Rabba p. 59 n. קפ"ח) misunderstood the expression. He also failed to note that all other editions of Eka
Rabba agree with the Pesiktha.

[131] See the unsuccessful attempts to explain these difficult words in
Grünhut's Sefer Ha-likkutim IV, p. ל and in the Hebrew periodical האשכול
VI, p. 210, note.

[132] As quoted in Aruch s. v. בלספימיסון.

[133] Euphemism for curse.

[134] See the Rabbinic interpretation of the verse in Tosephta Sanhedrin
I.2, 415₁₀ seq. (and parallels); TP Halla I.9, 58a; Sifre II, sec. 17, ed. Finkelstein p. 29 and elsewhere.

[135] בלספימיסון, βλασφήμησεν, ἐβλασφήμησεν.

[136] In TP Kiddushin III.4, 64a we find: איפרסן לוי, "Levi became poor"
(ἠπόρησεν, נתרושש), a grammatical form corresponding to ours, in an ordinary
phrase. However the real meaning of the word is not quite sure. See the
responsum of Ramban in ספרן של ראשונים ed. Assaf p. 94 and n. 2 ibid.; Me'iri
quoted in אוצר הגאונים on Gittin I p. 23. It is also probable that we have
there a quotation from a legal document (a legal term) designating a man
without means, from whom certain debts can not be collected.

[137] Both in our verse as well as in Job I.11; ibid. II.5.

εὐλογεῖν. The same Greek word is employed by Aquila as the equivalent of the euphemistic ברך[138]— a literal translation.

But the 'Εβραῖος translates יברכך (Job II.5): βλασφημήσει σε.[139] In the same way, Josephus in his account of the story of Naboth and Ahab[140] utilizes this verb: ὡς τὸν θεόν τε εἴη βλασφημήσας καὶ τὸν βασιλέα . . . βλασφημῆσαι τὸν θεόν τε καὶ Ἀχαβον.

Thus, the Rabbis used a translation (or translations) which rendered מובאים by ἐκάθισαν, יפה וברה by καλὴ καὶ ἀνδρεία, the euphemistic ברך by ἐβλασφήμησε etc.,[141] a translation which (unlike Aquila's) was both elegant, free and at the same time faithful to the text.[142]

Likewise TP Berakoth[143] reads: בשעה . . . המביט לארץ ותרעד שהקב״ה מביט בבתי תיטריות ובבתי קרקסיות יושבות בטח ושאנן ושלוה ובית מקדשו חרב הוא אפילון לעולמו להחריבו וכו'. " 'Who looketh on the earth, and it trembleth' (Ps. CIV.32) . . . When the Holy one blessed be He looks down on the theatres and circuses as they stand secure, at ease and in peace while His Temple is destroyed, He אפילון at His world to destroy it." The reading אפילון is absolutely sure. So also Shir-Hashirim Rabba (towards the

---

[138] In Job I.5, 11; ibid. II.5, 9.

[139] Comp. ps. Jonathan to I Kings ad loc. and Field, Hexapla Job II.9, n. 24.

[140] Antiq. VIII.13.8, 358 seq.

[141] See the following instances.

[142] These characteristic features correspond to the general character of the 'Εβραῖος (See Field Prolegomena p. LXXV seq.). It seemed to be more or less a free translation in the Jewish spirit. So he followed a Jewish tradition by rendering לדבורה (Isa. VII.18) by σφηκί — לצרעה —, as can be inferred from a Baraitha (quoted in TB Shabbath 121b) which mentions together זבוב שבארץ מצרים וצירעה שבנינוה, evidently in allusion to our verse (as correctly observed by R. Samuel Straschun — רש״ש — in his notes ad loc.). He again followed a Jewish tradition when he rendered מה אפעל לך (Job VII.20) by τί σε ἔβλαψα. The Rabbinic aphorism (Debarim Rabba ed. Lieberman p. 70) ואם תשנאהו מה אתה מזיקו, ואם תאהבהו מה אתה מהנו, "If thou hatest Him what harm dost thou to Him, if thou lovest Him how dost thou benefit Him", which was formed after the parallel verses (Job XXXV.6–7. See my note in Debarim Rabba ad loc.) confirms the translation.

[143] IX.3, 13c (and parallels).

end), ed. Pesaro:[144] אפילון להחריבו לעולמו. The dictionaries explain אפילון to mean ἀπειλῶν, threatening, but this interpretation is impossible. It is difficult to comprehend why in the middle of the Hebrew phrase the Talmud should have used a Greek word which was not current in Palestinian Aramaic, since it occurs only in this passage (and parallels). The use of the participle "הוא ἀπειλῶν" is also out of place. Jastrow must have realized these difficulties, for he remarked[145]: "probably taken from Aquila to Ps. CIV.32," but this free translation is hardly in the spirit of Aquila.

Therefore it seems to me that Ehrlich[146] was on the right track in taking[147] the word as ἐπιλλῶν (=ἐπιλλίζων), looking askance, winking.

The exact meaning of ἐπιλλῶ is not yet established[148]; it may also mean to look indignantly.[149] The gloss in Yalkut and Aruch,[150] which explained אפילון as מסתכל, seems to be correct, for מסתכל means also to look indignantly.[151] The Targum of Ps. CIV.32 translates indeed: דמסתכל לארעא. The Septuagint renders: ὁ ἐπιβλέπων ἐπὶ τὴν γῆν. But it is very likely that the Greek translation employed by the Rabbis rendered it: ὁ ἐπιλλῶν τῇ γῇ, "Who looketh (angrily) at the earth."

---

[144] read: לעולמו להחריבו. Yalkut I sec. 863 quotes from TP: הוא מסתכל, באפלון עולמו להחריבו, where the word מסתכל is a gloss to אפלון. The original reading, beyond any doubt, was: הוא אפלון בעולמו להחריבו. The same gloss is found in Aruch s. v. אפליון in a quotation from Yelamdenu: אותה שעה מסתכל אפליון של עולם והוא מזדעזע שנא' המביט לארץ ותרעד. The correct reading is: אותה שעה אפליון לעולם (See also Tanhuma ed. Buber I p. 8, n. 72). Midrash Tehilim XVIII.12, ed. Buber 142 reads: מחרה אפו בעולמו, but Yalkut II sec. 158 quotes from it: חרה אפו בעולמו which has to be corrected: הוא אפי' (=אפילון) בעולמו.

[145] Dictionary s. v. אפילון.

[146] Referred to by Loew in Krauss' LW, p. 106.

[147] MGWJ 1897, p. 480.

[148] See the long article on Ἴλλω and its derivatives in Stephanus' Thesaurus vol. VII, p. 11080 seq.

[149] See Steph. ibid.

[150] See above n. 144.

[151] See the material quoted in my הירושלמי כפשוטו I, p. 289, n. 2. Comp. also Pesiktha deR. Kahana 137a.

The translator of *Psalms* may have used this verb in the same sense as Homer in his *hymns*. Hermes exclaimed: "I shall avenge me on him for this pitiless accusation, mighty as he is" etc. Homer concludes the scene with:[152] ὧς φάτ' ἐπιλλίζων Κυλλήνιος Ἀργειφόντης· "So spake Cyllenian the Argus-slayer looking indignantly."

The Talmud quoted the Greek translation of the verse because ἐπιλλῶν was much more explicit than the ambiguous מסתכל. The participle "הוא אפילון" is now perfectly in place as a translation of המביט.

Again, we read in Vayyikra Rabba:[153] הצדא שדרך מישך ועבד נגו. מהו הצדא ר' אבא בר כהנא אמר אונטיס[154] וכו'. "'*Hazeda, O Shedrach, Meshach and Abed-Nego*' (Dan. III.14), what does 'Hazeda' mean? R. Abba bar Kahana[155] said: 'it means ὄντως'" (really, in truth). Although this word existed in Syriac it is not extant in Palestinian non-Greek literature (with the exception of the above). Thus it is most likely that R. Abba quoted an authoritative Greek translation in support of his view.[156] The Septuagint translates the word: διὰ τί, "why", but the Theodotionic version renders it: Εἰ ἀληθῶς which is the same as ὄντως.[157] Tanhuma[158] reads אמת instead of ὄντως; Aggadath Bereshith[159] reads קושטא[160] which is the equivalent of ὄντως.[161] Thus, the Greek version of Daniel used by the Rabbis in Palestine[162] during the third century was close to that of Theodotion.[163]

[152] Mercur. 387 seq.
[153] XXX.6 (and parallels).
[154] Read with parallels: אונטוס.
[155] Fl. III–IV c.
[156] As contrary to the opinion of R. Jose bar Hanina (See ibid. ad loc.).
[157] Comp. the expression ὄντως τε καὶ ἀληθῶς, really and truly. See Liddell and Scott s. v. ὄντως.
[158] נח sec. 10, ed. Buber sec. 15.
[159] VII, ed. Buber p. 16.
[160] See Buber ad loc., note 5.
[161] So Sym. to Gen. XLII.21, Ἑβραῖος to II Kings IV.14 translate אבל. Comp. BR. 11303.
[162] Comp. Swete, Introduction p. 46 seq.
[163] The verse (Esth. III.14) פתשגן הכתב (A copy of the writing) is explained by Midrash Rabba ad loc. as meaning: דאיגרתא (so ed. pr.) אנטיגרפון. The Septuagint translates it: ἀντίγραφα τῶν ἐπιστολῶν. I do not believe

Finally, we may refer to an anonymous statement in Midrash Shemoth Rabba,[164] which renders in Greek all the stones of the breastplate of the High Priest (Exod. XXVIII.17–20).

A. Epstein was the first to call attention[165] to the various Midrashic sources dealing with the definitions of the stones of the breastplate. W. Bacher published a long article[166] on this subject, where he compared the list in our Midrash to that of the Septuagint, of Josephus, of the Apocalypse[167] and the Targumim. Translations of the names of the stones, both oral and written, existed among the Jews until late mediaeval times.[168] Many glossaries containing such translations were discovered in various countries.[169] A large number of them were republished and commented upon by Blondheim[170] who also joined to them a comparative study on their relation to the Septuagint and the Vetus Latina. To these we may add the important list found in Hiskuni's[171] commentary[172] on the Pentateuch, which differs in some cases from all the glossaries[173] published by Blondheim. For our subject only the list of the Midrash (which differs entirely from all the glossaries) is of

that we have here a quotation from the Septuagint, for ἀντίγραφον seems to have been a term current in government offices for the copy of a document. Both the translators and the Rabbis employed independently of one another the official language prevalent at that time. The same can be said about many similar words which merely represented the current terms of the time.

[164] XXXVIII.8. R. Isaac who is mentioned in the Midrash ibid. has probably nothing to do with this statement.

[165] מקדמוניות היהודים p. 83 seq.

[166] REJ vol. XXIX (1894) p. 79 seq.

[167] XXI.19 seq. Comp. The Intern. Crit. Comment. ibid., p. 165 seq.

[168] See J. Perles, Beitraege zur Gesch. der hebr. und aram. Studien (Munich, 1884) p. 123, Blondheim, Les Parlers Judeo-Romans p. LXXIII, n. 1.

[169] See Blondheim ibid. and Bacher JQR OS XVII, p. 803.

[170] Ibid. p. LXXV and LXXVI seq.

[171] Fl. XIII c.

[172] Ed. Cremona 1559, p. 79b.

[173] Hiskuni does not mention the source he drew from, but it must have been a written one, since he twice states that he found a gloss to the interpretations he records. Most probably he had before him a glossary similar to those current in France.

importance. Bacher published it from a modern edition of the Midrash whose readings have no basis in fact. He, accordingly, reached the erroneous conclusion that in the interpretation of the Midrash seven names out of the twelve are identical with those of the Septuagint. We shall copy the passage from the ed. pr. of the Midrash and collate it with Cod. Oxford:[174]

ראובן שדרגנין. שמעון שומפוזין.[175] לוי דייקינתין.[176] יהודה כרכרינין.[177] יששכר סנפירינון.[178] זבולון אזמרגדין. דן כוחלין.[179] נפתלי אבא טיס.[180] גד הימיסיון. אשר קרומטסין.[181] יוסף פראלוקין.[182] בנימין מרגליטוס.

Bacher (following Mussaphia) corrects the first name to שרדנגין.[183] Kohut[184] identifies שרדנין with σαρδονύχιον,[185] a derivative of σαρδόνυξ, the name given to this stone by Josephus and the Apocalypse.[186] The Septuagint translates it: σάρδιον. The second name שומפוזין is correctly altered by Kohut[187] and Bacher into טומפוזין — τοπάζιον,[188] the name given by the Septuagint. The name of the third stone is דייקינתי—ὑάκινθος.[189] The Septuagint has: σμάραγδος. The fourth stone is כרכרינין (read: כרכדינין) — καρχηδόνιος, carchedonius, which is the same

[174] =א. I do not record the readings of cod. Oxford when they are literally the same as in ed. pr.

[175] א: שומיפזין.

[176] א: דייקנטין.

[177] א: ברקורינון.

[178] א: ספרינין.

[179] א: בירולין.

[180] א: אבא טוב.

[181] א: ברומשסין.

[182] א: פדלוקין.

[183] This correction is supported by some of the glossaries mentioned above. Hiskuni records: (alemandine) שרדנא. ומצאתי בהגהה אלמנדינא.

[184] Aruch Completum s. v.

[185] More probably σαρδονύχιν, the vulgar Greek suffix ιν for ιον. See Sophocles, lexicon, Grammatical observations, p. 35b; Jean Psichari, Bibliothèque de l'école des hautes études vol. 92 (Paris 1892) p. 160; E. Mayser, Grammatik der griechischen Papyri Band I, Teil II (Leipzig 1938) p. 15–16. In our transcriptions here we shall however adhere to the classical form.

[186] See Bacher ibid.

[187] Aruch Comp. VIII, 41b.

[188] For the m before p and b see Bacher ibid. Comp. also Blondheim, Les Parlers Judeo-Romans p. XXXI, n. 9; ibid. p. 126.

[189] See Bacher ibid., p. 84, n. 4.

as carbunculus,[190] or ἄνθραξ of the Septuagint.[191] The fifth is
סנפירינון (or as Cod. Oxf. ספרינין) — σαπφείρινον. The Septuagint
renders it σάπφειρος. Almost all translations agree with it.[192]
The sixth is אזמרגדין — σμάραγδος. The Septuagint has ἴασπις.
The seventh is בירולין[193]— βηρύλλιον. The Septuagint has
λιγύριον. The eighth is אבא טיס which was correctly altered by
the dictionaries into אכאטיס — ἀχάτης, the name recorded in the
Septuagint. The ninth is הימיסין. The word is corrupted. Very
probably the correct reading is אמטיסטון[194]— ἀμέθυστος, the rendering of the Septuagint and the glossaries. The tenth is
קרומטסין.[195] Ps.-Jonathan and Targum Yerushalmi ad loc. translate כרום ימא. It therefore seems to me that (קרומטסין) כרומטסין
should be changed into כרומט[ל]סין — χρῶμα θαλάσσιον[196] which
is exactly the semitized כרום ימא. The Septuagint translates the
name of this stone χρυσόλυθος. The eleventh is פראלוקין[197]—
παράλευκον or περίλευκον.[198] The Septuagint renders it: βηρύλλιον. The twelfth is מרגליטוס[199]— μαργαρίτης. The word in the
Septuagint is ὀνύχιον.

Thus, the Greek source of our Midrash translated the
names of the breastplate-stones: 1. σαρδονύχιον. 2. τοπάζιον.
3. ὑάκινθος. 4. καρχηδόνιος. 5. σαπφείρινον. 6. σμάραγδος.
7. βηρύλλιον. 8. ἀχάτης. 9. ἀμέθυστος. 10. χρῶμα θαλάσσιον.
11. παράλευκον. 12. μαργαρίτης.

---

[190] Vetus Latina, Vulgata, Glossaries and Hiskuni.

[191] Bacher and the dictionaries quoted the reading of the modern editions
ברדינין which cannot be considered seriously. Their interpretations are
accordingly to be eliminated from the lexicons.

[192] Because it is based on Hebrew ספיר.

[193] So cod. Oxford. The reading of ed. pr. כוחלין is a very natural corruption of this word.

[194] Bacher suggests: אמסיסטון.

[195] ברומשסין of cod. Oxf. is to be corrected into כרומטסין.

[196] Plut. (Moralia, de Pythiae orac. 2, 395b) describes the color of the
bronze as θαλαττίους τῇ χρόᾳ.

[197] Cod. Oxf. פדלוקין, an obvious mistake for פרלוקין.

[198] Bacher ibid.

[199] The spelling מרגליטוס instead of the usual מרגניתא, מרגליתא proves that
we have here a direct transcription of a Greek source into Hebrew characters,
whereas in all other places the Aramaic מרגליתא or מרגניתא is retained.

When we compare our list to those of the Septuagint and the glossaries (which on the whole followed the latter) we see how greatly it differs from them. The Rabbis drew from an old Greek translation of the Bible, which widely diverged from the Septuagint.

The dependence of the Jewish preachers in Palestine on Greek translations of the Bible was probably much greater than we can judge from the material preserved in Midrashic literature. It is only natural that a preacher in a synagogue where the Shema was read in Greek quoted verses of the Bible accompanied by their standard Greek translations.[200] The latter were probably eliminated either when the sermons were recorded in writing or when the Midrashim were compiled. Yet it seems to me that a remnant of such a quotation has been preserved in Pesiktha deR. Kahana 131a: פיסיאו[201] פיספיסאי תנחומא ר' אמר .אינון עבדין ואת עבד, אינון עבדין ועזבני והפר את בריתי ואנת עבדית וכו' "R. Tanhuma[202] said: פיספיסאי פיספיסאי, they act and You act, they act [as it is said]: '*And [they] will forsake me and break my covenant*' (Deut. XXXI.16) and You act" etc. Although the words פיספיסאי פיספיסאי (or פיסיאו of the printed ed.) are corrupted it is quite obvious that the passage contains a Greek phrase bearing on the words "they act and You act," that is, You will act as they acted. This connection between the two sentences was already noted by Jastrow in his dictionary s. v. פיספיסאי, but he missed the main point.

It is most probable that R. Tanhuma introduced here a verse from the Prophets corresponding to the verse of the Pentateuch. A very adequate verse to בריתי את והפר ועזבני (Deut. XXXI.16) is: להפר אלה בזית עשית כאשר אותך ועשיתי ברית (Ezek. XVI.59), "*And I will deal with thee as thou hast done who hast despised the oath in breaking the covenant.*" And it is the Greek translation of this verse, which R. Tanhuma inserted into his sermon. He said: "[ס]פוספיאי פיסווסאי, ποιήσω σοι ὅπως ποίησας,[203] '*I shall deal with thee as thou hast done*',

---

[200] Even when they were not necessary to support the preacher's interpretation.

[201] Cod. Oxf. פיספיאי.   [202] Fl. IV c.

[203] = ἐποίησας.

they act and You act" etc. The Septuagint translates this verse:[204] ποιήσω σοι καθὼς ἐποίησας.

But it is, of course, possible that the phrase, even if its source is the Bible, was current as a proverb, and was cited as such by R. Tanhuma.

Single Greek words were introduced by the Haggadists not because they wanted to show off, but for very good reasons growing out of rhetorical technique. In a fragment of an old Yelamdenu Midrash published by the late Prof. Mann[205] we read: ויהי בדרך במלון ויפגשהו ה' וגו'. למה ביקש לחונקו, אילא אמ' לו האי'ם: אני שלחתיך שתלך ותגאל את בניי שהן בצרה, וישבת לך במלון, ספאטאלון, לכך ויבקש המיתו. " 'And it came to pass on the way at the lodging that God met him' (Exod. IV.24) etc. Why did he want to strangle him (i. e. Moses)? God said to him: 'I have sent thee to go and redeem my children that are in distress, and thou sittest in a lodging ספאטאלון', and therefore 'He sought to kill him' (Exod. ibid.)." But what does ספאטאלון mean? Mann identified it with ὀσπιτάλιον — hotel.[206] He overlooked the important fact that this very passage of the Yelamdenu was quoted by R. Samuel Jama in his lexicon:[207] בילמדנו, בואלה שמות פ' (=) פסוק) ויאמר ה' אל משה בלכתך לשוב מצרימה: א ס פ ט ל י ן, מיד ויפגשהו ה' ויבקש המיתו. The editor remarks that Jama quoted only the word and not the sentence; he further observes that the word is not found in our editions of Tanhuma. O. H. Schorr in his review[208] of Buber's edition of Jama's lexicon concluded: There is no doubt that אספטלין means hospis, hospitalia.

If Schorr and Mann are right in their explanation of the word we should have to agree that the use of ὀσπιτάλιον instead of the Hebrew מלון displays bad taste on the part of the preacher. But, happily, we are able to trace the correct meaning of this word in the Hebrew-Persian dictionary of R. Solomon ben

[204] Cod. Al.

[205] The Bible as read etc., p. ק'ב.

[206] If that is true we have to suppose that the Hebrew word מלון was a gloss to the Greek ὀσπιτάλιον.

[207] Jubelschrift ... Graetz, p. 29.

[208] החלוץ Vol. XIII, p. 114.

Samuel (XIV c.), extracts of which were published by Bacher.[209]
The latter made a special list of the unidentified words recorded
in this dictionary, and he counted[210] among them[211] אספטלון. בי כאר
and[212] אפפטלון. באטל, בי כאר.

Despite Bacher's alleged failure to recognize the words[213] he
correctly conjectured that they must be of Greek origin. And
indeed, the correct explanation in the dictionary בי כאר (otiosus,
idle, at leisure) guides us towards the discovery of the Greek
original of the word. It is σπάταλος, σπαταλῶν, luxurious, idle.

The abstract form of this word can almost surely be traced
in other sources, although it was misunderstood by the modern
lexicons and commentaries. In BR[214] we read: כי גר יהיה
זרעך וגו'... אמר ר' יודן גירות עבדות עינוי בארץ לא להם. א ר ב ע[215]
מ א ו ת ש נ ה לאספטיה שלהם " 'That thy seed shall be sojourners'
etc. (Gen. XV.13)... R. Judan said:—גירות—the status of
sojourners in a land that is not theirs implies slavery and suf-
fering. 'Four hundred years' (Gen. ibid.) beginning with their
אספטיה." But the best ms. of BR, Cod. Vat., reads: לאיספטליא;
the margin of Cod. Brit. Mus. records: אספטילי which is σπατάλη,
leisure.

R. Judan explained that the four hundred years which are
not accounted for by the actual slavery of the Jews in Egypt
extend to the time when the seed of Abraham began to dwell in
a strange land.[216] From that time the Bible regards them as
slaves, even though they enjoyed leisure. The idea is more
explicit in the parallel sources. So Shir-Hashirim Rabba II
(towards the end): רבי יודן אמר גירות ועבדות בארץ לא להם. א פ י ל ו
באיספטלייה שלהם "R. Judan said: 'In a land that is not theirs'
(Gen. XV.13) their condition is that of aliens and slaves even

---

[209] Ein Hebraeisch-Persisches Woerterbuch, Budapest 1900.

[210] Hebrew part p. 47, No. 110.

[211] Bacher translates the Persian: otiosus, iners.

[212] Ibid. p. 48, No. 139. It is quite obvious that אפפטלון is a scribal error
for אספטלון, and the dictionary indeed assigned to it the same meaning as
to אספטלון.

[213] German part, p. 85, n. 5.

[214] XLIV.18, 440s.

[215] So cod. Vat. and Yalkut.

[216] I. e. from the time of the birth of Isaac.

when they are [free and] at leisure."²¹⁷ It is very noteworthy
that Aruch s. v. פלטיא II quotes from the Pesiktha:²¹⁸ אפילו על
פ ל ט י א שלהם. ס"א אספפלטיא פי' מנוחה. There is no doubt that we
have to read: ס"א אספטליא.²¹⁹ One ms. of the Aruch²²⁰ reads
indeed: ספר א' אספטליה. The Aruch's interpretation of אספטליה
(=σπατάλη) by מנוחה, rest, leisure is perfectly correct.²²¹

Since in all the above mentioned sources we find only the
abstract noun of σπαταλεῖν, whereas the Hebrew-Persian
dictionary quotes the adjective or the participle, we may assume
that the latter, like R. Samuel Jama, drew from the Yelamdenu.

Thus, the real meaning of אספטלון) ספאטאאלון) is not ὁσπι-
τάλιον — hotel, but σπαταλῶν, in luxury, in idleness, namely:
"Thou sittest in a lodging in luxury and idleness." The same
word was used by a contemporary of our preacher²²² to translate
the Syriac מפנקא. Eusebius quotes²²³ from Bardesan: ἀνδρείους
καὶ σπαταλούς. The Syriac original of Bardesan²²⁴ reads:
חליצא ומ"פקא which is an obvious mistake for חליצא ומפנקא, as
observed by many scholars.²²⁵ The Hebrew equivalent of σπα-

---

²¹⁷ See also Pesiktha deR. Kahana 47b n. 96 and Pesiktha Rabbathi ed.
Friedmann 71a.

²¹⁸ Ibidem.

²¹⁹ Like Pesiktha l. c., ed. pr.

²²⁰ Cod. Jewish Theological Seminary No. 0429.

²²¹ Jastrow, dictionary p. 53, identifies the word we are treating with the
Greek ἰσοπολιτεία, whereupon Loew remarks (LW p. 37) that this explanation is the best contribution of the whole book of Jastrow and that
the identification is undoubtedly correct. However, we cannot agree with
this remark: firstly, the contribution is not Jastrow's but Bruell's (Jahrb.
1883, Vol. V, p. 120); secondly, the identification is undoubtedly wrong, in
view of all the material adduced above. The word ἰσοπολιτεία has to be
eliminated from the Talmudo-Midrashic lexicons.

²²² The composition and the language of our Midrash-fragment show that
the "Derashoth" are most probably of the IV century.

²²³ Praep. Ev. VI, 10, 276a.

²²⁴ Book of the Laws of Countries, ed. Cureton p. ה"י. Composed in the
middle of the second century.

²²⁵ See Schulthess, ZDMG, 1910, p. 92. The latter contends that our
Syriac text is a translation from Greek; since חליצא (vigorous) and מפנקא
(lascivious) are almost antonyms he suggests that the translator was misled by
the wrong reading of the Greek: ἀνδρείους instead of ἀνάνδρους (effeminate).
Noeldeke, on the other hand, maintains (ibid. p. 555 seq.) that the Syriac

ταλῶν would be מתפנק, but the preacher preferred the Greek word on account of the alliteration — במלון ספאטאלון — which is much more rhythmical than במלון מתפנק.[226]

Finally, we have to question Loew's method of listing *all* rare Greek words occurring in the Midrash as foreign words and not as loan words. In Debarim Rabba (V.8) we read: כל מי שנשען בבשר ודם עובר, אף פרוסטיה שלו עוברת וכו'. Fürst (in his Glossarium) corrected פרוסטיה into פרוסטטיה — προστατεία, and his correction is corroborated by the reading in Debarim Rabba ed. Lieberman p. 99. The translation is therefore: "He who relies on a mortal man passes away, and his patronage passes away." Loew[227] classified the word προστατεία among the foreign words, since it is found only once in the whole Rabbinic literature.

text is undoubtedly the original, and that vigour and courage do not exclude lasciviousness; a person can be courageous, vigorous and lascivious at the same time. A careful reading of the Syriac text is sufficient to convince one that the truth lies with Noeldeke. See also below p. 99 n. 30. As for the reading חליצא ומפנקא it seems to me that חליצא here is synonymous with מפנקא. It is stated in VayR (XXXIV.15) that יחליץ is the same as ינח, "he will set at ease." חליצא ומפנקא means therefore: at ease and lascivious. The Latin translation in Recogn. IX.22 (see Schulthess ibid.): "effeminatos et dissolutos" is perfectly correct. It is the Greek translator who mistakenly took the word חליצא in its usual sense and translated it: ἀνδρείους.

[226] This Yelamdenu fragment published by Mann is one of the most important portions of this Midrash. Mann in his Foreword p. צ"ו pointed out its importance. He observed that we find in this short fragment Greek words that are not found anywhere else in Rabbinic literature. But he is wrong in the interpretation of some words. In addition to ספאטאלון we may cite the following: כבד פה וכבד לשון אנוכי (שמות ד' י') א' ר' לעזר פיקופסלום. Mann (n. 48) corrects the last word into פיקרופסלוס, πικροψελλός. In my opinion, there is no need to alter the text. פיקופסלום means πυκιψελλός, a thick stammerer. The form πυκι — instead of πυκνο — is usual in poetry and might have been familiar in the koiné (See A. Thumb, Die griechische Sprache im Zeitalter des Hellenismus p. 216 seq., on the poetic elements in the koiné). It may further be noted that this statement of R. Eleazar is already quoted (from our Midrash?) in Debarim Rabba ed. Lieberman p. 5. The description of the procedure in the Roman courts is already available in BR and elsewhere (see my note in Debarim Rabba p. 18 n. 18), a fact which Mann (p. צ"ו) overlooked. See also below p. 176 seq.

[227] In Krauss' LW p. 674.

But the idea of patronage was well known in those days, yet we find in Talmudic literature no other word conveying this concept. We have therefore no right to treat פרוסטטיה as a foreign word. Moreover, the Rabbis were quite consistent in their terminology in connection with patronizing. They always used the foreign word פטרון, πάτρων, patronus, which they even declined פטרוני, פטרונך, פטרונו.[228] But for the verb patronize they used the Semitic להתקיים על or the Hebrew לעמוד על. So, for instance, we read in TP Berakoth:[229] בשר ודם יש לו פטרון ... אמר אני מתקיים עליו "A mortal man has a patron ... he said I shall protect him" etc., and we find this expression seven times in that one page of TP.[230] Likewise, we read in Shemoth Rabba XI.2: שפלוני פטרונו עומד עליו, "That his patron such and such will protect him."[231]

Attention should also be called to the Epistle to the Hebrews V.1: πᾶς γὰρ ἀρχιερεὺς ἐξ ἀνθρώπων λαμβανόμενος, ὑπὲρ ἀνθρώπων καθίσταται τὰ πρὸς τὸν θεόν etc. The Vulgate translates it: Omnis namque pontifex ex hominibus assumptus, pro hominibus constituitur in iis quae sunt ad Deum etc. The usual English translation is: "For every high priest being taken from among men *is appointed* for men in things pertaining to God."

But in the Palestinian Syriac fragments[232] we read: כול גר ריש כהנין דמתנסב מן בנינשא על בנינשא הוא מתקים על לות אלהא. According to this translation "καθίσταται ὑπέρ" means מתקים על, עומד על in its usual Palestinian meaning: stands for, protects — "the high priest protects men before God." This is most likely the real meaning of the sentence. The author of the Epistle was alluding to the epithet of the high priest as προ-

---

[228] See ibid. p. 438.

[229] IX.1, 13a.

[230] Bacher in his ADPA III, p. 337 translates מתקיים על "feindselig verhalten"! In note 8 ibid. he maintains that judging from the context there can be no other translation of this expression! But he entirely misunderstood the context; see the right interpretation of it in the Hebrew Quarterly "Tarbiz" Vol. III (1932) p. 450 seq.

[231] See also BR LXIX.3, p. 792₈ and Theodor's note ad loc., Schulthess, Lexicon Syropalaestinum p. 177 s. v. מקמא.

[232] Ed. Schulthess, (Berlin 1905) p. 81.

στάτης τοῦ ἔϑνους.[233] Josephus[234] expresses himself: τὴν δὲ
προστασίαν τοῦ ἔϑνους οἱ ἀρχιερεῖς ἐπεπίστευντο.
"And the high priests were entrusted with the patronage over
the nation." The author of the Epistle to the Hebrews made
excellent use of this phrase. The high priest, the προστάτης
τοῦ ἔϑνους, is really entrusted with the protection of men
before God.[235]

The substantive of the verb להתקיים, the קיומא (patron) is
preserved in the Palmyrene bilingual inscriptions.[236] The Palmyrene reads: רחמה וקיומה and the Greek: φίλον καὶ προστά-
την. Thus קיומה is the Semitic translation of προστάτης, a term
which generally meant patron or something similar to it.[237]

Moreover, it is very noteworthy that we find the word קיומא
in the meaning of patron in the Palestinian Talmud:[238] ואמרתם
כה לחי לקיומא. ואתה שלום ונו'. The commentaries understood the
word לקיומא as לקיומא — "for life". But in my opinion we have
to vocalize it לקיומא, to the patron, and to translate: " 'And
thus shall ye say to the living one' (I Sam. XXV.6), [it means]
to the patron: 'Peace be unto thee' (I Sam. ibid.) etc." David
called himself (ibid. 8) the son of Nabal, which the Rabbis
understood as client of Nabal,[239] and it is only natural for them
to have felt that David called Nabal "patron". TP used here
the Semitic לקיומא and not the usual פטרון because לקיומא is the
Aramaic translation of the Hebrew לחי.[240]

Thus, the Rabbis retained the verb להתקיים על ("to patronize"), but dropped its substantive קיומא, substituting the Roman

[233] See Juster, Les Juifs dans l'Empire Romain I, p. 443, n. 4.
[234] Antiq. XX.10 (end), referred to by Juster ibidem.
[235] See Philo, de spec. leg. III, 131; Sifre I. 161, ed. Horovitz p. 22010, TB
Makkoth 11a, Seder Eliyyahu Zuta, ed. Friedmann p. 111 (bottom).
[236] De Vogüé No. 26.
[237] Comp. also Frey CIJ p. XCIV seq.
[238] Sanhedrin II.3, 20b.
[239] See BR XCIII.10, p. 11607: לאב לפטרון ("to a father means to a
patron").
[240] A very similar interpretation is found in R. David Kimchi's commentary on I Sam. ad loc. in the name of יש מפרשים ("some commentaries")
which explain לחי as לעשיר. It may be that this interpretation has its root
in some lost old source which was influenced by TP.

פטרון (πάτρων, patronus) for it. The idea of patronage was expressed by no other word than προστατεία. There is no reason whatever to list it among the foreign terms, for it was probably part and parcel of the language as spoken both by the learned Rabbis and the common people.

The acquaintance of the Rabbis with Greek culture was not limited to matters of language and to quotations from Greek sources. In their sermons they adopted the accepted literary forms of the civilized world of that time.

TB Megilla 6a records a eulogy on R. Ze'ira which was pronounced[241] in Tiberias. The preacher began thus:

ארץ שנער הרה וילדה
ארץ צבי גידלה שעשועיה
אוי נא לה אמרה רקת
כי אבדה כלי חמדתה[242])

This kind of style in a eulogy was very fashionable in the ancient world. Athenaeus[243] has preserved a similar formula in an inscription on the tomb of Laïs:[244]

... ἥν ἐτέκνωσεν Ἔρως, θρέψεν δὲ Κόρινθος·
κεῖται δ'ἐν κλεινοῖς Θετταλικοῖς πεδίοις.[245]

The same pattern is often found in ancient Greek epigrams.[246]

The Rabbis of Palestine were familiar with the fashionable style of the civilized world of that time. Many of them were highly educated in Greek literature as has been proved above. But they were conscious of the superiority of Judaism. They used their learning to spread Judaism among the Gentiles, to enlighten the pagans and open their eyes to see the truth. They discussed religion with Christians on the basis of the methods

---

[241] IV c.

[242] "The land of Shinear (=Babylonia) conceived and bore | The land of choice (=Palestine) brought up her darling | 'Woe is me', said Rakkath (=Tiberias) | For she lost her precious gem."

[243] Deipnos. XIII, 589b.

[244] IV c. B.C.E.

[245] "Whom Eros begot and Corinthus brought up; now she lies in the glorious plains of Thessaly."

[246] See Greek Anth. VII, 368, 417, 418.

accepted by the civilized world of that time. They spoke to the people in their language and in their style; they were understood and admired. We can perfectly understand the statement of the Midrash Shir Hashirim Rabba[247] which reads: בשעה שהזקן יושב ודורש הרבה גרים מתגיירים באותה שעה "When the elder (=the sage) sits and preaches many proselytes are converted to Judaism."

The style of the preacher was understood by the Gentile. It appealed to him and revealed the light of Judaism to him. The intelligent Rabbis were able to demonstrate the superiority of Judaism by the means and methods current among the cultured men of that time. They were able to compete[248] even with Gentile Christians, including those who got their education in Greek schools, in winning proselytes. They understood the mentality of the Gentile and they knew how to approach him. They were aware of his religious feelings and they directed those feelings towards the right channel of truth. They were conscious of the natural honesty ($\pi\iota\sigma\tau\iota\varsigma$) of the better Gentile and they extended this $\pi\iota\sigma\tau\iota\varsigma$ to the larger and higher concept of faith. These conclusions are consistently confirmed by the attitude of the Rabbis towards the Gentiles and the semi-proselytes.

---

[247] I. 15, ed. Romm 13a.
[248] Ceteris paribus, of course.

GENTILES AND SEMI–PROSELYTES

The title of this chapter may be very misleading, and a statement regarding the scope and limits of this inquiry is appropriate. It would require a whole treatise to deal with the attitude of the Rabbis towards the Gentiles and semi-proselytes. Much has been said about it in books and articles by distinguished scholars.[1] In this chapter we intend to discuss mainly those passages of the Talmudic literature, which have been either left unnoticed by scholars or misunderstood by them.

In order to appreciate the Rabbis' opinion of the honest Gentiles we must first appraise their view regarding the good qualities that a Jew ought to aspire to. A great part of the Mishna tract "Pirke Aboth" is devoted to ethics; it teaches the principles and ways one ought to follow in order to become pious. Rules and laws to regulate the proper behavior of the well intentioned Jew are scattered all over Talmudic literature.

Undoubtedly there were among the Jewish people a great many holy and pious men,[2] but we should like to establish what was the extent of piety commonly ascribed to the average Jew in Palestine, or, more exactly, with which qualities was it considered proper and possible to credit the average Jew in Palestine.

The best way to get this information is to visit the old Jewish tombs of Palestine, and to see what kind of virtues were attributed to the deceased by their surviving relatives. It is of no concern to us whether the deceased really possessed all the virtues ascribed to them after their death, or whether they were adorned with them by the fancy of loving relations. For

---

[1] See the long article on Gentiles in the JE Vol. V, p. 615 seq. and the bibliography ibid. p. 624. A useful book on proselytism in the Talmudic period by B. J. Bamberger has been recently (Cincinnati 1939) published, and we shall have the opportunity to refer to it subsequently.

[2] See A. Buechler, Types of Jewish-Palestinian Piety (from 70 B.C.E. to 70 C.E.), p. 13 seq.

us it is important to know what the people expected of a good person. Fortunately, the Excavations at Beth She'arim (Sheikh Abreiq) have uncovered one of the greatest cemeteries in Palestine of the II–IV centuries.[3] The inscriptions on the tomb-stones are highly instructive and are an excellent guide to the solution of our problem. Let us compare the virtues prescribed by the Mishna with the epithets preserved on the cold stones of the Jewish tombs in Palestine.

We read in the first Mishna of the supplementary chapter to Pirke Aboth, Perek Kinyan Tora:[4] ומכשרתו להיות צדיק חסיד ישר ונאמן, "And (the Tora) makes him fit to become righteous, pious, upright and faithful." These are the supreme virtues a man is apt to acquire after he has studied the Tora. Let us examine these virtues one by one.

צדיק. The old tombstones of Palestine do not crown their inhabitants with the title צדיק or δίκαιος. It is very instructive to note that the inscription on the tomb of one of the Rabbis in Jaffa[5] reads[6] זיכרונו לברכה ("His memory unto blessing") and does not quote Prov. X.7: זכר צדיק לברכה ("The memory of the righteous unto blessing"). It is true that on the tombstone of a Jew from Caesarea[7] who was buried in Italy this verse is quoted:[8] Μνία δικαίου εἰς εὐλογίαν,[9] yet it seems that this custom was limited to the Jews in the diaspora,[10] but was not in vogue in Palestine.[11]

---

[3] See the excellent report by Prof. M. Schwabe in the Hebrew Quarterly ידיעות החברה העברית לחקירת א"י vol. V, p. 77 seq.; Maisler ibid., p. 49 seq.; Klein ibid., p. 109.

[4] Printed in the majority of Prayer Books.

[5] Probably III c.

[6] Euting, Epigraphische Miscellen, 1885, No. 47; Klein Corpus Inscriptionum, No. 114.

[7] II or III c.

[8] Müller and Bees, Katakombe, No. 118; Frey CIJ, No. 370.

[9] See Deissman's illuminating note in Müller's book ibid., p. 109.

[10] See Frey ibid. Nos. 86 and 201. Comp. also No. 321.

[11] The quotation of this verse in Mishna Yoma III, 11 (and parallels), Tosephta Taanith IV, 22017 (and parallels), Mekiltha פסחא, ed. Horovitz p. 61 (and parallels), Tanhuma ed. Buber I, 18a and elsewhere has nothing to do with the invocation of the verse after mentioning the name of a deceased person (or engraving it on a tombstone).

The Jews in Palestine did bless the righteous person when they recalled his name,[12] but they did so without mentioning the word צדיק, and it made no difference whether the person was alive or dead. According to Pesiktha Rabbathi[13] a man who passes a cemetery in which he knows a righteous person to have been buried is obliged to mention him and his good deeds,[14] i. e. if the deceased was in the habit of giving charity he is to be praised as "the charitable" and so on.[15] But it is not suggested that the verse זכר צדיק לברכה be recited.[16] The usual custom in Palestine when mentioning a departed righteous person was to say[17] נוח נפש, "Whose soul is at rest,"[18] as is clearly stated by Resh Lakish:[19] מדכרין ומניחין מדכרין ומשחקין, "Some are mentioned and blessed (with the word נוח), others are mentioned and cursed (with the words שחיק טמיא or שחיק גרמיא).[20] This statement served as a recommendation for behavior only when talking of a dead person,[21] and the expression נוח נפש is indeed found on the Palestinian tombstones[22] of the first centuries C. E.[23]

[12] See BR IL.1, p. 496 seq.; Midrash Tehilim CXVIII (beginning).

[13] XII, ed. Friedmann 47a.

[14] אדם אם היה עובר בין הקברות והיה יודע שצדיק קבור שם צריך להזכירו במעשיו.

[15] See below.

[16] The presence of the phrase at the very end of Debarim Rabba is due to a later hand. Comp. מתנות כהונה ad loc.

[17] TP Erubin III (end), 21c and Pesahim IV.1, 30d.

[18] See BR IX.5, p. 715.

[19] Vayyikra Rabba XXXII.6.

[20] The honor of the correct interpretation of the phrase and its association with נוח נפש belongs to Bacher AdPA I, p. 404, n. 1. Comp. also מתנות כהונה ad Shemoth Rabba XLVIII,2. We may add the expression נשתחק (So edit. princ. of Eka Rabba I.16 and IV.19. Ed. Romm 17c and 29d reads: נשתחק. Ed. Buber reads: ומית), died, as contrary to נח נפשיה.

[21] See TP Megilla III.8, 74c (and parallels. Comp. also Theodor ad BR, p. 497 n. 3).

[22] Klein CI Nos. 110, 114, 166 and elsewhere.

[23] The blessing זכור לטוב seems to have been used in Palestine mainly for a living person, or for Elijah the Prophet who never died, or for Harbonah who was identified with Elijah (See Prof. L. Ginzberg's note in his Legends of the Jews vol. VI, p. 316 n. 1 and 325 n. 45). The adequate Aramaic דכיר לטב is found in the inscriptions of the synagogues (See Klein CI, p. 69, 75, 77 and 82; L. Sukenik in the Hebrew Quarterly Tarbiz I, fasc. 1, p. 150 and elsewhere) as a blessing on a living person. Comp., however, TB Baba Bathra 21a.

Finally, we may note the important fact that the word
צדיק (or δίκαιος) has not yet been found on the numerous
tombstones of Beth She'arim. This shows that the Jews in
Palestine were not too eager to confer this title even on a
deceased person, that in practical life this epithet was not
abused in the first centuries C. E., despite its frequent appear-
ance in Rabbinic literature.

חסיד וישר. The Septuagint translates both חסיד and ישר:
ὅσιος, an epithet found very often on the tombstones of Beth
She'arim as well as on those of Italy.[24] The old Jewish eulogy[25]
similarly consisted of the formula: הוי עניו הוי חסיד, "Alas! The
humble man, alas! The pious man," חסיד and עניו being interchangeable.[26] Thus, the epithet חסיד was readily and easily con-
ferred on a person who more or less deserved it.[27]

To the epithet נאמן we shall return below.

The sixth Mishna of the same chapter[28] teaches that a man
cannot acquire Tora unless he is אוהב את הבריות אוהב את הצדקות,
"A lover of mankind and a lover of charity." It seems to me
that we have two fixed epithets here which were quite current
in Aramaic among the people.

The first was originally רחים כל עמא,[29] "Lover of mankind"[30]
which was subsequently condensed to רחים עמא in adaptation to
the current epithet.[31] Likewise, the attribute אוהב צדקות was
used by the people in Aramaic: רחים מצוותא, "Lover of charity.[32]"

---

[24] See Prof. M. Schwabe's report (mentioned above n. 3), p. 83.

[25] Tosephta Sota XIII, 319₄ and parallels, TB Berakoth 6b.

[26] See Rabbinovicz, Variae Lectiones ad Berakoth, p. 19, n. ת; Buechler,
Some Types of Jewish-Palestinian Piety, p. 15, n. 2.

[27] On the relation between צדיק and חסיד see TB Nidda 17a and commentaries ad loc. Comp. also Aboth deR. Nathan VIII, ed. Schechter,
p. 38 (top).

[28] See above p. 69.

[29] As quoted in the minor tract Kalla, ed. Coronel, p. 7b in the name of
Ben Sira.

[30] כל עמא in Palestinian Aramaic is equivalent to כולי עלמא (every body)
in Babylonian Aramaic. See my remarks in הירושלמי כפשוטו I, p. 504.

[31] See Schürer, Geschichte etc. I³, p. 738; Cooke, North-Semitic Inscriptions, Oxford 1903, p. 244.

[32] See on מצוה and ἐντολή as צדקה in Blondheim's Les Parlers Judeo-
Romans, p. LXVI and Debarim Rabba ed. Lieberman, p. 36 n. 10.

In TP[33] an anecdote is related about a certain woman who was
a great lover of charity, and she is described as רחמא מצוותא סני.
An inscription on a tombstone in Italy[34] styles the woman in
the tomb σπουδέα φιλέντολος. Frey translates it: "Diligent
and loving the Law."[35] It is more probable that we have here
the expression of the Palestinian Talmud and it ought to be
translated: "The zealous lover of charity." Another inscription
in Italy[36] describes the man in the tomb as φιλόλαος φιλέντολος.
In my opinion, this is the translation of the original רחים עמא
רחים מצוותא,[37] namely אוהב את הבריות אוהב את הצדקות of our
Mishna.[38]

חלק טוב. A very common term of praise in the epitaphs
uncovered in the cemetery of Beth She'arim is εὔμυρος
(=εὔμοιρος), of good fortune.[39] Moreover, on fifteen of these
epitaphs we read[40] εὐμύρι (=εὐμοίρει), indicating a wish in
behalf of the dead. Prof. Schwabe[41] accepts Deissmann's[42]
explanation that εὔμοιρος is equivalent to μακάριος, the happy,
the blessed, as commonly said of deceased persons.

Since εὔμοιρος was so frequently used in Palestine it is
natural to expect to find it in the Jewish sources of that time.
Now, the exact equivalent of εὔμοιρος is חלק טוב (good lot,

[33] Terumoth VIII.5, 45c.

[34] Frey CIJ No. 132.

[35] He accordingly alters it into σπουδαία.

[36] Frey No. 509.

[37] It is very probable that epithets like רחים מצוותא, רחים עמא were not
limited only to the diaspora. We have already quoted (above n. 14) the
statement of the Pesiktha that a dead man should be mentioned together
with his good deeds. Further excavations in Palestine may uncover more
material of the same nature. So far these epithets have not been found on
the comparatively scarce Jewish tombstones inscriptions of Palestine.

[38] Comp. however the famous inscription on the tombstone of Regina
(probably of the II c., see Frey CIJ No. 476) in Italy which reads: hoc et
amor generis hoc observantia legis, "This also thy love of thy people, this
thy observation of the Law." See also Müller and Bees, Katakombe, p. 135.

[39] See Prof. Schwabe's report (mentioned above n. 3) p. 91, 92 (end) 93
(top).

[40] Schwabe ibid. p. 83.

[41] Ibid. p. 92.

[42] Light etc., p. 176, n. 4.

good share) in Hebrew. This is indeed found among the various virtues required by R. Jose (II c.) of a person before he is qualified to be appointed as a judge.[43] Thus, חלק טוב was used in Palestine in the second century as a term of a certain quality. Moreover people prayed for the privilege of becoming a חלק טוב. TP[44] records a prayer:[45] יהי רצון מלפניך ה' אלהי שתתן לי לב טוב חלק טוב וכו', "May it be thy will, my Lord God, that thou endow me with a good heart, a good lot" etc. Thus, חלק טוב occurs both as an attribute and as a wish, just as on the tombstones of Beth She'arim.

But what exactly does חלק טוב mean? In Tosephta Sanhedrin[46] the required virtue[47] is פרק טוב instead of חלק טוב. In a Baraitha quoted in TB[48] the quality פרקו נאה is mentioned. Abaye[49] explained[50] that פרקו נאה means a man whose youth was unblemished. Yet there can be no doubt that in Palestine this term also retains its plain sense, a man's happy lot, both materially and spiritually.

Mishna Aboth[51] teaches: ממהר לשמוע וקשה לאבד זה ח ל ק; here חלק טוב and ט ו ב, קשה לשמוע וממהר לאבד זה ח ל ק ר ע;[52] חלק רע are taken in the plain sense of the word. This double meaning of the epithet was also current among the Greeks. Damagetus (III c. B. C. E.) said[53] about Praxiteles of Andros that he was Μουσέων ἱκανὴ μερίς ("well endowed by the Muses"); ἱκανὴ μερίς is very near the Hebrew פרק טוב, חלק טוב and means literally "good lot," whereas κακὰ μερίς[54] which is equivalent to the Hebrew חלק רע means "bad lot" in the sense of bad behavior.

[43] TP Sanhedrin I.7, 19c. See below.
[44] Berakoth IV.2, 7d.
[45] In the name of the "House of R. Jannai" (III c.).
[46] VII, 425₁₇.   [47] See above n. 43.
[48] Taanith 16a.
[49] A Babylonian sage of the IV century.
[50] Taanith 16b.
[51] V.18, according to the reading of the Prayer Books.
[52] "Quick to understand and slow to forget, this is a *happy lot;* slow to understand and quick to forget is an *evil lot.*"
[53] Greek Anth. VII, No. 355.
[54] Ibid. No. 433.

The expression פרק טוב is also included among the virtues enumerated in the minor tract Kalla:[55] איש, חשבון יפה ופרק טוב, הבטחה איש אמת "Of good account and good lot, a man who keeps his promise, a truthful man." The "Gemara" explains חשבון יפה to refer to a man of good account, a man who is not counted among the licentious persons. פרק טוב is the opposite of פרק רע, as explained by the "Gemara"[56] in conformity with the opinion of Abaye[57] (a fact overlooked by the commentaries).

Since we have tried to prove that the latter explanation does not exhaust the implication of the epithet פרק טוב as used in Palestine, we may similarly assume that חשבון יפה has a wider connotation than that assigned to it by the "Gemara". We have seen that פרק יפה was very common among the Greeks[58] and the Jews in the form of εὔμοιρος; its synonym was ἱκανὴ μερίς[59] which would be rendered in Hebrew חלק טוב, חתיכה טובה.[60] Now, an anonymous Baraitha[61] requires a leader to be חתיכה ופסיפס. One of the meanings of פסיפוס (ψῆφος) is also חשבון in a sense very near to חכמה (wisdom). The Septuagint[62] translates חכמה וחשבון: σοφίαν καὶ ψῆφον. Hermes was said[63] to be the cause of συνέσεως, ψήφου etc., ψῆφος coming immediately after σύνεσις (intelligence). Hermes made:[64] γραμματικούς, ψηφιστάς, φιλοσόφους etc., the ψηφιστής[65] standing between the

---

55 IV (and parallels), ed. Higger p. 256. See ed. Coronel 10a.

56 Ibid., p. 234.

57 TB Taanith 16b. See above p. 73.

58 Deissmann, Light etc., p. 176, n. 4.

59 See above p. 73.

60 The Septuagint translates the Hebrew נתח by μερίς.

61 Sifre Zuta, ed. Horovitz, p. 320; Sifre Deut. sec. 13, ed. Finkelstein, p. 21 (and parallels. See Prof. Finkelstein's note ad loc.). Comp. Appendix, below p. 185 seq.

62 Eccl. VII.25.

63 Catalog. Codic. Astrol. Graec. III, ed. Boll etc. (Bruxelles 1900), p. 178.

64 Ibidem.

65 Accountant. This word is also found in Rabbinic literature. In Midrash Tehilim LXVIII, ed. Buber, p. 319 (and parallels) we read: עד מקום שיכול פסיפפטס לחשוב ("as far as the accountant can count"). Krauss (LW 377) hesitated to accept this meaning of the word, not being sure of its existence

γραμματικός and φιλόσοφος. Libanius in a letter of recommendation[66] mentions ψῆφον ὀρθήν[67] among the various virtues of his protegé.

Thus, it is very probable that חתיכה ופסיפס is the contracted form of something like (ἱκανή) μερὶς καὶ (ὀρθή) ψῆφος, which correspond exactly to חשבון יפה ופרק טוב (חתיכה טובה) of the tract Kalla mentioned above.[68]

נ א מ ן. The last two virtues mentioned in the minor tract Kalla are איש הבטחה, איש אמת, "A man who keeps his promise, a truthful man."[69] In the Mishna in Aboth[70] these two virtues are comprised in the one word נאמן which means faithful, loyal, trustworthy, akin to the Greek πιστός. This excellent quality which is the basis of human society was highly esteemed by the Jews. The Almighty Himself is very often termed נאמן in Rabbinic literature.[71]

These form the highest standard virtues set by the Rabbis for the Jews, and duly appreciated by the latter, as can be seen from the various inscriptions in Palestine and from the popular eulogies.

Now, these virtues are ascribed by the Rabbis to the honest Gentiles as well. They are termed צדיקים[72] (righteous), טובים[73] (good) etc. We shall not dwell in detail on such descriptions, since it is very probable that the Rabbis had semi-proselytes[74]

in Greek; Loew (ibid., 681) marked it with two question marks. But we have seen that it was current in Greek; see also Sophocles and Preisigke s. v. ψηφιστής.

[66] Epist. XIX.10. Written about 360.

[67] "correct judgment".

[68] The statement of R. Eleazar ben Shammua in Aboth deR. Nathan XXVIII, ed. Schechter, p. 86 is only a play of words based on the double meaning of ψῆφος (pebble), a play very usual in Rabbinic literature.

[69] The reading יש הבטחה, יש אמת does not alter the general meaning.

[70] Mentioned above p. 69.

[71] See Tosephta Hullin II, 503₂₁; Sifre Deut. 357, ed. Finkelstein, p. 428; Tanhuma וישב sec. 5. Comp. also Mishna Aboth II (end) and elsewhere.

[72] Tosephta Sanhedrin XIII, 434₁₀; Mekiltha de'arayoth in Sifra אחרי מות, ed. Weiss, p. 86b.

[73] Sifra ibidem.

[74] See, for instance, Bemidbar Rabba VIII.2.

in mind, whereas we are mainly interested in the honest Gentiles
who remained loyal to their faith.

Deissmann[75] very convincingly emphasizes the general fund
of real morality of the honest heathen. Faith, loyalty, πίστις
was a virtue highly esteemed by the heathen.[76] In Rabbinic
literature[77] a Gentile judge is credited with the just acquital of
a Jew, in whose favor a Roman officer bore testimony. The
judge motivated his verdict by saying: נאמן מנאמן[78] קביל, "The
loyal received from the loyal," calling both the Jew and Roman
officer נאמן; a נאמן has to be believed and cannot be condemned;
this title is a compliment both to the Jew and the Gentile.

Deissmann[79] laid special stress on the love of labor as a
very common virtue of the lower classes of heathen society.
The tombstones of the heathen relate with pride that the deceased had labored much, or had gained his livelihood by the
labor of his hands. Paul's concepts of the virtue of labor were
borrowed from the workshop morality[80] of both the Jews and
the pagans. Finally, Deissmann calls attention[81] to the inscription in honor of a heathen,[82] which reads: ἄνδρα ἀγαθὸν γενό-
μενον καὶ διενένκαντα πίστει . . ., emphasizing that the man
was good (ἀγαθός) and faithful (πιστός).

We find a striking parallel to this inscription in a statement
of a Rabbi who lived some three hundred years later. In the
minor tract Semahoth[83] the eulogy that is to be pronounced on
a dead Gentile or slave is recorded. We read there: ר' יהודה אומר
הוי טב הוי נאמן[84] אוכל מעמלו. אמרו לו אם כן מה
הנחת לכשרין. אמר להם אם היה כשר מפני מה אין קורין עליו, "R. Juda

[75] Light etc., p. 310 seq.
[76] Ibid., p. 309 seq.
[77] Koheleth Rabba XI.1.
[78] BR XCIV.9, 1182₉: אני היא שהשלמתי נאמן לנאמן etc.
[79] Ibid., 312 seq.
[80] Ibid., 314.
[81] Ibid., 318.
[82] Dittenberger, Orient. Gr. Insc. Selectae No. 438 (from Asia Minor,
I c. B.C.E.).
[83] I, ed. Higger, p. 100.
[84] This is the reading of Cod. Adler recorded by Higger in his variants.
I have consulted the manuscript; there is no doubt about the reading.

(II c.) said: [the eulogy on a Gentile is] *'Alas! The good, alas! The faithful who eats [the fruit] of his own labor'*. [The sages] said to him: 'What then did you leave for the worthy'? He replied: 'If he (i. e. the Gentile or slave) was worthy why should he not be lamented in this manner'."

The virtues enumerated in this eulogy are purely secular; there is no trace of religion in them. The man was good, faithful and enjoyed the fruits of his labor. The Gentile spoken of is a heathen; he is neither semi-proselyte nor even a Christian; no mention is made of his fear of God. This picture of the honest Gentile portrayed incidentally by the Rabbi of the second century coincides perfectly with the actual state of pagan morality; it corresponds to the description by the pagans themselves of their own better men; it is in accordance with the qualities the masses of the heathen thought to be good.

The Rabbis understood the heathen society and credited it with the virtues it was not devoid of. They came in constant contact with this society; they tried to influence it and to enlighten it. The better men of this pagan society began to see the light of Judaism. Many of them were entirely converted to Judaism and many more became conscious of Judaism, supplying masses of semi-proselytes of various kinds.

Semi-proselytes. It was already intimated[85] that the so-called semi-proselytes were held by the Rabbis in high esteem. They were called טובים, צדיקים etc., were promised their share in the future world and were compared to high priests. Many Jewish and non-Jewish scholars have dealt with the problem of the semi-proselytes. Graetz[86] was the first to discover the many references to them in Rabbinic literature under the name of יראי שמים, יראי ה' which he correctly identified with the θεο-σεβεῖς, σεβόμενοι, Ἰουδαΐζοντες mentioned by Josephus and others. The material bearing on the semi-proselytes has recently been collected by Bamberger,[87] Proselytism, p. 134 seq.[88]

---

[85] Above p. 75.
[86] Die jüdischen Proselyten im Römmerreiche, p. 13 seq.
[87] See above n. 1.
[88] The various articles on the subject are indicated in the bibliography ibid., p. 307 seq.

But despite the ardent interest of scholars in this subject
some pertinent passages have remained obscure and misunderstood. We read, for instance, in the Palestinian Talmud:[89]
מליהון דרבנן אמרין דאתגייר אנטונינוס דאמר ר' חזקיה ר' אבהו בשם
ר' ליעזר אם באין הן גרי צדק לעתיד לבוא אנטונינוס בא בראשם, "The
words of the Rabbis indicate that Antoninus[90] was converted,
for R. Hezekia and R. Abbahu said in the name of R. Eleazar
(III c.): 'If true (full) proselytes come into the future [life],
Antoninus will come at the head of them'." This interpretation
of the passage by all the commentaries is entirely impossible.
No Rabbi ever questioned the right to a future life of the full
proselyte. The latter is equal to a Jew by birth in the eyes of
God. R. Eleazar could never have said "*if* true proselytes etc.";
there could be no doubt about it.

The misinterpretation of the passage bearing on Antoninus
in that place of TP is based on the erroneous reading of the
text as it was "corrected" by the editor of the Palestinian Talmud in Bomberg's printing house. We shall quote the whole
passage according to Cod. Leyden:[91]

[אית מילין דאתגייר אנטונינוס ואית מלין דלא אתגייר אנטונינוס][92] ראו אותו
יוצא במנעל פחות ביום הכיפורים. מה את שמע מינה שכן אפילו יריאי שמים
יוצאים בכך. אנטולינוס אמר לרבי מייכלתי את מן ליויתן בעלמא דאתי. א"ל
אין. א"ל מן אימר פיסחא לא אוכלתני. ומן ליויתן את מייכל לי. א"ל ומה
נעביד לך וכתיב ביה כל ערל לא יאכל בו. כיון דשמע כן אזל וגזר . . . הדא
אמרה דאיתגייר אנטולינוס. מיליהון דרבנן אמרין ד ל א אתגייר[93] אנטולינוס,
דאמר ר' חזקיה ר' אבהו בשם ר' לעזר אם באין הן גירי צדק לעתיד לבוא
אנטולינוס בא בראשם.

"There are some things that indicate that Antoninus was
converted and vice versa. He was seen going out on the Day of

[89] Megilla III.2, 74a.

[90] See Bamberger, Proselytism, p. 264, n. 108.

[91] The basic ms. for the printed edition. See my Introduction to הירושלמי
כפשוטו I, p. ט"ו seq.

[92] The bracketed phrase was completed on the margin by the editor.

[93] The editor corrected: דאתגייר. Likewise in the parallel passage, TP
Megilla I.13, 72b, in cod. Leyden: ל א נתגייר, but the editor deleted the
word לא!

Atonement wearing a broken sandal.[94] What can you deduce from that? Even 'fearers of Heaven' ($\vartheta\epsilon o\sigma\epsilon\beta\epsilon\tilde{\iota}s$, semi-prose-lytes) go out wearing such a sandal.[95] Antoninus asked Rabbi: 'Will you let me eat of leviathan in the next world? He answered: 'Yes'.[96] But he objected: 'You will not let me eat of the Paschal lamb, how then will you let me eat of leviathan'? He replied: 'What can I do for thee, since it is written: *no one that is un-circumcised may eat thereof*'[97] (Ex. XII.48). When he heard this,

---

[94] Indicating that he was converted, as correctly interpreted by I. Levi in REJ, vol. L, p. 8. The usual interpretation is that from the fact that Antoninus wore broken sandals on the Day of Atonement the Rabbis inferred that he was not converted. No talmudist would ever accept this interpreta-tion, for TP Yoma VIII.1, 44d records many cases of leading sages who wore slippers on the Day of Atonement because they were sensitive and could not walk barefooted. True, the Mishna (Yoma VIII. 1. Comp. Or Zarua II, 277, p. 127a) releases the king from the prohibition of washing his face on this day, but, seemingly, not from that of wearing shoes (Juvenal, Sat. VI, 159 remarks: observant ubi festa mero pede sabbata reges, "where [even] *kings observe the sabbath festivals* — a term mistakenly used by the heathen writers for the Day of Atonement — *barefooted*"), yet in the eyes of the Rabbis sensitiveness could easily be claimed by the Roman Emperor, and it would never occur to them to infer that he was not converted because he wore shoes on the Day of Atonement. The interpretation seems to be all the more preposterous in view of the fact that the Emperor wore *broken* sandals, which behavior is in perfect accordance with the law (See the following sentence in TP. Comp. also Tosephta Yebamoth XII, 255₂₅; TB ibid., 103a).

The commentaries ad loc. offered a forced interpretation because until recently the real meaning of ירא שמים (in the subsequent phrase) was not known.

[95] Here we have the important evidence to the effect that the "fearers of Heaven" did not wear shoes on the Day of Atonement, as noted by I. Levi, ibid.

[96] See above p. 77.

[97] It is very noteworthy that the Jews in their missionary activity ad-mitted the God fearing Gentile to the future life, even to their share in leviathan, but not to any share in the Paschal lamb. When it came to this the Gentile had to become a full proselyte; there is no compromise with the Law of Moses. Perhaps a remnant of the Jewish missionary terminology has been preserved in Shir-Hashirim Rabba I.12 (and parallels): כך אמר לי הקב״ה סינטומוס כל ערל לא יאכל בו, "So said God to me briefly — $\sigma v v\tau\acute{o}\mu\omega s$ — '*no one that is uncircumcised may eat thereof*'" (Ex. XII.48). When the question of the Paschal lamb arose no further arguments were advanced. The strict law of the Bible was quoted, and the Jewish missionary cut the arguments short declaring the Law $\sigma v v\tau\acute{o}\mu\omega s$.

he went and circumcised himself . . . This indicates that Antoninus was not converted, for R. Hezekia and R. Abbahu said in
the name of R. Eleazar אם באין הן גירי צדק לעתיד לבוא etc."

As said above, the usual interpretation of R. Eleazar's
statement is totally untenable. He could have never questioned
the future life of the full proselyte. In my opinion, the word
באין is a shortened technical term for coming to embrace a new
faith (or new principles). So, for instance:[98] יתרו שמע הוא ו א ת א
ואתיא   רחב שמעה, "Jethro heard and came [to be converted],
Rahab heard and came [to be converted]." Likewise:[99] כל
ה ב א   צריך לקבל עליו, "Whoever comes [to follow the principles
of Haberuth] must take upon himself [the obligations of a
Haber]." We have here but a part of R. Eleazar's saying. It
can be understood only in connection with the other part which
reads.[100] אין מקבלין גרים לימות המשיח . . . אמר ר' א ל ע ז ר   מאי קרא
הן גור יגור אפס מאותי. מי גר אתך עליך יפול, אבל אידך לא "No proselytes will be accepted in the days of the Messiah . . . R. *Eleazar*
said: what Scriptural [support is there for this view]? *'Behold he
shall be a proselyte who is converted for my own sake; he who lives
with you shall be settled among you'* (Isa. LIV.15); [only he who
'lives with you' in your poverty shall be settled among you] but
no other." In accordance with his opinion R. Eleazar said: "If
full proselytes come [to be converted] in the Messianic future
(i. e. if proselytes are accepted) Antoninus will come at the
head of them," for only the Gentiles who had nothing to do
with the Jews during their bitter past will not be admitted to
conversion, but those "fearers of Heaven" who lived with the
nation of Israel in its period of poverty have a chance to
be accepted as full proselytes in the Messianic future, and
Antoninus will be at the head of them.[101] This, of course,

---

[98] Shir Hashirim Rabba I, 15.

[99] TP Demai II.3, 22d (bottom).   [100] TB Yebamoth 24b.

[101] This statement of R. Eleazar implies, of course, that the "fearers of
Heaven," like Antoninus, will rise from the dead in the Messianic future.
The problem of their resurrection may have occupied the Jewish missionaries.
We may incidentally point to the Psalms of Solomon (III.16) which read:
οἱ δὲ φοβούμενοι κύριον ἀναστήσονται εἰς ζωὴν αἰώνιον. "They that *fear
the Lord shall rise again* into life eternal." But it is very doubtful if these
"φοβούμενοι κύριον" have anything to do with our "fearers of Heaven."

indicates that Antoninus was *not converted*[102] during his earthly life.

This passage of the Palestinian Talmud is very instructive. The "fearers of Heaven" did not wear shoes on the Day of Atonement; they were expected to participate in the "Leviathan Festival" of the future life and to arise from the dead in the Messianic future when they will become full proselytes.

The question arises: Who were these "fearers of Heaven"? Did all of them adhere to the same code of behavior? We can certainly answer in the negative. The "fearers of Heaven" renounced their old religion of idolatry and accepted the principle of monotheism. But they were not entirely converted to Judaism; they sympathized with only some of the Jewish precepts. And, of course, it can never be expected that different individuals who have not embraced the Jewish faith as a whole should evince exactly the same interest in the same laws and precepts. It is natural and human for one to have liked the Jewish Sabbath, for another to have been attracted by the Jewish holidays, while still others were impressed by the Jewish Day of Atonement (and the ideas associated with it), by the Jewish family life and so on.

In practice, all the "fearers of Heaven" must have accepted monotheism and the moral laws, whereas in questions of religious ceremony and ritual they may have widely differed. The Rabbis disagree completely as to the requirements made of a legitimate גר תושב mentioned in the Bible[103]; their opinions on the number and character of the Noahide laws diverge,[104] a clash which mirrors the facts of actual life. There were in existence (as could be expected) different groups of semi-converts, each of whom adopted different parts of the ceremonies and rituals of Judaism. The Rabbis had to face the actual situation and to decide what type of semi-convert is to be con-

---

[102] In accordance with the genuine, indeed the only possible, reading of cod. Leyden (here and in the parallel passage): ד ל א אתנייר.

[103] See TP Yebamoth VIII.1, 8d; TB Aboda Zara 64b, 65a; Kerithoth 9a.

[104] See TB Sanhedrin 56b; Hullin 92a (comp. however TP Aboda Zara II.1, 40c); BR XVI.6, 149₆ (and parallels noted therein) and Theodor's long note ibidem.

sidered the legitimate גר תושב mentioned in the Bible. But all
these groups were considered "fearers of Heaven" as soon as
they rejected idolatry, accepted monotheism and the moral
laws. Perhaps this variety of the character of "fearers of Heaven"
led one Rabbi to decide[105] that the law of גר תושב was valid
only when the Jubilee law was in force, i. e. was valid only in
the far gone past. In other words, he identified none of the
various groups of the "fearers of Heaven" with the גר תושב mentioned in the Bible.

Thus, the existence of various groups of "fearers of Heaven"
according to their respective relation to the Jewish ceremonial
and ritual law can be considered as a well established fact. The
question is, however, whether the Jews included all these groups
under the one name of "fearers of Heaven" (and their equiva-
lents). Were the groups that accepted all the precepts of Judaism except the dietary laws[106] and the groups that considered
their status as only transitory to full Judaism[107] designated by
the same name as those which accepted only monotheism and
the moral laws[108]? It is very probable that the people employed
different names for the various groups of semi-converts, but in
the comparatively scarce material on them clear evidence of the
existence of such distinct definitions is not forthcoming.

However, it is possible that remnants of these different terms
have been preserved in Talmudic literature. In Vayyikra
Rabba[109] we read: א"ר ה', יראי ה'. יראי ה' הללוהו כל זרע יעקב כבדוהו.
ר' יהושע בן לוי אלו יראי שמים. ר' ישמעאל[110] בר נחמן אמ' אלו גירי צדק.
חזקיה ור' אבהו בשם ר' אלעזר אמרי אם באין הן גירי צדק לעולם הבא
אנטונינוס בא בראש כלן. ומה תלמוד לומר כל זרע יעקב כבדוהו אלו ע ש ר ת י[111]
שבטים וכו'. " 'Ye that fear God, praise Him; All ye the seed of
Jacob glorify Him' (Ps. XXII.24). 'Ye that fear God', said R.
Joshua ben Levi,[112] 'refers to fearers of Heaven'. R. Samuel bar
Nahman[112] said: 'It refers to full proselytes'. R. Hezekia and

[105] Arakin 29a.
[106] TB Aboda Zara 64b and tract Gerim III, 1.
[107] See my little booklet מדרשי תימן p. 8.
[108] TB Aboda Zara and Gerim ibidem.
[109] III.2.
[110] Read שמואל, as in Midrash Tehilim XXII.29, p. 195.
[111] So ed. pr. and mss.   [112] III c.

R. Abbahu said in the name of R. Eleazar: 'If full proselytes will be admitted in the future world[113] Antoninus will come at the head of them'. And what is implied by '*All ye the seed of Jacob glorify Him*'? It refers to the Ten Tribes.''[114]

According to this reading, the opinion of R. Eleazar is more closely related to the statement of R. Joshua ben Levi, who speaks of semi-converts, than to that of R. Samuel bar Nahman who speaks of full proselytes. But the reading of Cod. Brit. Mus. in the statement of R. Samuel is: אילו גירי הארץ, and the word הארץ was subsequently altered into הצדק. This reading is too original to be a mere scribal error. And although it is hard to define what גירי הארץ ("the proselytes of the earth") really means[115] it seems that we have here a special name for a certain category of semi-converts.[116]

Similarly, we find in Aboth deR. Nathan:[117] ובשם ישראל יכנה אלו גרי אמת "'*And he shall surname himself by the name of Israel*' (Is. XLIV.5) refers to the true proselytes." Schechter (ad loc.) did not record any other reading, but his text is corroborated only by Yalkut Hamakiri[118] and הגהות אבות דר"ן in

[113] See above p. 80.

[114] The Palestinian tradition seems to have compared the fate of the "fearers of Heaven" to that of the Ten Tribes. R. Eleazar apparently uttered his opinion on the semi-converts in connection with the future life of the Ten Tribes (See TP Sanhedrin X.6, 29c). Likewise, in Midrash שכל טוב, ed. Buber, p. 181: צאן אלו עשרת השבטים...ועבד ושפחה אלו יראי שמים. "'*Sheep*' (Gen. XXXII.6) refers to the Ten Tribes ... '*and men-servants and maid servants*' (ibid.) refers to the fearers of Heaven." This passage was overlooked by the scholars who collected the material bearing on the "fearers of Heaven."

[115] The Septuagint twice mentions (Ex. XII.19 and Is. XIV.1) the word γειώρας as equivalent to the Hebrew גר. Basilius of Caesarea in Cappadocia (IV c.) in his commentary ad Is. XIV.1 (Migne P. G. XXX, 608a) remarks that "the proselyte who cultivates the earth is the one called γειώρας." (ὁ περὶ τὴν γῆν διαπονούμενος, ὁ προσήλυτος οὗτός ἐστιν ὁ γειώρας). Basilius, however, is not in favor of this explanation. See also Sophocles, Lexicon, s. v. γειώρας and Hort, the first Epistle of St. Peter, 155 n. 1. Comp. also Sachs, Beitraege II, p. 155.

[116] Perhaps by גרי ארץ the Palestinian semi-converts were designated as a contrast to גרי חוץ לארץ.

[117] XXXVI, ed. Schechter p. 107.

[118] Is. p. 146.

תמת ישרים 65d (as a varia lectio), whereas the editio princeps has: אילו גירי אומות העולם. This is also the reading of Aboth deR. Nathan Cod. New York[119] and Yalkut ms. quoted by Schechter.[120] Thus, the reading אילו גירי אומות העולם is backed by far more reliable authority than the reading אילו גירי אמת; it has also the advantage of the lectio difficilis,[121] and is therefore the genuine reading. Graetz[122] considered the reading גירי אומות העולם as "reiner Unsinn" (sheer nonsense), but in view of the material adduced above his opinion has to be completely disregarded.

We may conclude that גירי אומות העולם as well as גירי הארץ are special names for the different categories of semi-proselytes, the exact meaning of which cannot yet be established.

The attitude of the Rabbis to all these groups was very favorable; if they only feared God, they were thereby entitled to their share in the future world, they were regarded as צדיקים (righteous) and טובים (good).

Moreover, the attitude of the Rabbis towards the Gentiles who remained faithful to their religion was very tolerant and liberal. Talmudic literature is full of venomous remarks against the immoral behavior of the heathen Gentiles. The people are warned not to imitate the bad manners of the heathen. But the attack of the Rabbis is directed more against their religion than against its followers. The Roman Gentile, for instance, as a peaceful citizen is pictured in a rather pleasent light.

[119] Of the Jewish Theological Seminary No. 0816, p. 28b.

[120] Ibid., p. 148. Rashi, quoting Aboth deR. Nathan in his commentary (Is. XLIV.5), reads: אלו הגרים. This reading is also reported (in the name of Rashi) by Raymundus Martini in his Pugio Fidei, ed. Carpzov p. 458 and 544. But he translates it (p. 459): isti sunt advenae vel *conversi de gentibus*; on p. 544: isti erunt *conversi de gentibus*. Since Martini does not ordinarily translate גרים "conversi de gentibus" (see ibid. p. 457 seq.) we can only assume that he translated the phrase אלו גירי אומות העולם which his Rashi text carried. Although his Hebrew quotation from Rashi reads אלו הגרים, his translation followed another Hebrew text, a very common occurrence in Pugio Fidei, as I showed by force of many instances in my booklet שקיעין p. 47 seq. One Rashi version, then, supports the reading גרי אומות העולם.

[121] The expression גרי אמת is very frequent in TB. Comp. Nidda 56b and מסורת הש׳ס in the margin.

[122] Die jüdische Proselyten etc., p. 13, n. 2.

The Palestinian Talmud[123] relates an episode about R. Jonathan[124] who was renowned as a just judge. It happened that the branches of a tree belonging to R. Jonathan spread into the territory of a Roman Gentile whose house and field adjoined his. Once a case of a tree spreading in somebody else's premises came before R. Jonathan, and he put off the decision to the following day. The Roman said: "It is on account of me that the decision was postponed; tomorrow I shall waste the whole day[125] to see what decision will be rendered. If he judges others but does not judge himself he can not be called a man." At nightfall R. Jonathan had all the branches of his tree which spread into the Roman's premises cut off.

The Palestinian Talmud wanted to portray the justice of R. Jonathan, but incidentally we learn the good neighborly relations between him and the Roman. The latter resented the encroachment of R. Jonathan's tree on his premises, but he did not say a word about it. Only when a similar case was brought before the Rabbi he allowed himself to pass a remark about it. Upon discovering that the tree was cut down, he said: "Blessed be the God of the Jews." A very friendly and goodhearted human being, indeed!

Of course, we must not disregard the fact that the rapid spread of Christianity brought the heathen nearer to the Jews. The common dangerous enemy had to be fought by both Jews and heathens; it was desirable to have a united front and a joint program. The Jews were aware of the heathen philosophy regarding change of religion. So, their philosopher Celsus (II c.), according to Origen,[126] maintained that it is the duty of every nation to adhere to the religion of its ancestors. Origen[127]

---

[123] Baba Bathra II (end), 13c.

[124] Ben Eleazar. (fl. in the III c.). See Tanhuma שופטים sect. 3; Genizah Studies in memory of Schechter I, by L. Ginzberg, p. 130; Hadar Zekenim שופטים 68d; Gaster, Exempla, p. 111.

[125] The text reads: אנא מבטל אילו מדידי. The meaningless אילו מדידי was correctly altered by J. N. Epstein (Tarbiz vol. V, p. 272) into אולי מרידי, ὁλημερίδιον (a diminutif of ὁλημέρα), a whole day.

[126] Contra Celsum V. 25; ibid., 34 and 41.

[127] Ibid. 25, Migne P. G. XI, 1220a.

summed up Celsus' opinion briefly by saying: φησὶ καὶ συμ-
φέρειν τούτοις καὶ πάτρια θρησκεύειν, ὁμοίως τοῖς ἄλλοις
ἔθνεσι τὰ ἴδια περιέπουσι, "He (i. e. Celsus) says that it is to
their (i. e. the Jews') advantage to observe their ancestral worship, as other nations honor theirs." This opinion of the heathen
philosopher of the II century is ascribed by the Palestinian
Talmud[128] to a Gentile who resided in Rome in the IV century.[129]
It is related (ibid.) that R. Abba bar Zemina (IV c.) was employed in Rome as a tailor by a Gentile. The latter offered him
meat of an animal slaughtered not according to Jewish ritual,
having threatened him with death in case he refused to eat it.
R. Abba, however, rejected the demand saying: "If you want
to kill me, do so, but I shall not eat forbidden meat." Then the
Gentile said to him: "Who informed you that if you had eaten
I should have killed you"? או יהודיי יהודיי או ארמאי ארמאי, "If you
are a Jew stay a Jew; if a heathen, a heathen,"[130]—almost
word for word like the argument of Celsus!

It goes without saying that the Jews could not adopt the
view that a heathen has to remain loyal to the faith of his
fathers; it is entirely foreign to the Jewish ideology.[131] But at
the same time it protected the Jewish cult from attacks by the
Gentiles[132]; the heathen unintentionally became a protector of
the Jews.

It is, however, hard to believe that the philosophy preached
by Celsus played a great part in the attitude of the Jews towards
the heathen. R. Juda who was most probably a contemporary
of Celsus and who was not as yet aware of his opinions pictured
the honest heathen as "good, faithful and enjoying the fruits of

---

[128] Shebiith IV.2, 35a (and parallel).

[129] As correctly observed by Juster. (Les juifs dans l'empire romain I,
34, n. 6. But instead of TP "Sabbat 6.4." read: "Chebiith 4.2").

[130] The Roman Gentile probably employed the word Ἕλλην in contrast
to Ἰουδαῖος. So Gal. III.28: "οὐκ ἔνι Ἰουδαῖος οὐδὲ Ἕλλην" is translated
into Palestinian Syriac: לית יהודיי ולא ארמיי or (Horae Semit. VIII, p. 148):
לית יודיא ולא ארמיא.

[131] This philosophy may have been somewhat of a factor in the abate-
ment of the Jewish zeal to win new proselytes. See TB Yebamoth 47b.

[132] See Juster I, p. 35 seq.

his own labor."[133] This simple and plain phrase speaks much
more eloquently than any elaborate theoretical doctrine. It
represents the feelings of both the Rabbis and the people. If
the sages were opposed to the opinion of R. Juda it was not
because they were unaware of the existence of such Gentiles.
They merely objected to such a eulogy over a heathen Gentile
because they wished to preserve it for the worthy Jew. They
believed that a distinction should be drawn between the righteous Jew who believed in the true God and the worthy heathen
who worships idols. But they admitted the fact that the honest
heathen may be "good, faithful and enjoying the fruits of his
own labor." The very admission of this fact mitigated the
natural animosity between the Jew and the heathen Gentile. If
they happened to be neighbors, if they knew each other, they
could not help but become friendly and trusting.

The same can be said about the relation of Jew and Christian
at the time of R. Juda. Christianity was abhorred, Christians
were persecuted, but the Gentile (we are not speaking of Jewish
apostates) Christian who happened to be an acquaintance, or a
neighbor, was not only tolerated like the Gentile heathen, he
could be accepted as a real friend.

A good illustration of this is afforded us by the portrayal,
by Justin Martyr,[134] of the character and manners of his opponent Trypho.[135] After quite a lengthy discussion between Justin,
on the one hand, and Trypho and his Jewish friends, on the
other, the group had to separate. Neither of the disputants
won his opponents over to his convictions; both remained con-
fident that they were right. But the Jew and the Gentile learned
to know each other. They are no longer abstract representatives
of two different religions, but human beings of flesh and blood
facing each other and speaking to each other. What was the
result? When Justin was about to embark Trypho asked him:[136]

[133] See above p. 77.

[134] He was born in Palestine and probably knew the character of the
Palestinian Jews well.

[135] He fled (from Palestine) to Ephesus on account of the war (about
135). See Dialogue ch. I.

[136] Dial. CXLII.

μὴ ὄκνει ὡς φίλων ἡμῶν μεμνῆσθαι ἐὰν ἀπαλλαγῇς, "Do not
shrink from remembering us as your friends when you make
your departure." And Justin himself declares[137] that the Jews
departed εὐχόμενοί τέ μοι σωτηρίαν καὶ ἀπὸ τοῦ πλοῦ καὶ ἀπὸ
πάσης κακίας, "Praying for my deliverance from the dangers of
the sea and from all evil." Not only the polite and courteous
Trypho but his friends, the more common Jews, join in prayer
for the deliverance from all evils of the Gentile Christian.
Justin was no longer a symbol of a hostile faith; he became a
living honest man for whom even the common Jew prays to
God. Thus a Palestinian Jew was portrayed; a Jew who fled
to the diaspora after experiencing the persecutions of the Roman
conquerors in his own country.

True, not all religious discussions ended in such a cordial
spirit. But in the great majority of discussions the parties
regarded one another as enemies from the very beginning. A
religious debate (especially in public) is not the proper occasion
for learning to know the real character of the disputants. It
seems that this lovely Epilogue to the discussion was possible
only thanks to the exceptional circumstances under which it
began. The Gentile and the Jew met accidentally in the Colon-
nade. The discussion was conducted privately, without any
ambition on the part of the discussers to win the applause of
the onlookers; both display a great amount of eagerness to
learn, but not a previously formed decision to defeat and to
conquer. This was a very natural occasion to learn to know
each other and therefore brought about the natural result.

It makes no difference whatever whether this dialogue is real
or imaginary; Justin, most probably, went through the experience of a private conversation under the conditions he describes.
And it goes without saying that Justin did not invent the
character of the Jew from Palestine whom he depicted. He
surely pictured a type he knew in Palestine or one of the ref-
ugees from Palestine. The results of the acquaintance between
Jew and Gentile in this discussion could not be more satisfactory than those of the acquaintance between two laborers

[137] Ibidem.

working together or two landowners in the same neighborhood.
The relations between R. Jonathan and his Roman neighbor
were not the exception but the rule.

The Jewish, the heathen and the Christian communities in
Palestine were not insulated and walled-in; they lived together
in the big cities and met in the smaller villages. True, a very
wide gap, perhaps an unbridgeable chasm separated the Jewish
concepts of religion, morality and ethics from those of the
Gentiles. Gaius of Gadara and Lucius of Susitha (Hippos) were
adulterers and murderers[138]; but these were Gaius and Lucius
the symbols[139] of אומות העולם; as such they were adulterers and
murderers. But the individual Gaius and Lucius, the neighbors
and friends, were "good, faithful and enjoying the fruit of their
labors."[140]

The Jew is allowed to criticise the behavior of Gaius and
Lucius, the symbols of the Nations — אומות העולם, but he is not
permitted to gossip about the affairs of the persons Gaius and
Lucius. In the Midrash[141] we read: תשב באחיך תדבר בבן אמך
תתן דופי אמר ר' יוחנן אם הרגלת לשונך לדבר באחיך שאינו בן אומתך סוף
בבן אומתך תתן דופי. " 'Thou sittest and speakest against thy brother;
thou slanderest thine own mother's son' (Ps. L.20). R. Johanan[142]
said: 'if you have accustomed your tongue to speak against
your brother who is not of your own nation, you will eventually
slander the son of your own nation'."[143]

The learned Rabbis were conscious of their great task of
guarding the true faith, the high ethics and the pure family
life of the Jews against any outside contamination; they made

[138] Pesiktha Rabbathi XXI, ed. Friedmann, 107b, 108a.

[139] These two names are always taken only as symbols in Palestinian
Talmudic literature. See TP Terumoth X.7, 47b (and parallel); Gittin I.1,
43b.

[140] See above p. 77.

[141] Debarim Rabba VI.9.

[142] One of the most prominent scholars of Jewish Palestine in the 3rd
century. He was the head of the school in Tiberias, and the Jewish tradition
ascribed to him the editorship of the Palestinian Talmud (See Frankel מבוא
הירושלמי p. מ"ז–מ"ח). His opinion has therefore exceptional weight.

[143] See Redal ad loc., n. 29 and Tanhuma פקודי sect. 7.

hedge upon hedge around the Law in order to protect it and to preserve it in its entire purity. But they were not blind, nay they refused to close their eyes to reality. They observed attentively and studied carefully the non-Jewish Hellenized world; they were quite conscious and well aware of it; they knew its shortcomings and failures. But they never denied the great virtue of the individual in that world. He was a human being with all his weaknesses and failings, but one who, in course of times, began to aspire towards the better and the higher.

PLEASURES AND FEARS

In the previous chapters we sought to prove that all Rabbinic literature displays a wide knowledge and thorough understanding of the Gentile cultural world. This literature reflects but incidentally the actual life of the Jews in Palestine. The Rabbis were not interested in leaving us records of events and descriptions of life in Palestine. We possess only occasional remarks and incidental observations on events and facts in so far as they touched upon halachic questions or as they were utilized by the Haggadists for teaching the people a lesson in morality.

The cultural influence of Hellenism on the people was even larger and deeper than could be inferred from the facts recorded in Rabbinic literature. The middle class of the Jewish people lived together with heathens and Christians in the big cities of Palestine; they traded together and they worked together. The people could not help admiring the beautiful and the useful; they could not fail to be attracted by the external brilliance and the superficial beauty of Gentile life. The learned and pious Rabbis did their utmost to prevent the people from becoming thoroughly Hellenized; they persisted in stressing to the people the superiority of the spiritual over the physical and the final victory of the soul over the body. But it is hardly possible that the great masses of the Jewish people in the big towns conducted themselves in conformity with the idealistic views of the Rabbis. It is very unlikely that they kept consciously refusing to imitate the manners and life-pattern of their neighbors, so attractive at first sight. The ignorant people of the country, on the other hand, whose economic status made it impossible for them to emulate the middle class in the pursuit of pleasures and elegance, adopted their neighbors' belief in magic, astrology and all kinds of superstitions in defiance of Written and Oral Laws.

The Rabbis faced the situation admirably. They exerted themselves to the utmost in their struggle against that part of the foreign influences in the life of the people, which, in their view, threatened the existence of the Jewish religion and the Jewish nation. They strove perforce to eliminate such elements entirely from the Jewish mode of life. On the other hand, they tried to legalize strange customs which could be tolerated without endangering the vital principles of Judaism. But their fundamental work was that of Judaizing the foreign elements.

It is very hard to remove certain practices adopted by the people. It is particularly difficult to eliminate practices which have their roots in popular beliefs and superstitions. The Rabbis were compelled to tolerate the practice, but they succeeded in endowing it with Jewish character. They had to adapt a Gentile custom adopted by the ignorant masses so as to suit Jewish requirements. They sometimes had to draw upon heathen folk-lore popular among the masses and recast it in a Jewish form in order to instruct and edify those same masses.

The mirror of Rabbinic literature reflects a continuous war between the Rabbis and the masses. The Rabbis warned the townspeople not to follow the way of the Gentiles, not to adopt the Hellenistic manner of life, but most bitterly they fought the superstitions of the ignorant country people. The history of this fight of the Rabbis against the Gentile manner of life and popular superstitions is recorded in almost every branch of Rabbinic literature. But we shall deal here mainly with foreign manners, customs and superstitions tolerated by the Rabbis or legalized and Judaized by them.

Physical exercise. The care of the body played a prominent part in the everyday life of the Gentile, and undoubtedly it began to occupy an important place in Jewish life also.[1] The Rabbis, of course, felt a deep contempt for the one who pays excessive attention to the development of the body, but there is no Biblical law forbidding physical training. The Rabbis did not miss the opportunity to condemn sport as an occupation.[2] They even cursed the man who behaved during the ritual

[1] See Krauss, Talmudische Archaeologie I, 209 seq.; III, 113 seq.

[2] See my article on water-sports in the Hebrew monthly סיני, טבת תרצ"ט, p. 54 seq.

immersion, טבילה, as if he was indulging in water-sports.[3] Nevertheless they did not forbid sports outright, tolerating them when they did not contradict or interfere with the Law.

We shall quote an interesting Mishna[4] which deals with the exercises in the wrestling arena, and which may shed light on the manner of life of the Jews in Palestine.[5] We read there: סכין וממשמשין בבני מעים אבל לא מתעמלין ולא מתגרדין. אין יורדין לקורדימה ואין עושין אפיקטויין. "They may oil and massage their stomach, but not exercise (the body)[6] and not scrape. They may not go down to קורדימה (see below) and may not use artificial emetics."[6a] The commentaries, the translators and the dictionaries did not comprehend all the implications of this Mishna. There can be no doubt that what we have here is a list of the different exercises of the wrestlers. They used to oil themselves, to grapple and trip each other and to wallow in the clay.[7] But what does קורדימה mean? When we examine the readings of the mss. and the old editions we realize that two different readings — both well supported — have been preserved. The Palestinian reading, beyond any doubt, is פילומה.[8] Lewy, Kohut and Krauss

---

[3] See סיני ibid., p. 57 and my remarks in Tosefeth Rishonim IV, p. 27–28.

[4] Shabbath XXII.6.

[5] Second century?

[6] See Maimonides' commentary ad loc.

[6a] On the Sabbath-day.

[7] Lucianus Samoset. in Anacharsis I (883) writes: Ταῦτα δὲ ὑμῖν ὦ Σόλον, τίνος ἕνεκα οἱ νέοι ποιοῦσιν; οἱ μὲν αὐτῶν περιπλεκόμενοι ἀλλήλους ὑποσκελίζουσιν, οἱ δὲ ἄγχουσι καὶ λυγίζουσι καὶ ἐν τῷ πηλῷ συναναφύρονται κυλινδούμενοι ὥσπερ σύες. καίτοι κατ' ἀρχὰς εὐθὺς ἀποδυσάμενοι—ἑώρων γάρ—λίπα τε ἠλείψαντο καὶ κατέφησε μάλα εἰρηνικῶς ἄτερος τὸν ἕτερον ἐν τῷ μέρει κτλ. "Why do your young men behave like this, Solon? Some of them grappling and tripping each other, some throttling, struggling, intertwining in the clay like so many pigs wallowing. And yet their first proceeding after they have stripped — I noticed that — is to oil and scrape each other quite amicably etc." (Translation by Fowler, Oxford, 1905). On the exercises in the sand see also Philostr. περὶ γυμναστικῆς, ed. Jüthner, p. 178 and notes ibid., p. 303–304.

[8] See Rabbinovicz, Variae Lectiones ad loc., p. 351, n. 30. Add: Mishna, ed. Lowe, cod. Kaufmann, Geniza ms. (In Festschrift... Israel Lewy's etc., Hebrew part, p. 198. The latter reads: פולומה), R. Hananel ad loc. in the name of ס'א (other books) and Rabiah I, p. 284₃.

take פילומה to mean πήλωμα — mud. Krauss[9] refers to Sophocles, Lexicon, who quotes this word from Charisius[10] and translates it "mud". Accordingly, the lexicons[11] explain that our Mishna does not permit one to bathe in mud.[12] Loew,[13] however, doubts the very identification of פילומא with πήλωμα. It is indeed difficult to understand why the Mishna should use the exceedingly rare Greek word πήλωμα for the general term "mud".

But in reality πήλωμα means not "mud", but a *place* which has something to do with mud. Charisius,[14] enumerating the feminine nouns that are used only in the plural, mentions: "Lutinae πήλωμα". Lutinae like πήλωμα is a very rare word[15] and their exact meaning is obscure.[16] It seems to be a local technical term from the vocabulary of a certain profession. Since the exercises of the wrestlers form the subject of our Mishna it is probably to the profession of wrestlers that the word belongs. πήλωμα will be the place where the wrestlers exercised themselves in πηλός (mud), and the Mishna used the technical word prevalent during a certain period in certain districts of Palestine. The Rabbinic literature once more[17] explains the special terms of the professionals.

The other reading קורדימא of the editions also has some support.[18] Stronger evidence favors the reading קירומא,[19] and קורדימא is most likely a corruption of קירומא, קורומא. Jastrow[20] gives the

[9] Byzant. Zeitschrift II (1893), p. 548.

[10] P. 33₁₆.

[11] See Kohut and Lewy. Krauss, as usual, explains only the word but not the whole phrase.

[12] On the Sabbath. Jastrow s. v. פילומא translates: "you must not go down to the clay ground (of the brickyard etc.)"!

[13] In Krauss' LW, p. 673a.

[14] Art. Gramm. I, Lipsiae 1925, p. 364.

[15] Neither word is recorded in any dictionary from any other source than Charisius.

[16] See Forgellinus, Totius latinitatis lexicon III, p. 820, s. v. Lutina.

[17] See above p. 32, n. 21.

[18] So Maimonides and Me'iri ad loc.

[19] R. Hananel, Aruch (In the latter we read erroneously: קורימא), Rashi ms. and the Hebrew-Persian dictionary (see above p. 60), ed. Bacher, Hebrew part, p. 72 Nos. 957 and 958.

[20] Dictionary, s. v. קירומא.

correct Greek equivalent κήρωμα and explains: "You must not
go down (on Sabbath) to a wrestling ground." But he did not
realize the relation of this word to the Mishna as a whole,[1] nor
did he explain the exact meaning of the term in our Mishna
correctly.

The question, however, is: How was the well established
Palestinian reading פילומה altered into קירומא? Our answer is that
קירומא (κήρωμα), equivalent to פילומא (πήλωμα), presents an old
different tradition. And just as πήλωμα means the place in the
wrestling ground where the wrestlers performed their exercises
in mud and clay, so κήρωμα designated the same place,[2] and to
go down to the κήρωμα means not to go to the wrestling ground
to wrestle but to exercise the body.

Plutarch mentions the πηλός and κήρωμα together. He
says:[3] μόνον τῶν τῆς ἀγωνίας εἰδῶν πηλοῦ καὶ κονίστρας καὶ
κηρώματος τυγχάνει δεόμενον. "It (wrestling) happens to be
the only kind of exercise in which clay, dust and κήρωμα (wax
and clay mixed with oil) are used."

The original reading in the Mishna seems to have been
פילומא which was subsequently explained and changed to the
more common קירומא — κήρωμα. The latter was retained by the
Babylonian Amoraim, whereas the Palestinian preserved the
former.

In Midrash Sechel Tob[4] we read: אין יורדין לקורדימא[5] דהיינו
פילומא וכו', "You may not go down to the 'Kordima' (read:
Keiroma, κήρωμα) which is the same as πήλωμα etc." Finding
פילומא in the Mishna and קירומא in the quotation (פיסקא) of
TB, the author drew his own conclusion that the two words
mean the same.[6]

---

[1] As it can be seen from his explanations of פילומא and עמל.

[2] See Liddell and Scott s. v. κήρωμα.

[3] Quaest. conviv. II.4 (Moralia 638c).

[4] Ed. Buber, p. 312. The author fl. in the XII c.

[5] Read: קירומא.

[6] This supports again the theory advanced by me in the bibliographical
Quarterly קרית ספר vol. XIV p. 324 and the Introduction to Tosefeth Rishonim
IV, p. 13. Comp. our note above p. 43 n. 76.

Happily, we find the same word קירומא in a Palestinian
Syriac Homily. We read there:[8] אתליט לא מעמיל הוא אברוי
במישחא להון ומרכרך בקירום. The editor translates: "An
athlete doth not smear his limbs in wax, but softeneth them
with oil." This translation is wrong; the correct rendering is:
"Doth not the athlete exercise his limbs in the Ceroma ($κήρωμα$)
and doth he not soften them with oil"? Thus, the passage contains a striking parallel to our Mishna.

The following clause of the Mishna ואין עושין אפיקטוזין — "And
they may not use artificial emetics" — also had some connection
with the practice of the athletes. In ancient times artificial
emetics played an important part both in controlling the weight
of the body and in providing the gluttons with more opportuni-
ties to eat.[9] The life of the athletes was constantly dedicated
to the cult of the body.[10] They exerted special care to keep their
bowels clean and were in the habit of purging their body frequently. Oribasius[11] mentions incidentally: $καὶ μάλιστα ἐπὶ τῶν$
$ἀθλητῶν διὰ τὸ πρὸς τὸν κλυσμὸν ἔθος κτλ.$ "And especially by
the athletes, due to their habit of resorting to intestinal irriga-
tions etc." They were likewise in the habit of using artificial
emetics. We may quote a most instructive passage[12] from the
epistles[13] of Seneca: Aeque luctatores et totam *oleo ac luto*
constantem scientiam expello ex his studiis liberalibus . . . Quid
enim, oro te, liberale habent isti *ieiuni vomitores*, quorum cor-
pora in sagina, animi in macie et veterno sunt? "From the
liberal studies I also exclude the wrestlers (wrestling) and all
knowledge that consists of oil and mud . . . For what of the
liberal, prithee, is there in these contemptible vomitors, whose
bodies [find pleasure] in cramming whereas their minds are in
a state of meagerness and sluggishness?"

[7] Not recorded in any Syriac dictionary.

[8] Horae Semiticae VIII (Cambridge 1909), p. 200.

[9] On artificial vomiting in general see Oribasius Med. (IV c.), Collect.
Med. VIII.19–23, ed. Daremberg, p. 195–205 and on artificial vomiting
after the meal in particular ibid. p. 202 seq.

[10] See Dictionnaire des antiquités etc. par Daremberg et Saglio I, p. 517b.

[11] Ibid. VIII.24, p. 220.

[12] Referred to by the Dictionnaire etc. ibidem.

[13] LXXXVIII.18.

Thus, Seneca calls the wrestlers, whose knowledge consists of oil and mud, "contemptible vomitors", vomiting being closely associated with the oiling of the body and the exercises in mud — just the same as in our Mishna. Both sources shed mutual light upon each other, and Seneca is easily understood without any reference to the drunkards who drink wine on an empty stomach[14]; he calls the wrestlers vomitors because of their habit of using artificial emetics. The Rabbis could have no greater respect for the "contemptible vomitors" than Seneca, yet they did not forbid physical exercises. They prohibited certain exercises on the Sabbath, but they allowed them on ordinary days.

From this Mishna we learn that, like their Gentile neighbors, the Jews used to perform all kinds of exercises of the body, and that the Rabbis tolerated it.

Astrology, magic and superstition. The close relations between the Jewish people in Palestine and their Gentile neighbors created another problem. Like the latter, the Jews believed in Astrology and magic and they borrowed from them many superstitions entirely alien to the Jewish religion.[15] The Rabbis had to face the situation as it was. They had to regulate, to legalize, to Judaize foreign elements, to exploit the false religious feelings of the ignorant populace and turn them to the channels of true religion and, finally, to eliminate what could be neither utilized nor tolerated. It is very instructive to see how the Rabbis treated the problem of Astrology.

There is a tradition[16] in the name of R. Jose of Huzal (II c.): מניין שאין שואלין בכלדיים שנאמר תמים תהיה עם ה' אלהיך "How do we know that you must not consult Astrologers? Because it is said (Deut. XVIII.13): *'Thou shalt be whole-hearted with the Lord thy God'*." Already the Sibylline books praise the righteous who

---

[14] Ep. XV.

[15] L. Blau published a valuable book, Das altjüdische Zauberwesen, 1898, in which he dealt with the large subject of superstitions, magic and demonology in the Jewish world. Even now this remains the standard work on the subject. We shall dwell here, as in the previous chapters, mainly on sources either not recorded or misunderstood by Blau and other scholars.

[16] TB Pesahim 113b.

do not study the predictions of Chaldean Astrology, nor do they astronomize.[17] Likewise an old anonymous Baraitha[18] teaches: " '*Do not* ובכוכבים בעופות בחולדה מנחשים שהם אילו כגון תנחשו לא divine' (Lev. XIX.26), like those who divine by means of a weasel,[19] birds and stars."[20]

But Astrology was a highly respected art in olden times; in the Midrash[21] we read: כתיב ותרב חכמת שלמה מחכמת כל בני קדם ומכל חכמת מצרים ומה היתה חכמתן של בני קדם שהיו יודעין במזל וקוסמין בעופות ובקיאין בטייר. "It is written (I Kings V.10): '*And Solomon's wisdom excelled the wisdom of all the children of the East and all the wisdom in Egypt*'. What, then, was the wisdom of '*the children of the East*'? They were skilled in Astrology and divination from birds and expert in Augury."[21a] The wisdom of the East (adopted by the Greeks and Romans) could not be entirely ignored. A learned and cultured man of those times could not reject the science of Astrology, a science recognized and acknowledged by all the civilized ancient world. To deny at that time the efficacy of Astrology would mean to deny a well established fact, to discredit a "science" accepted by both Hellenes and Barbarians. Some of the Rabbis did not indeed deny the efficacy of Astrology.[22] One of the later Rabbinic authorities, the great Nahmanides, dealt at length[23] with these differences of opinions in Rabbinic sources; he even concludes

[17] Sibyllina III, 227: οὐδέ τε Χαλδαίων τὰ προμάντια ἀστρολογοῦσιν οὐδὲ μὲν ἀστρονομοῦσι.

[18] Sifra Kedoshim VI.2, ed. Weiss 90b.

[19] On the weasel as a bad omen see Liddell and Scott s.v. γαλέη. Dio Cassius (LVIII. 5) mentions both weasel and birds among the bad omens which foretold Sejanus' fall. On the attitude of the Jews towards augury see Joseph., Against Apion 1.22, 203–204; Sybill. ibid., 224.

[20] See Rabbinovicz, Variae Lectiones ad Sanhedrin, p. 187, n. 4. However, the reading דנים seems to be preferable. See Blau, Zauberwesen, p. 45, n. 2.

[21] Koheleth Rabba VIII.23 (and parallels).

[21a] Comp. Jos. (Ant. VIII.2.5) who speaks of the knowledge of Solomon of the art used against demons. See also Ginzberg, Legends of the Jews, VI.291.

[22] See TB Shabbath 156a–b.

[23] "Ascribed" responsa No. 283, quoted in ארחות חיים II, p. 620.

that the diviners from stars are not the same as Astrologers.[24]
The real fact seems to be that not all Rabbis maintained the
same negative attitude towards Astrology.[25]

Some Rabbis reached a remarkable compromise between the
power of Astrology and the proper Jewish attitude to it. In
Mekiltha[26] we read: ר' יונתן אומר אילו ואילו נתנו לגויים שנאמר כה אמר
ה'. אל דרך הגוים אל תלמדו ומאותות השמים אל תחתו. "R. Jonathan (II c.)
says: All these signs (of the planets) were given to (i. e. were
valid for) the Gentiles, for it is said (Jer. X.2): 'Thus saith the
Lord: Learn not the way of the nations, and be not dismayed by
the signs of heaven'."

Even more explicitly R. Johanan declares: אין מזל לישראל[27]
"There is no planet for Israel," i. e. Israel is not dependent on
the planets. The power of Astrology is not denied, but it is
confined to the Gentiles only, having no influence on Israel.

According to Tanhuma[28] this maxim was accepted even by
the Gentile Astrologers; they said: יהודים אתם, אין דברי האיסטרולוגין
מתקיימים בכם, שאתם יהודים "You are Jews, the predictions of the
Astrologers have no effect on you, for you are Jews." We possess
independent evidence confirming the words of the Rabbis.
Bardesan maintains:[29] יהודים ... ולא דבר להון בקטירא כוכבא דמשלט
בקלמא "And the Jews ... nor does the star, which has authority
in the Clime, govern them by force."[30] The words of Bardesan

---

[24] ואלו המנחשים בכוכבים דקתני, לאו באיצטגנינות קיימא. Comp. also Me'iri ad
Sanhedrin 65b.

[25] Comp. also Debarim Rabba VIII.1 and commentaries.

[26] Bo, פסחא I, ed. Horovitz, p. 720 (and parallels).

[27] TB Shabbath 156a and parallels.

[28] Shoftim sec. 10.

[29] "Book of the Laws of Countries," ed. Cureton, p. י"ט. See above
p. 63 n. 225.

[30] Eusebius in his Praep. Ev. VI.10, 279c, ed. Gifford, p. 357 (See also
Bardesan ed. Cureton p. 30) quotes: οὐ κλίματος ἐξουσίαν ἐντρεπόμενοι —
"nor do they heed the influence of the clime." This is an obvious paraphrase
of the original Syriac, as is revealed by comparison of the Syriac with the
Hebrew saying of the Rabbis — a fact which again refutes the opinion of
Schulthess that the Syriac text published by Cureton is a translation from
the Greek. See above p. 63, n. 225.

are almost literally the same as those reported by the Rabbis
in the name of the Gentile Astrologers.[31]

The pious Jew instructed by the Rabbis used to defy the
signs of the stars,[32] and the Gentile Astrologers had either to
discredit the force of Astrology or to admit that the stars have
no power over the Jews; they preferred the latter course. Astrology is a "science", but only for the Gentiles,[33] not for the pious
Jews. The opinion of the Rabbis finally prevailed even on the
Gentile Astrologers.

Charms. The Rabbis had to face the same problem regarding
all kinds of charms. The civilized world believed in charms;
observation proved that they sometimes helped and cured; the
ancients did not yet discriminate between real medicine and the
magic of the "medicine-man", between charms and experi-
mental science. The charms recorded in the Talmud were
accepted all over the civilized ancient world,[34] and even the
foremost scholars of the time were not able to mark the definite
limits between superstition and science; they were aware of the
fact that there are some grains of scientific truth in the accepted

[31] Bardesan further emphasizes (ibid.) that the Jews perform their religious rites regardless of the country and the clime which have no influence
over them. This view seems to be an outgrowth of the general opinion of the
Gentiles that the local gods have no power over the Jews, whereas the Gentile
is subject to the gods of the locality (See Deissmann, Light etc., p. 185,
n. 4. Comp. also Pap. Oxyr. 936, 2; 1296, 4; 1664, 5).

TP Berakoth (IX.1, 13b) records a similar opinion held by Gentile
sailors who maintained that their gods can help them only in their respective
places, whereas the Jewish God is powerful everywhere (כל אהן דאת אזיל אלהך
עמך, "Wherever thou goest thy God is with thee).

This concept of the Gentiles, supported by the observation of the
Astrologers probably helped to continue in force the "privilegia iudaica" in
matters of worship.

[32] See the story of the proselyte in TP Shabbath VI, 8d and the explanation in הירושלמי כפשוטו I, p. 115. Comp. Epiphanius, de mens. et pond. 15
(about the Astrology of Aquila). See also below p. 149 seq.

[33] Who believe in it, as well as for the Jews who practice it. See the
opinion of R. Levi in TP ibidem.

[34] See the illuminating remarks thereon by קיל"ר in the Hebrew periodical
ציון, ed. Creizenach and Jost, 1842, p. 82.

charms, but they were not mature enough to distinguish truth from fiction.[35]

The Rabbis left us a whole chapter (פרק אמוראי) dealing with the Amorite practices[36] in which they rejected them as forbidden superstitions. But at the same time TP[37] records the law laid down by R. Johanan that the use of whatever possesses a remedial character (in contrast to magic) is not forbidden even if it is part of the ways of the Amorites.[38] Thus, whenever the Rabbis were convinced from observation and experience that an application of magic contains some natural basis,[39] they did not forbid it.

The Tosephta[40] teaches: אין תולין תחובין בתאינה ואין מרכיבין מפני שהיא עבודה "Branches (of a wild fig) must not be hung on a fig tree, nor may it be inoculated (in the Sabbatical year), for it is considered cultivation."[41] The process whereby the quality of a fig tree was improved by attaching to it a branch of a wild fig tree was known to the Ancients.[42] It is possible that the author of this Halacha understood the natural causes of this process of caprification, as the word תחובין shows.[43] But Loew[44] and Blau[45] failed to note that the peasants of Palestine took it as a charm. For TP[46] enjoins: אין תולין תובין[47] בתאינה. כיצד הוא עושה מייתי יחור דתאינה שטר[48] ותלי בה ואמ' לה הדא עבדא ואת לית את

[35] See קיל'ר ibidem.

[36] TB Shabbath 67a. See my remarks in Tosefeth Rishonim I, p. 126–127.

[37] Shabbath VI, 8c: כל שהוא מרפא אין בו משום דרכי האמורי.

[38] Comp. also TB ibid., 67a.

[39] Divinatio naturalis? See Colson's notes to Philo's de spec. leg. III.100, in the Loeb classical Library vol. VII, p. 636.

[40] Shebiith I.9, 61:30.

[41] Which is forbidden during the Sabbatical year.

[42] See Arist., de anim. hist. V.32, 557b; Theophr., de causis plant. II. 9.5; Plin., nat. hist. XV.79.

[43] See the correct explanation by Loew in Flora I, p. 233.

[44] Ibidem.

[45] Zauberwesen, p. 165.   [46] Shebiith IV.4, 35b.

[47] =תחובין. See Loew ibidem.

[48] Read: שטי=שטיא (On the similarity of 'י and 'ר see שו"ת הרא"ש XLV.2). שטיא here means wild, like שוטים in the Mishna Shebi'ith IX.1 (See Aruch s. v. ירבוח). The word שטר is missing in Cod. Vat.

עבדה "Branches must not be hung on a fig tree (in the Sabbatical year). How is it done? One gets a shoot of a wild fig tree and, suspending it on the barren fig tree, he says to the latter: 'This one (i. e. the wild) bears fruit, but thou dost not' "! Perhaps, even the more enlightened men of the people still attached more importance to the charm of the remedy than to its natural causes. The Jewish peasant who believed in the "magic" of caprification could not be expected to be better informed than Plutarch. The latter discusses[49] strange phenomena the causes of which are unknown to us, and he writes there:[50] καὶ τὸ τῶν ἀγρίων ἐρινεῶν, ἃ ταῖς ἡμέροις περιαπτόμενα συκαῖς ἀπορρεῖν οὐκ ἐᾷ τὸν καρπὸν ἀλλὰ συνέχει καὶ συνεκπεπαίνει. "And that wild fig trees, being bound around garden fig trees, will [not only] prevent the fruit from falling, but they will keep them and promote their ripening." Plutarch mentions this wonder among two other strange phenomena: that the blood of a mole or the rags of women — ῥάκια γυναικεῖα — avert hail[51] and that deer shed salt tears when they are taken captive. He admits, then, that he does not know the causes of these "supernatural" phenomena, although he mentions Theophrastus' discourses in the same chapter.[52] If the learned Plutarch did not know the scientific explanation of caprification which was known to Aristotle and Theophrastus,[53] and he considered it to be supernatural like the averting of hail by the blood of a mole and similar "wonders", what could be expected of the peasant in Palestine?

The attitude of the Babylonian Rabbis towards a similar "magical act" performed on a barren date tree is quite edifying.

[49] Quaest. conviv. VII.2.
[50] 700 f.
[51] The Mishna (Nidda VII.3) teaches: כל הכתמים הבאים מרקם טהורים, "All blood-stains (on women's garments) that come from Rekem are clean." Tanhuma (וארא, ed. Buber, p. 27) quotes a proverb: יש מוליכין תבן לעפרים, כתם לרקם? "Would anyone import straw to Afarayim or a blood-stain to Rekem?" This proverb indicates that blood-stains on women's rags were exported from Rekem. Perhaps for the purpose of charms and magic.
[52] 700d.
[53] See above n. 42.

According to the Babylonian Talmud[54] תלינן כובסי בדיקלא "We suspend a cluster of dates[55] on a barren date-tree." The Rabbis explain that this process is not one of the ways of the Amorites, but has its roots in the Bible, for it is written (Lev. XIII.45): וטמא טמא יקרא, *"And he* (i. e. the leper) *shall cry, 'Unclean, unclean';"* he must advertise his grief, so that the public may pray for him. Similarly, the public exhibition of the sterility of the tree may arouse pity in the hearts of passers-by who will then pray for it.

The Babylonian Rabbis were confronted with a practice current among peasants from time immemorial. They had either to uproot it or to legalize it. They chose the latter because they may have had some vague notion of its natural course,[56] and especially because they were able to attach to this practice a genuine Jewish idea. They kept to the rule that there is no need to fight the superstition of the people when it is possible to transform it into true religion.

We shall quote one more example of a popular superstition which was not eliminated by the Rabbis, but rather Jewishly interpreted and sanctioned.

Midrash BR portrays in lively colors how Laban deceived Jacob, giving him Leah instead of Rachel. The Midrash tells us:[56] ברמשא אתון מעלתא וטפון בוצינא. אמר להון, מהו כדין? אמ' לי' מה את צבי דאנן דביוין דכוותכון וכו'. "In the evening they came to bring her [to the bridal canopy] and extinguished the light. He (i. e. Jacob) asked them: 'What does this mean?' They replied: 'Dost thou want us to . . .[57] like you?' " The commentaries offer no satisfactory explanation of the extinguishing of the light at the wedding — apparently a regular practice. The text can not be understood unless we presume that the Rabbis supposed Laban to have followed an Aramaic practice which was not familiar to Jacob, the Palestinian. Let us examine

---

[54] Shabbath 67a.

[55] Or a branch of a date-tree. See Mei'ri ad loc. and Lewy Chald. Woerterbuch über Targumim, p. 351, s. v. כבוסין.

[56] LXX.19, ed. Theodor-Albeck, p. 8184.

[57] The meaning of the word דביוין is not clear and the reading is not sure, see the variants ad loc.

whether the extinction of lights at weddings might have been practiced by the Babylonian Jews.

We read in IV Ezra X.1:[58] Et factum est, cum introisset filius meus in thalamo suo cecidit et mortuus est. Et euertimus omnes lumina, et surrexerunt omnes ciues mei ad consolandum me, et quieui usque in alium diem usque noctem. "And it came to pass that when my son entered into his wedding chamber he fell down and died. Then we turned over all the lamps, and all my fellow townsfolk rose up to comfort me; but I remained quiet until the night of the next day."

We have here a true record of the mourning customs followed by the Jews. The mourner remained quiet[59] for one day. The Ethiopic version which reads: "till the night of the second day"[60] seems to agree with later Jewish customs.[61] But what is the meaning of "evertimus omnes lumina"? The Ethiopic version has: "We extinguished the lights," but the Latin seems to be more original. Its Hebrew equivalent would be: כפינו את המנורות,[62] "We turned over the lamps," an action parallel to the turning of the beds by the mourners.[63] To turn over the lamps required, of course, that they be first extinguished. And although there is no direct law directing the mourner to put out the lights, there is good evidence to the effect that the Jewish mourner did so.

In the Midrash[64] we read: היאך בני אדם מתאבלים, אמרו לו אבל קורע את בגדיו . . . האבל יושב לעצמו ומראה פנים . . . האבל כופה את מטתו . . . האבל מכבה פנסין וכו'. "How do men mourn? They told Him: The mourner rends his garments . . . the mourner sits by

---

[58] Ed. Gry, p. 300.

[59] דומם. See TB Berakoth 19a and Pesiktha deR. Kahana, p. 120a.

[60] The Vat. ms. of the Arabic version reads: till the third day.

[61] See the minor tract Semahoth VI.2–7, ed. Higger, p. 131 seq. (and parallels). Comp., however, Ben Sira XXXVIII.17.

[62] In פיוטי יניי edit. Zulay p. קפ'ט we read: נרות ציון לוכדו ונתכפו "The lights of Zion were seized and turned over." Comp. also the expression (Sifre בלק, ed. Horovitz, p. 17314, and parallels): כפה סייח את המנורה and eversores luminum canes (Tertul., Apol. VII.1, Migne PL I 358a and n. 44 ibid.).

[63] See TP Berakoth III.1, 5d–6a and parallels.

[64] Eka Zuta vers. I, ed. Buber, p. 66.

himself[65] and shows his face[66]... the mourner turns over his bed ... the mourner extinguishes the lamps."[67] Thus, we have authentic proof that the Jewish mourner used to extinguish the lights[68] (or to turn over the lamps, as in IV Ezra) in order to express his mourning.

From TB[69] we learn further that the Jews (probably Babylonian) used to put ashes upon the head of the bridegroom. This seemed originally to have been a bit of magic for the purpose of averting the demons. We may agree with Prof. Lauterbach, who concludes:[70] "The third method, i. e. the one of fooling the demons by making them believe that the people are sad and mourning and therefore not to be envied, is represented by in the ceremonies of putting ashes upon the head of the bridegroom or a piece of black cloth upon the heads of both the bride and the groom, thus making them appear to be mourners."[71] Since there is no hint of such customs at weddings

[65] Keeps silent. See the verse quoted in the parallel sources.

[66] To the comforters. The usual meaning of להראות פנים is that the comforters show their face to the mourner, see Jastrow, dictionary, p. 1436. In BR C.7, ed. Albeck 1292 l. 1 and l. 3 למחזייה אפין means to show the face and not to see the face.

[67] In the parallel passages these are listed as acts of a king in mourning (Comp. Pesiktha deR. Kahana 119b n. 16) and not of ordinary mourners. Comp. also Eka Zuta Vers. II, ed. Buber, p. 139. But our source speaks only of the ordinary man, and there is no hint of the purple cloak (פורפורין) of the king, mentioned in all parallel sources.

[68] See Buber's note ad Pesiktha deR. Kahana, 120a, n. 17.

[69] Baba Bathra 60b.

[70] H. U. C. A. vol. II, p. 359.

[71] We may also mention Tanhuma תולדות ed. Buber 126: שמקדם היו מכניסין על האבל עדשים, ולבית המשתה עדשים "Formerly they used to serve lentils to the mourner as well as at weddings." Since the first practice was quite current in Talmudic times (See TP Berakoth III.1, 6a and Ratner ad loc. 68–69) we may conclude that the adverb "formerly" alludes to the lentils at weddings. Comp. also RR LXIII.14, 699i and Loew Flora II, 447.

In our opinion, it is very possible that the author of this Palestinian statement speaks of a practice which he regarded as obsolete because it was never known to have been used in Palestine and which came to him from a Babylonian source. The reason for this practice was again probably to mislead the evil spirits by pretending that a mourning occasion was being observed in the house. This practice at the weddings seems to have subsequently disappeared even in Babylonia.

in the ancient Palestinian literature, we have to assume that
this practice was confined to the Babylonian Jews only. The
Midrash BR related a Babylonian custom of putting out the
lights at the wedding ceremonies (so as to appear like mourners)
which was not known to Jacob, the Palestinian. But Laban
took advantage of this practice, substituting Leah for Rachel in
the darkness.

The Rabbis of Babylonia did not fight this superstition,
but, on the contrary, sanctioned it by endowing it with religious
character. The Jew should remember the destruction of the
Temple even at the time of his greatest joy. A Jewish bridegroom has to put ashes on his head in order to bear in mind
that even now he is a mourner for Zion.[71a] The same may be
said of many other ceremonies treated in Lauterbach's article[72];
they may have had their origin in popular superstitions, but
the Rabbis reinterpreted them until they were transformed into
ceremonies with true religious content.[73]

The Rabbis also tried to attach a Jewish interpretation to
formulas of obscure origin which were current among the
people. In the Midrash[74] we read: דבריתא מ ש ת ב ע י ן ואמרין
במאן דאקים עלמא[75] על תלתא עמודים. אית דאמר, אברהם יצחק ויעקב אינון
ואית דאמרין אלו הן חנניה מישאל ועזריה. "The people swear and say
'By Him Who established the world on three pillars.' Some say
they are Abraham, Isaac and Jacob, and some say they are
Hananiah Mishael and Azariah."

The simple meaning of the oath implies that the world is
standing on three pillars, in its ordinary sense. In TB[76] is
recorded: ר' יוסי אומר . . . הארץ על מה עומדת על העמודים . . . וחכמים
אומרים על י"ב עמודים . . . ויש אומרים ז' עמודים . . . ר' אלעזר בן שמוע
אומר על עמוד אחד וצדיק שמו, "R. Jose said . . . on what does the
world stand? On pillars. The sages said on twelve pillars . . .

[71a] TB Baba Bathra 60b.

[72] Ibid., p. 361 n. 19, 263 n. 23.

[73] Comp. Maimonides מורה נבוכים III.32.

[74] Shir Hashirim Rabba VII.8 (ed. Romm 38a).

[75] Midrash Tehilim I.15, ed. Buber, p. 15 reads: והוא ד א מ ר י ברייתא
על מאן קאים עלמא which is a "corrected" reading.

[76] Hagiga 12b.

Some said on seven pillars ... R. Eleazar ben Shammua said
on one pillar whose name is righteous."[77] However, the parallel
passage in TP[78] does not mention that the world stands on
pillars, nor is any reference to it in the older Palestinian sources
known to me, although TB quotes a Tannaitic Baraitha dealing
with it. That the world is standing on *three* pillars is not stated
explicitly in any other Rabbinic source.

But Plutarch[79] writes: μίμημα τῆς γῆς ἡ τράπεζ᾽ εἶναι, "The
table is a copy of the earth." Martin[80] asserts that Plutarch
undoubtedly had in mind the three-legged Roman table[81] and
that he assumed the world to be standing on three legs, which
gave it perfect stability. This idea of the world standing on
three legs seems to have been popular among the Jews, and the
Haggadists made use of it. So we find in Tanhuma:[82] אמר ר'
שמואל בר נחמן עד שלא נבנה בית המקדש היה העולם עומד על תרנוס של שני
רגלים, אבל משנבנה בית המקדש נתבסס העולם, "R. Samuel bar Nahman
said: before the Temple was built the world was standing on a
two-legged chair,[83] but after the Temple was built the world
became firm" (i. e. a third leg was added). Thus, the world is
stable only when it stands on three legs.[84]

Yet it is hard to believe that in their every-day life the
people (ברייתא) used such an elaborate oath as "By Him Who
established the world on three pillars." This oath gives the impression of having been taken from a literary source which the
Rabbis tried to comment and interpret. The most plausible
literary source for such a phrase is likely to be an incantation.
Accordingly, we have to translate דברייתא משתבעין "that the

[77] See also the sources referred to in Ginzberg's Legends of the Jews
vol. V, p. 12 n. 28.

[78] Hagiga II.1, 77a.

[79] Quaest. conviv. VII.4, 704b.

[80] In his article on Astronomy in Daremberg et Saglio's Dictionnaire des
Antiquités etc., vol. I, 478b.

[81] See fig. 579 ibid.

[82] תרומה sec. 9 (ed. Buber sec. 8, p. 94).

[83] Is ϑρόνος used here in the Astrological sense? See Liddel and Scott's
lexicon s. v. ϑρόνος 6.

[84] See also the same R. Samuel bar Nahman's conception of three pillars
in Midrash Tehilim I, ed. Buber, 15, l. 2/3.

people adjure,"[85] i. e. the people use this formula of adjuration in incantations, for the latter abound in all kinds of elaborate oaths.

Let us quote, for example, one of the most famous Jewish love-charms. It is a marvelous love-spell which is scratched upon a lead-tablet, found in 1890 at Adrumentum, the capital of the region of Byzacium in the Roman province of Africa. Its text published several times, was finally edited by Deissmann[86] with improved readings, fac-simile and commentary. It was written in the III c.,[87] but the original text from which it was copied was probably much older.[88] The spell begins with an adjuration of the demon in the name of God, the God of Abraham, Isaac and Israma.[89] It continues the adjuration, mentioning all kinds of miracles performed by Him. Deissmann remarks:[90] "This heaping up of attributes of God appears to have been a favorite custom, especially in prayers." For our purpose it is sufficient to quote the following phrases from this incantation: Ὁρκίζω σε τὸν θεὸν . . . (l. 34) δι᾽ ὄν ὁ λέων ἀφίησιν

---

[85] משתבעין may be a scribal error for משביעין. But it is unnecessary to emend the text, for this form is met with in the same Midrash (Shir Hashirim Rabba VII.9, ed. Romm 38c): אישתבע לציצא, "He adjured the frontlet," as correctly explained in מתנות כהונה s. v. מיסלק. Moreover, according to Jewish law the forms משתבעין or אישתבע are perfectly natural in adjurations, for the adjured is not bound by any oath unless he agrees to it (See TB Shebuoth 29b and Maimonides, Mishne Thora, hilkoth Shebuoth V.2). If a Jew wished to adjure an angel in an incantation he might instead bind himself by an oath according to which the angel should and will act. If the angel acts differently he causes the swearer to perjure himself (See Maimonides ibid. V. 3), which is not compatible with piety. In this way R. Joshua ben Levi adjured the angel of death (TB Kethuboth 77b), see also Mishna Taanith III.8.

[86] Bibelstudien, p. 26 seq. From there it was reprinted by Blau, Zauberwesen p. 97.

[87] See Deissmann ibid., p. 33.

[88] Deissmann, p. 48 surmises that the date of its composition may go as far as the second century.

[89] An obvious mistake for Israel, as proved by Deissmann (p. 36) and Blau (p. 101). The invocation of the God of Abraham, Isaac and Jacob is very usual in incantations. Deissmann (ibid.) refers to Origen (Cont. Celsum V, 45) who confirms this fact.

[90] P. 52, Bible Stduies, p. 297.

τὸ ἅρπαγμα, "I adjure thee by God . . . through Whom the lion parts with its prey." Blau[91] correctly proves that we have here an allusion to Daniel.[92] In line 11 we read: Ὁρκίζω σε τὸν διαχωρίσαντα τοὺς εὐσεβεῖς, "I adjure thee by Him Who separates the devout ones." Blau[93] sees here an allusion to Korah.[94] Finally, we shall point to line 18 which reads: Ὁρκίζω σε τὸν συνστρέφοντα τὴν γῆν ἐ[πὶ τ]ῶν θεμελίων αὐτῆς.[95] If we suppose that the Rabbis had before them a similar incantation which read: ἐ[πὶ τῶν τρι]ῶν θεμελίων αὐτῆς — "I adjure thee by Him Who holdeth the earth upon her three foundations" — we shall have exactly the same formula as found in our Midrash.

Now, since Abraham, Isaac and Jacob are mentioned in the incantation, Daniel is alluded to[96] and a faint allusion to Korah is, possibly, included, it is only natural that the Rabbis drew their exegesis from the same document and concluded that the three pillars are none other than either Abraham, Isaac and Jacob, or Hananiah, Mishael and Azariah, or the three sons of Korah.[97] The Rabbis were wont to interpret even secular written documents by the method they employed in the interpretation of Scripture,[98] and it is quite understandable why they interpreted that the three pillars are the righteous men mentioned in the same document. It is much more in the Jewish spirit to treat the pillars as allegoric than to take them literally as physical entities. This was also the reason which prompted R. Eleazar ben Shammua to say[99] that the world stands on a pillar whose name is righteous. The Rabbis did not reject, they did

[91] Ibid. p. 108, n. 2.

[92] Comp. the prayers for rain in Mishna Taanith II, 4 and סדור רב עמרם II, 21a, where the miracle of Hananiah, Mishael and Azariah are also mentioned.

[93] P. 107 n. 2 and p. 108.

[94] See Num. XVI.21.

[95] Probably an allusion to Ps. CIV.5.

[96] Hananiah, Mishael and Azariah are also mentioned in an incantation recorded in TB Shabbath 67a.

[97] So Midrash Tehilim I, 15, ed. Buber p. 15: ואית דאמרי תלתא בני קרח.

[98] See Tosephta Kethuboth IV, 265 and parallels in TP Yebamoth XV, 14d (and parallel) and TB Baba Mezia 104a.

[99] TB Hagiga 12b.

not even modify the formula of the incantation, but they interpreted and transformed it into a Jewish phrase.

"Superstitions" in Palestinian literature. It is fundamentally
an error to generalize and say that in Palestinian Talmudo-
Midrashic literature fewer "superstitions" are found than in the
Babylonian.[100] To adhere to this view would mean to maintain
that the Palestinian Jews were less civilized than the Babylonian,
that they were not men of their time and place. Palestine,
situated between Egypt on the one hand and Babylonia on
the other, could not escape the influence of the wisdom of that
time. The Rabbis did their utmost to combat the superstitions
which were forbidden by the Written Law, to eliminate the
magic which smacked of idolatry, but they had to accept those
charms which were sanctioned by the "scientists" of that time.
The power of love charms was recognized by all nations of the
ancient world, and the Palestinian Jews were no exceptions.

TP[101] records the opinion of Resh Lakish who said that a
man can plead: נאנסתי מפני כשפים שעשת לי, "I was forced (to commit adultery) by the sorcery she performed upon me." According to TB,[102] however, a man can never be forced to commit
adultery. Similarly, the Palestinian Targumim Pseudo-Jonathan
and Yerushalmi (ad Deut. XXIV.6)[103] speak of the "binding"
(by charms) of brides and bridegrooms,[104] a belief that seems to
have its roots in the Palestinian Talmud.[105]

True, the Babylonian Talmud records many incantation-
formulas, whereas the Palestinian Talmud mentions only a
few,[106] yet this fact does not prove that the Palestinian Jews
resorted to incantations less frequently than the Babylonian.
The Palestinian Talmud is much shorter than the Babylonian.

---

[100] So Rapoport ערך מלין s. v. ארץ ישראל and many other scholars.

[101] Nazir VIII.1, 57a.

[102] Yebamoth 53b.

[103] Referred to by Blau, Zauberwesen 158, n. 2.

[104] Comp. also דרשות ר׳י בן שועיב ed. Krakow, p. 48d; תורתן של ראשונים
ed. Horowitz II, p. 47, l. 1 and Ginzberg, Geonica II, p. 152, n. 5. Bar
Hebraeus, Nomocanon, Cod. Hunt 67v (as quoted by Payne Smith s. v.
אסר I, 5), mentions: הנון דאסרין נבוא מן נשיהון.

[105] Kethuboth I.1, 24d. Comp. the comments of חתם סופר in TP ed. Rom

[106] See Rapoport ערך מלין s. v. ארץ ישראל No. 25.

There is much of Halachic material in the latter, recorded in
the name of Palestinian sages, of which there is no trace in the
Palestinian Talmud. Moreover, many passages in that Talmud
have so far remained obscure, and we may hope, that, in the
course of time, when these will be elucidated, more facts and
ideas bearing on Palestinian "superstitions" will also be revealed.

The following passage[107] is of interest for our discussion:
אמר ר' ינאי קרוח קריחה, קפוח קפיחה, שפוך צנינים על מאן דעדי[108] ליה,
"R. Jannai said: Make bald the baldhead, rob him that has been
robbed, pour cold water on him who is cold." We have here
quotations from different popular sayings which R. Jannai
applied to the situation of a man who is compelled to find
apartments at his expense for the former tenants of his house
which happened to collapse.[109] It seems to me that the phrase
קרוח קריחה קפוח קפיחה is taken from an incantation.[110]

A similar incantation-formula is preserved in TB:[111] קרח
קרחייקי פרח פרחייקי, but the reading is not sure.[112] Moreover, it
seems that the Palestinians read: קדח קדחייקי. The Hebrew-
Persian dictionary of R. Solomon[113] cites the phrase בפדחית
קדחית (בפרחית?) in the name of the Palestinian "Paytan"
חדותא.[114] In an incantation published by C. Gordon[115] we read:
ויפרח ויקדח.[116]

[107] TP Shabbath XX.5, 17d.

[108] Read with the Geniza ms. (Tarbiz III, 245): דעדי.

[109] See my הירושלמי כפשוטו I, p. 215 (and note 1 ibid.).

[110] Comp. the text of the incantation in TB Shabbath 67a: בו בזייה מס
מסייא כס כסייה וכו'.

[111] Pesahim 110a (bottom).

[112] See דקדוקי סופרים and אוצר הגאונים ad loc.

[113] See above p. 60.

[114] See the illuminating note of Prof. J. N. Epstein in Tarbiz XII, 78.

[115] Archiv Orientální, VI (1934), p. 470, l. 12.

[116] Epstein, in REJ, LXXIII (1921), p. 42 n. 2, took the phrase in TP
Shabbath to be a cursing-formula (he also referred to the reading of the
Hebrew-Persian dictionary), but in Tarbiz III, p. 245 n. 4 he, following my
explanation of the whole subject, accepted the interpretation of the פני משה,
that the phrases are popular proverbs. However, his original interpretation
seems more plausible than the latter, although it has probably nothing to do
with the wording of the formula in TB Pesahim.

On the other hand, the incantations teach us the methods
by which sorcerers could be conquered. In a Mandaic incantation[117] we read: ומצרינין בעדקיא דנידוליאתין ואמר לין כרוך דלאטתין,
"And he seized[118] them by the tufts of their braids and said to
them: 'Remove[119] what you have cursed'."[120] It is very remarkable that in the Palestinian Talmud we find the same method
applied to sorcerers. We read there:[121] עד דאסק חדא איתא בקלעיתא
דשערה. אמר לה שריי מה דעבדתין, "Until he[122] brought up a woman
by the tresses of her hair and said to her: 'Loose what you
have done' "— almost verbally identical with the incantation.
Likewise, we read in Midrash Abkir:[123] הקב"ה תופס לשרו בציצית
ראשו, "The Holy blessed be He seized its angel by the hair of
his head." In another quotation from the same Midrash[124] we
find: תפשן מיכאל בציצת ראשן, "Michael seized them (the sorcerers)
by the hair of their head." Thus the sorcerers once they have
been seized by their hair become subject to the seizer and lose
their power.[125] This motif of seizing by the hair is also extant
in erotic "Hellenistic Magic" dating from the second to the
fifth century. In Pap. Par.[126] we read: ἕλκε τὴν δεῖνα τῶν
τριχῶν, "He dragged such and such by the hair."[127]

Finally, we may recall that the author of the famous general
rule[128] כסא דחרשין ולא כסא דפושרין was a Palestinian sage (R.
Johanan). Montgomery[129] translates this phrase: "The cup of
the sorcerers and not the cup of those who break sorcery."

[117] Lidzbarski, Ephemeris I, p. 96.
[118] See below p. 167 seq.
[119] A similar text published by Pognon has שראי (loose). Comp. Litzbarski
ibid., p. 92, n. 4.
[120] See also Gordon, Archiv Orientální IX (1907), p. 96, l. 8–11.
[121] TP Sanhedrin VII.19, 25d.
[122] R. Joshua. I–II c.
[123] Quoted in Yalkut I sec. 133.
[124] Ibid. sect. 235 (ed. pr. 236).
[125] See S. Eitrem in Gaster Anniversary Volume, p. 107 seq.
[126] Bibl. Nat., Suppl. Gr. 574, p. 376 (=Pap. Gr. Mag. I, p. 84), quoted
by Eitrem ibid.
[127] And gained power over her. The expression in Ezek. VIII.3 has, of
course, nothing to do with our subject.
[128] Baba Mezia 29b and parallel.
[129] Aramaic Incantation Texts, p. 43, n. 19.

This translation is correct beyond any doubt, the uncertainty expressed by Blau[130] and Montgomery notwithstanding; the כסא דפושרין mentioned in Tanhuma[131] has nothing to do with our כסא דפושרין. As a matter of fact already R. Hananel[132] records: ויש אומרים פושרין הן הלוחשין, "And some say that פושרין are charmers." He clearly realized that פושרין here has not the usual meaning of "tepid". There are many other statements regarding incantations and charms in the Babylonian Talmud in the name of Palestinian sages, and we have to admit that Palestine was not behind the ancient world of that time in matters of magic and charms.

The Rabbis displayed the same intelligent attitude towards magic and charms as towards Astrology.[133] Magic is effective in the case of the ordinary man only, but not in that of the really righteous, whose merit is great (דנפישא זכותיה); it is powerless in face of the virtuous man. So TB[134] relates: ההיא איתתא דהוה קא מהדרא למישקל עפרא מתותי כרעי דר' חנינא אמר לה שקילי לא מסתייעא מילתיך. אין עוד מלבדו כתיב, "A woman tried to take the sand from under the footsteps of R. Hanina.[135] He said to her: Take it; thy sorcery shall not succeed, for it is written: 'There is none else besides Him' " (Deut. IV.35). However, the popular belief that a spell can be cast upon a man by using the sand of his footprints was not rejected by the Rabbis. It was too deeply rooted among the ancient nations.[136] On the contrary, they made use of it and explained events mentioned in the Bible with the aid of this popular belief.

In this the Rabbis utilized this belief in their explanation of how the Jews made a *living* golden calf. The Jews supposedly took the sand from the footprints of "the ox of the Merkabah" and threw it into the fire (or into the calf) whereupon a *living*

[130] Zauberwesen 157, n. 2.
[131] וישב sect. 4.
[132] Fl. XI c. See also שיטה מקובצת ad loc.
[133] See above p. 99.
[134] Hullin 7b (and parallel).
[135] A Palestinian sage of the III c.
[136] See Thompson, Semitic Magic, p. 146.

calf jumped out etc.[137] Further light is shed on this belief by the author of עץ חיים Cod. Monacencis,[138] quoted by Güdemann,[139] who maintains that the sorcerers who know the order of the "Merkabah" take sand from under the legs of the corresponding מערכה and create whatever they want. Even at present they follow this practice in India and Turkey and convert men into animals. Adjured, the demon brings the sorcerer some sand from under the appropriate מערכה, which he serves to whomever he wants. The latter thereupon immediately assumes the form of the being from under whom the sand was taken.[140]

Thus, by taking sand from the footprints of an object one can recreate that object. This was the method employed by the Jews when they made the golden calf; they took the sand from the footprints of the "ox of the Merkabah" and recreated him. The explanation seems to have been very natural and understandable to the audience of that time.

The Rabbis did everything in their power to attract the people to the word of the Tora. They drew their material from the vast stores of popular belief; they used it, modified it and offered it to the people in a more suitable form. They made the events related in the Bible more understandable to the man of the people; they used the "scientific methods" of their time and place; they were the "modern" men of their time.

---

[137] See L. Ginzberg, Genizah Studies I p. 243, Legends of the Jews VI, p. 52, n. 271 and the new material adduced in my lecture on the Yemenite Midrashim (מדרשי תימן) p. 17 seq.

[138] On the author and his work, see Steinschneider, Catalogus... Monacencis, p. 88, No. 207.

[139] Geschichte des Erziehungswesen etc., I, p. 169, n. 1.

[140] וכל המכשפים וחרטומי מצרים שבוראים הבריאות יודעים על ידי שדים או על ידי חכמה אחרת סדר המרכבה ולוקחין עפר מתחת רגלי אותה המערכה ובוראים מה שהם רוצים... היו יודעין הסוד ולוקחין עפר מתחת רגלי המרכבה ומזכירין עליו השם... והיום הזה עושים כן בארץ הודו ובארץ ישמעאל, מן בני אדם עושים בהמות, מפני שמשביעים שם השד ומביא מן העפר השיד שתחת אותה מערכה ונותן לבעל הכישוף, ואותו המכשף נותן לשתות למי שהוא חפץ ומיד הוא כמוה. ורב סעדיה יודע זה המעשה וכו'.

OATHS AND VOWS[1]

Generally speaking, popular oaths and vows are an expression of piety, in the sense that the simple man thereby invokes the Lord as his witness. But the natural tendency to swear was carried to excess; the populace swore always and everywhere, not contenting themselves with the name of God and His attributes, or with the component parts of the universe or with the lives of persons one holds dear, but turning to the strangest and most varied objects to serve vicariously as surety for their veracity. The learned Rabbis were confronted with a double task. On the one hand they had to emphasize the sacredness of the oath, the necessity of avoiding it and the evil consequences of transgressing it. On the other hand they had to keep the unbridled zeal of the populace in check, to teach them to distinguish between valid oaths and meaningless outbursts of supposedly holy words.

The Rabbis constantly and repeatedly preached that it is preferable entirely to abstain from swearing; even he who pronounces a true oath, when there is no urgent need for it, is considered a sinner.[2] True, the Rabbis themselves often swore, but they were entitled and qualified to decide whether their oaths were justified by necessity.[3] The people, on the other hand, swore in their houses, in the streets and in the markets,

---

[1] In ordinary speech.

[2] See the illuminating note of Prof. Louis Ginzberg in his book "Eine unbekannte jüdische Sekte" p. 130, n. 3; comp. also the sources quoted and referred to by Strack and Billerbeck, "Kommentar" I, p. 329 seq. In addition we may note the statement of R. Bahya (XI c.) in his חובת הלבבות (VIII. 3, ed. Ziphroni p. 226): ואמר א' מן החסידים לתלמידיו התורה התירה לנו להשבע בשם הבורא באמת ואני איעצכם, שלא תשבעו בו לא באמת ולא בשקר, אמרו: הן או לאו. Comp. also below, n. 74.

[3] They swore mainly to confirm the true tradition of the Law. See "Kommentar" ibid., p. 334–336.

both in general conversations and in business matters,[4] and they had to be checked in one way or another.

The old Rabbinic sources speak of "substitutes" for the actual formulas of vows and oaths. They mention "handles" (abbreviations) of vows,[5] hoping thereby to eliminate the pronunciation of holy words in the vow-formulas. But the question arises: Were these "substitutes" and "handles" artificial inventions by the Rabbis for the purpose of preventing the people from abusing the sacred formulas, or were they expressions used by the people, which the Rabbis had only to select, to regulate and to sanction? The correct answer is given by the Talmud itself, as we shall see below.

But, even more than in our previous chapters, our method of procedure should be to consider the oaths and vows of the Jewish populace in the light of the manners and customs of their Gentile neighbors in respect of swearing and vowing.

The Gentile populace in Greece resorted to oaths in their ordinary talk in the streets and the markets, even for purposes of cheating and out of mere verbosity.[6] The populace of Alexandria in Egypt did not behave any better. Philo[7] remarks: "As it is, so highly impious are they that on any chance matter the most tremendous titles are on their lips and they do not blush to use name after name, one piled upon another, thinking that the continual repetition of a string of oaths will secure them their object." Exactly the same can be said of the populace of Palestine. The people swore and adjured on every occasion; they affirmed their statements by an oath in business affairs,[8] in formulas of courtesy when they invited their friends, accepted invitations or rejected them,[9] and in support of stories which strained credulity.[10]

---

[4] See below.

[5] See Mishna Nedarim I. 1; TP ibid., 36d; TB ibid., 2b.

[6] See L. Ott, Beitraege zur Kenntniss des griechischen Eides, p. 24.

[7] De spec. leg. II. 8. The English is copied from the Loeb Class. Library.

[8] See Mishna Nedarim III. 1.

[9] Ibid. I. 3; Tosephta ibid., II. 1, 2774; Minor tract Kalla VIII, ed. Higger, p. 322; Tanhuma מטות, ed. Buber, p. 157, sect. 1 (end).

[10] Mishna Nedarim III. 2.

The formulas of the oaths and vows employed by the people were strange and capricious. The Mishna, Tosephta, TP and TB[11] abound in all kinds of oaths and vows in vogue among the people. We shall limit our discussion mainly to expressions either not noticed or misunderstood.

We shall try first to define the distinction between נדר (vow) and שבועה (oath). The differences between them which the Mishna[12] establishes are essentially theoretical. An oath, according to it, is a personal obligation to do or not to do something (I swear I shall do something, shall abstain from something), whereas a vow makes an item forbidden to the person[13] (this shall be forbidden to me). The vow is a development from the original vow — εὐχή, votum — when the man dedicated an object to God, which he could not consequently enjoy any more.

But in practice the people seem not to have discriminated between these two terms. In the Mishna[14] we read: היה חייב לחברו שבועה ואמר לו דור לי בחיי ראשך[14] "If a man was under the obligation of an oath to his fellow, and the latter said to him: 'Vow to me by the life of thy head'." דור (vow) is used here in the sense of swear.[14] We find the same meaning of נדר in Mekiltha:[15] והיה נודר בחיי הבן, "And he used to swear by the life of the son." Aggadath Shir Hashirim[16] states clearly: משביע[17] ... אותן כמלך שהוא נודר בחיי בנו "He adjures them ... like a king who swears by the life of his son."[18] The introduction of a נדר-formula into formulas of שבועה did not

---

[11] Nedarim, Shebuoth and elsewhere.
[12] Nedarim II. 2; Tosephta ibid. I. 5.
[13] See TB Nedarim 2b.
[14] Sanhedrin III. 2. Comp. also Tosephta ibid., V. 1.
[14a] Comp. also TP Berakoth V. 2, 9a (bottom): חי ה ' אם יהיה ... איכן הותר נדרו של טל ... לך והתר נדרו של טל טל.
[15] פסחא XVI, ed. Horovitz, p. 59.
[16] II. 7, ed. Schechter, p. 30.
[17] Matt. V. 33 uses "τοὺς ὅρκους σου" in the sense of "thy vows," a similar example of popular indiscrimination between oaths and vows.
[18] Comp. also Philo, de spec. leg. II. 12 seq.; TB Nedarim 28a; Mekiltha Mishpatim XX, ed. Horovitz p. 331. See also Mishna Sanhedrin VII. 6, and Genizah Studies I, ed. Ginzberg, p. 48, l. 14/15.

invalidate the obligation, since the vow was considered as a
substitute (or "handle") for an oath.[19]

Yet, we find in Sifre[20] a very interesting discrimination
between vow (נדר) as an oath and an oath proper: מה הפרש בין
נדרים לשבועות, בנדרים כנודר בחיי המלך בשבועות כנשבע במלך עצמו,
"What is the difference between vows and oaths? The former is
like vowing by the life of the king, the latter is like swearing
by the king himself." We are offered here a clear distinction
between a vow and an oath, yet for both of them the example
of swearing by the king is adduced. In the former one swears[21]
by the life of the king, in the latter by the king himself. Thus,
the ancients discriminated between נדר as a substitute for שבועה
and שבועה proper; they also distinguished between swearing by
the life of the king and swearing by the king himself. The
Rabbis have not revealed to us wherein is the difference between
an oath by the life of the king and one by the king himself,[22]
but they do teach us the very important fact that such a distinction existed.

In reality these two kinds of oaths are well attested by
documents of that age: we come across formulas like: ὀμνύω
βασιλέα, ὀμνύω Τιβέριον, ὀμνύω Νέρονα, ὀμνύω τὴν τύχην . . . ,
but also ὄμνυμι τὴν νίκην καὶ διαμονήν . . .[23] I have not been
able to trace the practical implications of the difference between
these two kinds of oaths, but the Jews and Christians of the
time were apparently aware of the distinction. So Tertullian[24]

[19] See Ramban, Ritba and Me'iri to TB Nedarim 16b; Ran ibid., 2b
s. v. איידי.

[20] I, sect. 153, ed. Horovitz, p. 199₁₂.

[21] By employing the verb נדר. That נודר בחיי המלך means "swearing" etc.
is confirmed by Tosephta Sota (VI. 1. TP ibid., V. 7, 20c): הרי הוא אומר
חי אל... שאין אדם נודר בחיי המלך אלא אם כן אוהב את המלך, "Behold
it is said (Job XXVII.2): 'As God liveth . . .', teaching us that none swears
by the life of the king unless he loves the king." To the oath חי אל the Tosephta
applies here the phrase נודר בחיי המלך. See however below p. 192 ff.

[22] It is a matter of profound regret that the commentary of the ראש ישיבה,
interpolated into הלכות גדולות (ed. Hildesheimer, p. 483), from the margin,
stops abruptly at the very point of explaining our passage.

[23] See Preisigke, Woerterbuch etc. s. v. ὄμνυμι, s. v. τύχη (p. 630) and
s. v. διαμονή.

[24] Apolog. XXXII.

writes: Sed et iuramus sicut non per genios Caesarum, ita *per
salutem eorum*, quae est augustior omnibus geniis... et pro
magno id iuramento habemus.[25] "But although we do not swear
by the genii of the Caesars, we swear *by their safety*, which is
worth far more than all genii... and we count an oath by it
a great oath."

Perhaps the insistence by the Romans that the Christians
swear by the genii of the kings (במלך עצמו) is due among other
reasons to the fact that they felt it to be more enduring and more
binding than an oath by the welfare or the safety of the king
which is connected with the life-span of an individual. The
Jews may consequently have drawn the conclusion that במלך
עצמו is weightier than בחיי המלך.

The verb נדר for swearing was only one of the substitutes
used by the people. Actually they resorted to the entire terminology of curses and adjurations in their search of substitutes
for oaths. This practice has its roots in the Bible, as noted by
the Babylonian Talmud. אלה and ארור, on the one hand, were
considered to be oaths,[26] נדר and שבועה, on the other, serve as
curses and bans. The magic incantations include curses like
ὅρκοι, מומיתא (i. e. oaths), חרימא, לוטתא and נידרי.[27] TP mentions[28]
the exclamation of R. Joshua (I–II c.): הותר הנדר, "The ban is
lifted." The curses found in incantations and the popular oaths
contain the same terminology.

This infiltration of the specific incantation-terminology into
the vocabulary of oaths and vows will explain an obscure
Baraitha[29] in which the adjuration אוסרכם אני קבלכם אני
occurs. Abaye (IV c.) interprets[30] it to mean: אוסרכם אני
בשבועה[31] כובלכם אני בשבועה "I bind you by oath, I

---

[25] See also Hirzel, der Eid, p. 16, n. 3 (who referred to Tertullian and
Mommsen, Staatsrecht II[3], 810[3]), p. 33, n. 2 and 34, n. 2.

[26] TB Shebuoth 35b–36a.

[27] See Montgomery, Aram. Incant. Texts, p. 52, p. 84 and p. 294 s. v.
נידרא. Comp. also Acts XXIII.12.

[28] Shabbath II. 7, 5b; TB Sanhedrin 68a.

[29] Tosephta Shebuoth III. 7, 450[6].   [30] TB ibid., 35a.

[31] The expression לאסור בשבועה is very usual in Rabbinic literature. See
Vayyikra Rabba XXIII.2; ibid. XXXI.4 (and parallels), Genizah Studies
ed. Ginzberg I, p. 48. Comp. also פיוטי יניי, ed. Zulay, p. 4.

chain you by oath." But TP[32] records it without any interpretation:[33] אוסרכם אני כובלכם אני, treating it as a valid adjuration
without adding any comments to it.

Now אסר[34] as well as בכל (=כבל)[35] are typical terms in
magical texts and are very frequent in ancient incantation formulas. אוסרכם אני כובלכם אני is nothing other than a phrase
borrowed from the incantation vocabulary upon which the
people drew liberally for their oaths.[36]

The Rabbis did their utmost to check the irrelevant terminology employed by the people in oaths. They permitted,
legalized and encouraged the use of certain substitutes and
"handles" of vows and oaths, but they banned and nullified
the validity of certain others. The Mishna, Tosephta and both
the Palestinian and Babylonian Talmuds of Nedarim and
Shebuoth abound in substitutes and "handles," discussed by the
Rabbis. It is certain that Talmudic literature preserved only
part of the popular swearing vocabulary. Actual stories recorded
in the Talmud incidentally show that the people resorted to
substitutes for oaths which were not otherwise considered by
the Rabbis. For instance, TP[37] relates that a man swore by
איפופי ישראל[38] which is a substitute for אלהי ישראל.[39]

---

[32] Ibid. IV. 14, 35d.

[33] The preceding clause of the Baraitha quoted in TP will be explained
in my הירושלמי כפשוטו ad. loc.

[34] See Blau, Zauberwesen 157, n. 8, 158, n. 2, Montgomery, Aram.
Incant. Texts, p. 52 and 282 s. v. אסר.

[35] Montgomery ibid., p. 79.

[36] The spelling in the Tosephta קבלכם אני (ed. pr. and Cod. Vienna read:
קובלכם אני) is not to be disregarded. קיבלי and איסרי are both common in
incantation terminology (See Montgomery ibid., p. 86 and אוצר הגאונים
Berakoth, נספחים, p. 70 n. 1).

[37] Nedarim XI. 1, 42c.

[38] Epopé Israel. R. Benjamin Mussafia (s. v. פופי) associated it with πιπι,
a substitute for the name of God, which is found in a few Hexaplaric mss.
The Hexaplaric Syriac uses it even with prepositions — לפיפי. See Swete,
Introduction, p. 39 n. 3. The Sword of Moses (ed. Gaster, p. V, l. 2 and
IX, l. 17) records פיפי and (ibid. l. 22) אפופיני. Comp. also Eugarius in
Onomastica Sacra, ed. Lagarde p. 205–206.

[39] As correctly explained by R. Samuel Jama (Jubelschrift ... Graetz
p. 23). This explanation is corroborated by TB (ibid., 22b) which records

Moreover, it seems possible to discover that the learned men[40] and the common people employed divergent substitutes and "handles."

We come across a very frequent oath in the Palestinian Talmud and Midrashim namely, יבוא עלי אם, "May [it] befall me if . . ." This oath is ascribed to King David,[41] to Hillel the Elder,[42] to the pious mother of seven high priests,[43] to R. Akiba,[44] to R. Simeon ben Johai,[45] to Rab,[46] to R. Joshua ben Levi,[47] to R. Eleazar[48] and to a disciple of R. Johanan.[49] The Aramaic form ייתי עלי is ascribed to R. Tarphon,[50] to R. Ze'ira[51] and to a disciple of R. Mana.[52]

This יבוא עלי is nothing other than the "handle" (abbreviation) of a curse which was originally part of an oath. So we read in Tosephta:[53] משביע אני עליך ויבוא עליך, משביע אני עליך זו שבועה, ויביא[54] עליך זו אלה, "I adjure thee and may it come upon thee, I adjure thee implies the imposition of the oath, may it come upon thee, that of the curse."[55] The curse was an integral part of the oath in ancient times, as can be seen from the Bible and other old sources. The regular practice in the Greek legal

the same story, mentioning אלהי ישראל instead of איפופי ישראל. Another substitute for His name is probably preserved in Pesiktha deR. Kahana, ed. Buber 104a, n. 81.

[40] See TB Nedarim 14a and 20a. Comp. also the sources quoted and referred to by Strack and Billerbeck, "Kommentar" I, p. 334 seq.

[41] TP Berakoth II. 1, 4b.

[42] TP Pesahim VI. 1, 36a.

[43] TP Yoma I. 1, 38d (and parallels).

[44] Yelamdenu quoted in Yalkut II sect. 146. But in parallel Tanhuma Jethro sec. 15: העבודה.

[45] TP Shebiith IX. 1, 38d (and parallels in Midrash).

[46] TP Gittin IX. 9, 50c.

[47] See below p. 123 n. 71.

[48] TP Sota III. 4, 19a (and parallel).

[49] TP Pe'a I. 1, 15c (and parallels).

[50] TP Shebiith IV. 2, 35b.   [51] TP Berakoth III. 8, 5c.

[52] TP Shebiith VI. 1, 36c (and parallel). TB also frequently mentions the similar expression ייתי לי which sometimes implies a curse and sometimes a blessing (See the Hebrew periodicals בית תלמוד II, p. 107 seq., התחכמוני, ed. Dr. Lewin I, p. 62; II, p. 63).

[53] Sota II. 1, 294₁₃.

[54] Read: ויבוא.   [55] See also TB ibid. 18a.

adjuration was to impose an oath which included a curse.[56] The
Egyptian papyri[57] very frequently contain the formula: Ὀμνύω...
εὐορκοῦντι μέν μοι εὖ εἴη, ἐπιορκοῦντι δὲ τὰ ἐναντία. "I
swear ... if I swear truly may it be well with me, but if falsely,
the reverse." In Tosephta[57a] we read: כן ייטיב לך ... ייטיב לך
... אם, ... אל ייטיב לך אם, "So may He do well with thee ... may
He do well with thee if ... may He not do well with thee if ..."

The same practice was followed by the Jewish Courts in
Palestine, as stated:[58] בכל השבועות שבתורה שלא יהו אלא באלה
ובשבועה, "That all the oaths imposed by the Thora should consist of an oath and a curse." Another source[59] decides: אם השביעה
באלה לא יצא, "If he (the priest) adjured her (i. e. the woman
suspected of faithlessness) by means of a curse[60] only, the procedure is not valid." But TB[61] quotes a Baraitha[62] which asserts
that a curse alone is binding. The same opinion is recorded[63] in
the name of the Palestinian R. Abbahu. There can be no doubt
that in ordinary speech the curse was looked upon as an oath by
the Jews of both Palestine and Babylonia.

Thus, יבוא עלי אם "May it come upon me if ..." is not only
an abbreviation of a curse but a "handle" of a real oath. This
expression is recorded in the name of learned (or otherwise
distinguished) persons only. I am not able to find a single

[56] See the material of early sources adduced and referred to by L. Ott,
Beitraege etc., pp. 29, 40, 59; Hirzel, der Eid, pp. 26 (note) and 137 seq.
(esp. 138 n. 3); Daremberg et Saglio, Dictionnaire Des Antiquités etc., III,
p. 752.

[57] Tebtunis Pap. 7817, all the papyri referred to in Ox. Pap. II, p. 348
s. v. εὐορκεῖν and elsewhere.

[57a] Shebuoth II. 15, 44831. Comp. Mishna ibid. IV (end).

[58] Sifre I. 12, ed. Horovitz 196. Comp. the parallels referred to in the
notes ibidem.

[59] Sifre Zuta, ed. Horovitz, p. 2361.

[60] It is very noteworthy that TP (Sota II. 3, 18a) terms this curse תנאין
"a stipulation," in accordance with its external form: "If I did not ... if I
did ..." Comp. the Greek formula mentioned above and Sifre I, 12, ed.
Horovitz p. 24 (and parallels).

[61] Shebuoth 36a (top).

[62] According to the reading of the editions, Rabad ad Sifra, ed. Weiss,
22c, Rashba ad Shebuoth 35b.

[63] Ibidem.

passage in Talmudic literature in which a commoner uses this expression.

On the other hand we come across a special "handle" of an oath which is attributed mainly to the common people. So we read:[64] ‎שהיו דור נח אומרים כך מכך אם‎ ..., "For the generation of Noah used to say 'so and so if'..." The same expression (‎כך מכך, כך וכך‎) is attributed to the generation of Abraham,[65] to Esau,[65a] to the Egyptians,[66] to the Jewish masses in the time of Moses,[67] to the uneducated father of R. Eliezer,[68] to a vulgar husband who maltreated his wife[69] and to an ignorant rich man who bragged of his wealth.[70]

It is evident that the oath ‎כך וכך‎ or ‎כך מכך‎ is ascribed to the common folk only.[71] True, the Tosephta[72] ascribes this oath to a dyer who cited a law connected with his profession and was rewarded for it by an appointment to some honor in the Rabbinical School. But the Tosephta itself adds that everybody was surprised at this appointment.[73]

[64] Sifre II, 337, ed. Finkelstein p. 386₁₄. Comp. also the variants in BR, ed. Theodor 294₆.

[65] BR XLVII. 9, 476₂ (in the variants).

[65a] Tanhuma ‎תולדות‎, sect. 8.

[66] Sifre ibid., 387₁.

[67] Ibid., 387₅; ibid. sect. 1, p. 34. Comp. also Debarim Rabba, ed. Lieberman, p. 5 n. 7.

[68] Tanhuma ‎לך לך‎, ed. Buber 68 (bottom).

[69] TP Sota I. 4, 16d (and parallels).

[70] TP Nedarim IX. 3, 41c. In our edition we read: ‎כך אין אתין כל גמלייא‎, but the correct reading is found in ‎מעלות המדות‎ by R. Yehiel Harophe (the scribe of TP Cod. Leyden, from which edition Venice was printed. See ‎הירושלמי כפשוטו‎ I, Introduction p. ‎ט'ו‎ seq.), ed. Cremona 62a: ‎כך וכך דאן‎ ‎אתין כל גמלייא‎.

[71] In Midrash Tehilim XXII.19, ed. Buber, p. 189 we read: ‎אמר ר' יהושע‎ ‎בן לוי יבא עלי כך וכך אם‎..., "R. Joshua ben Levi said: 'May it so and so befall me if'..." But the other editions read simply ‎יבא עלי‎ (without ‎כך וכך‎) which is the only correct reading, and is corroborated by ‎רי"צ גיאת‎ in his ‎מאה שערים‎, Laws of ‎הלל‎ p. 2; Yalkut Hamakiri Ps. XXII, p. 150; Midrash Haggadol Gen., ed. Schechter p. 379 and Exempla, ed. Gaster, p. 186. The reading of Buber's edition has no support whatever.

[72] Eduyyoth III. 1, 459₁₈.

[73] The story of the pious man (Midrash fragment published by Prof. L. Ginzberg in his Genizah Studies I, p. 47, l. 1), who said: ‎כך וכך איני עולה‎

Thus, the ignorant masses were sometimes more afraid[74] of
an oath than the learned men; they used a shorter "handle" of
an oath — כך וכך — than the learned who were not afraid to
mention the verb and the person — יבוא עלי.

This fear of the oath was not characteristic of the Jews
only; the whole ancient world was afraid of the evil consequences
of abusing an oath. Philo[74a] advises the people not to swear by
the name of the Lord. He says: κἄν εἰ ὀμνύναι μέντοι βιά-
ζοιντο αἱ χρεῖαι, πατρὸς ἢ μητρὸς ζώντων μὲν ὑγείαν καὶ
εὐετηρίαν, τετελευτηκότων δὲ τὴν μνήμην ὅρκον ποιητέον,
"And if certain urgent circumstances should force you to swear,
you should take the oath by father or mother, by their health
and welfare if they are alive, by their memory[75] if they are dead."
Or one should swear[76] by earth, sun, stars, heaven, the whole
universe (γῆν, ἥλιον, ἀστέρας, οὐρανόν, τὸν σύμπαντα κόσμον).[77]

אצלו, may be disposed in a similar manner. Since the name of the pious man
is not given (comp. the parallels noted by Prof. Ginzberg) we may take him
to have been a man of the people in whose mouth the Midrash put a popular
expression.

[74] It is among these pious men of the people (see above p. 115 n. 2) that
the proverb בין זכאי בין חייב לשבועה לא תיעול ("Right or wrong do not involve
yourself into an oath") was current. The Midrash (VayR VI.3. Comp. the
parallels in TP Shebuoth VI. 6, 37b and Pesiktha Rabbathi, ed. Friedmann,
p. 114a) introduces it explicitly as a popular adage (הדא דברייתא אמרין). In
the collection of proverbs by Maximus Planudes (E. Kurtz No. 181, cited by
O. Crusius in Rheinisches Mus. f. Phil. XLII, 1887, p. 414) we similarly find:
δικαίως, ἀδίκως, τὸν ὅρκον φεῦγε (Right or wrong avoid the oath), literally
the same maxime as in our Midrash. This confirms its proverbial character.
See below p. 154 n. 58.

[74a] De spec. leg. II. 2.

[75] See Prof. Ginzberg's note referred to above p. 115, n. 2 and S. Belkin,
Philo and the Oral Law p. 141, n. 8. Comp. also Montgomery, Aramaic
Incant. Texts, p. 158, n. 6.

[76] Philo, ibid., 5.

[77] In Midrash Shir Hashirim Rabba II.7 we read: השבעתי אתכם בנות
ירושלים. במה השביען ... בשמים ובארץ ... בצבא של מעלה ובצבא של מטה ... באבות
ובאמהות ..., "'I adjure ... ורבנן אמרי השביען בדורו של שמד ... ששופכין דמן על קדושת שמי
you O daughters of Jerusalem' (Song of Sol. II.7). By what did he adjure
them? By heaven and earth ..., by the hosts above and by the hosts below ...,
by the Patriarchs and Matriarchs ... The sages say: By the generation of
the persecutions ... which suffered martyrdom for the sanctification of My
name." This passage offers a good parallel to the oaths recommended by

He further[78] lavishes high praise on the people who, when forced to swear, say only: "*νὴ τόν*" ἤ "*μὰ τόν*", "Yes, by —" or "No, by —". Dr. S. Belkin[79] is quite justified in considering this kind of oaths as binding from the Halachic point of view, but Prof. Goodenough[80] is perfectly right in asserting that the Jews of Egypt adopted the same practice in their oaths as was followed by their Gentile neighbors. The oath "*νὴ τόν*" or "*μὰ τόν*", "By the —", without mentioning the name of the deity invoked, was very current among the Greeks.[81] As a direct consequence of the fear of the oath in the ancient world, they avoided the mention of the name of the deity. The Jews were no less pious than their neighbors. They adopted the general practice which happened to be in perfect accord with the spirit of the Jewish concepts of the fear of Heaven.

If we adopt this principle of considering the Jews in some of their behavior-patterns as part and parcel of the ancient Mediterranean world, if we regard certain expressions current among the Jewish masses as generally accepted during that time, we shall understand many difficult passages in Jewish literature which hitherto remained unexplained. Many obscure statements so far undeciphered will become fully intelligible.

One of the strangest oaths of the Greeks was the so called 'Ραδαμάνθυος ὅρκος. Socrates swears:[82] "*μὰ τὸν κύν*'," "No, by the dog." Lampon swears:[83] *τὸν χῆν*, "By the goose." This kind of oaths was quite common in ancient Greece,[84] and Christian apologetic literature very often ridiculed it.[85] But the pagan

Philo. For the last adjuration — by the martyrs — comp. IV Maccab. X.15: μὰ τὸν μακάριον τῶν ἀδελφῶν μου θάνατον . . ., "By the blessed death of my brothers . . ."

[78] Philo ibid. 4.

[79] Philo and the Oral Law, p. 142.

[80] The Jurisprudence of the Jewish Courts in Egypt, p. 43 seq.

[81] See Goodenough ibid., p. 43 n. 46, p. 47 n. 48. Comp. also Liddell and Scott, Lexicon, s. v. μά (IV); add Greek Anth. VII. 552.

[82] Aristoph. Wasps 83. See Starkie's notes in his edition, p. 124.

[83] Id. Aves 521. See Kock's notes ad loc.

[84] See the abundant material adduced by P. Meinhardt, De forma et usu iuramentorum, p. 74 seq. and p. 77; Hirzel, der Eid, p. 96 n. 2.

[85] See J. Geffcken, Zwei Griechische Apologeten, p. 251, n. 1.

philosophers defended the ancients, asserting that they never
intended to swear by the dog, goose etc. as gods, but as substitutes for gods. Philostratus the Sophist[86] says:[87] ὤμνυ γὰρ
ταῦτα οὐχ ὡς θεούς, ἀλλ' ἵνα μὴ θεοὺς ὀμνύοι "He (Socrates)
swore by these (objects) not as gods, but in order to avoid
swearing by the gods."[88] This idea in itself of employing "substitutes" in order to avoid mention of His name could be easily
understood by the Jews, for they themselves were inspired by
the same motive,[89] but to resort to the dog as a substitute for
the name of the gods must have seemed more than preposterous
to them. As a token of contempt the Jews themselves nicknamed the idols — dogs.[90] The dog was abhorred by the Jews,[91]
and they could not grasp that a pious Gentile should make the
dog a substitute for his god.

Indeed, we read in Mekiltha:[92] . . . שאל פלוסופוס את רבן גמליאל
אלא יש כח בעבודה זרה להתקנאות בה אמר לו: אלו אדם קורא לכלבו בשם
אביו, וכשהוא נודר, נודר בחיי כלב זה, במי האב מתקנא, בבן או בכלב?
"A certain philosopher asked R. Gamaliel (I–II c.) . . . but has

[86] Fl. in the beginning of the III c.
[87] Vita Apollonii VI. 19.
[88] See Meinhardt and Hirzel ibidem.
[89] TB Nedarim 10a.
[90] Tosephta Aboda Zara VI, 46924 (and parallels) recommends: פני מלך
קורין אותה פני כלב, "[If its name is] 'Molekh's Face' it should be nicknamed
'Dog's Face'." Comp. also Debarim Rabba, ed. Lieberman, p. 63, n. 1.
[91] True, in TP Terumoth VIII. 7, 46a (and parallel) we read touching
stories of the devotion of the dog to man, but it seems quite certain to me
that the Rabbis drew these stories from all kinds of Oriental Fables current
in the ancient world (See, for instance, Aesop., ed. C. Halm, No. 120). In
this connection it is especially instructive to quote the words of the Pesiktha
deR. Kahana (בשלח 79b), where the self-sacrifice of a dog for the sake of the
shepherds is related. In their gratitude they buried him and made a mound
on his tomb. Plutarch in his Lives (Themist. X. 10) records the same in
compensation of a dog's devotion. Both the Pesiktha and Plutarch (Cato
Major V. 4) conclude the story with the same words.

Plutarch:	Pesiktha:
ἦν Κυνὸς σῆμα	עד כדון מתקריא
μέχρι νῦν καλοῦσιν.	נפשא דכלבא

See also Aelianus, de natura animalium X. 41. Comp. however Euripides,
Hecuba, 1271. Comp. also Aelian. ibid. VI.17, TP and Pesiktha ibid.
[92] Jethro VI, ed. Horovitz, p. 226, Lauterbach II, p. 245.

the idol any power that one should be jealous of it? He (i. e. Rabban Gamaliel) said to him: Suppose a man would call his dog by the name of his father, so that when he is swearing[93] he would swear by the life of his dog, whom is the father jealous of, the son or the dog"? There can be no doubt that the Jewish Patriarch ridiculed here the Greek Sophists who tried to defend the ancient philosophers by asserting that they took the dog as substitute for the gods in their oaths, pronouncing "By the dog" and meaning "By Zeus".[94]

Thus, we possess authentic evidence that the Palestinian Jews knew of the Ῥαδαμάνθυος ὅρκος of the Greeks. The question is however whether they knew if from literary sources only, or learned it in the streets of Palestine from observation of the behavior of their neighbors. It seems to me that the Jews not only heard this kind of oaths from their neighbors in Palestine, but resorted to the same practice themselves.

We know that the Greeks swore by whatever happened to be close at hand:[95] by the caper-plant (τὴν κάππαριν), by the almond (τὴν ἀμυγδαλῆν), by the cabbage (τὴν κράμβην) and by other objects.[96] Now, the Tosephta[97] records the following fact: ומעשה באחד שנתחייב לחבירו שבועה בבית דין ונדר לו בחיי הקייץ וקיבל עליו "And it happened that a man who was obliged to take an oath in court swore by the life of the fig-picker[98] and his opponent

---

[93] On נדר in the meaning of "swear" see above p. 117 seq.

[94] Prof. A. Marmorstein (Tarbiz V, p. 145) called attention to this passage in the Mekiltha in connection with the Christian polemists, but he failed to see that the point of R. Gamaliel's attack was the use of the dog as a substitute for the gods and not the oath itself. He also overlooked all the Greek pagan sources which mention this oath.

[95] ἀνὰ χεῖρας· ἐκ τοῦ παρατυχόντος. See Hirzel der Eid, p. 25 n. 1. Comp. BR XCI. 7, p. 1129₃.

[96] See P. Meinhardt, de forma et usu iuramentorum, p. 76–77.

[97] Sanhedrin V. 1, 423₁.

[98] The reading of the mediaeval authorities (quoted in my Tosefeth Rishonim II, p. 155) הקרן seems to be a mere corruption of הקיץ, the final ץ having been split into י, and subsequently corrupted to רן, a very common mistake in Hebrew mss., see above p. 101 n. 48. The reading הקייץ of ed. pr. is supported by the mss. of the Tosephta, and is, beyond any doubt, the genuine one.

accepted it."[99] This is very reliable evidence that the Jewish populace used the same fanciful oaths as their Gentile neighbors, despite the teachings of the Rabbis who did not attach any importance to them.

Again, we read in the Mishna:[100] נדר בחרם ואמר לא נדרתי אלא בחרמו של ים. The accepted interpretation: "if one vows by the 'Herem' and then says 'I vowed only by a fishing net' " makes no sense. This is not a hypothetical case, but a fact taken from actual life; TP[101] records explicitly: חד בר נש נדר באילין מילייא "A certain man happened to vow by these objects" (mentioned in the Mishna). It is hard to believe that a man would take a vow by the common word חרם (הריני עליך חרם), which he later interprets to mean "a fishing net." In our opinion נדרתי here means "*I swore*"[102] by one of the popular worthless oaths. Aristophanes mentions[103] indeed among the oaths of the bird: μὰ δίκτυα "By the nets." From the Mishna we may infer that there existed a popular oath τὸν δίκτυον, "By the fishing net," which Aristophanes skilfully applied to the bird that swore ironically by the traps and nets. The Mishna did not concoct artificial oaths, but quoted life itself.

All the commentaries of Nedarim, both mediaeval and modern, lost sight of the important fact that the popular oath is often referred to in Talmudic literature as נדר.

In order to gain a clear conception of the opinions of the Rabbis we must bear in mind that they differentiated between a distinct "vow-formula", or a distinct "oath-formula", and a vague formula which may represent either of them. The ex-

---

[99] The Tosephta (ibid. 422₂₈) mentions also: בקייטא ובמקטייא דנקיטי. The term בקייטא is the same as בקייץ, and מקטייא etc. are, in turn, "substitutes" for קייטא. Ed. pr. and ms. Vienna read: בקיטא; TP (ibid., III. 4, 21a) reads: קיטה, which may correspond to בקיץ, "by the figs" (See II Sam. XVI.1, 2; Jer. XL.10, 12; Mishna Nedarim VIII. 4; Tosephta ibid., IV. 1; Mishna Baba Bathra III. 1 and elsewhere), i. e. if a man swore "by the figs." Suidas s. v. 'Ραδαμάνθυος ὅρκος writes: πολλοὶ γὰρ πρὸς λάχανα ὀμνύουσιν, "For many people swear by vegetables."

[100] Nedarim II. 5.

[101] Ad loc., 37c.

[102] See above p. 117. The man said: חרם שאיני נהנה לך.

[103] Aves 194.

pression ... מה שאני, "that which I shall ..." is considered a distinct vow-formula, with the meaning that what he may eat or enjoy is forbidden to him (איסור חפצא — a forbidden object); the expression שאני (or ... ש) as a negative answer to an offer is equal to [מה] שאני,[104] meaning "what I may enjoy is forbidden to me." The expression ... ש in an affirmative clause (promissory sentence) is a distinct oath-formula (איסור גברא — personal obligation).

But the expression שאיני in a negative clause may serve either as a vow-formula (meaning that he cannot accept it, for it is forbidden to him)[105] or as an oath-formula (meaning that the man swears that he shall not enjoy ...).

On the other hand, the Rabbis differentiated between a distinct oath-term (בשבועה, האלהים etc.) or a distinct vow-term with a כ (כקרבן, like a sacrifice, which could only mean that the object is forbidden like ...) and certain vague terms which could represent either oaths or vows, as we shall presently see.

The most usual term of vows is קרבן and its substitute קונם.[106] By using one of these terms a man can prohibit to himself the enjoyment of any object in the world as he is prohibited to enjoy a קרבן (before the sprinkling of its blood). In addition to its usual meaning "sacrifice" the term קרבן included money for sacrifices or money for the Temple.[107] If a man said[108] הרי עצמי קרבן, "May I myself be a Korban," he is obliged to give, in value, the equivalent of himself to the Temple.[109] Likewise, if a man said[110] הרי נטיעות האלו קרבן, "Let these plants be Korban," he is obliged to redeem them and to give the money to the Temple.

---

[104] See TB Nedarim 16a.

[105] See תוספות Nedarim 2a s. v. שאני.

[106] This word has nothing to do with the Phoenician קנמי. See Z. Harris, A Grammar of the Phoenician Language, p. 144. Prof. H. L. Ginsberg called my attention to Professor Torrey's article (Zeitschrift für Assiriologie vol. XXVI, p. 84), in which as far back as 1911 he dissociated קנמי from the Talmudic קונם.

[107] See Joseph., Bell. Jud. II. 9. 4; Matt. XXVII, 6.

[108] Mishna Nedarim II. 5.

[109] See ps. Rashi ad loc. and BR LX. 3 (and parallels) 642₅.

[110] Mishna ibid., III. 5.

But the noteworthy fact is that we can prove that the term
קרבן served also as an oath. The Tosephta[111] records: מודים
חכמים לר' יהודה באומר קרבן עולה[112]... שאיני[113] אוכל לך שמותר שלא
נתכוין לידור אלא לקרבן[114] עצמו. TB[115] reads in this Baraitah
.ה א קרבן ו ה א עולה... שאוכל לך שמותר שלא נדר זה אלא בחיי קרבן
But the Palestinian Talmudic literature makes no distinction
between הא קרבן and הקרבן. TP[116] states repeatedly: הקרבן מותר,
if a man said "the Korban" his vow is null, for this term implies that the man *swore* by the Korban itself ("τὸν κορβάν").
That the term "the Korban" was employed by the Jews as an
oath is also expressly recorded by Josephus[117] who asserts:
λέγει γὰρ ὅτι κωλύουσιν οἱ Τυρίων νόμοι ξενικοὺς ὅρκους
ὀμνύειν, ἐν οἷς μετά τινων ἄλλων καὶ τὸν καλούμενον ὅρκον
κορβὰν καταριθμεῖ. παρ' ουδενὶ δ'ἂν οὗτος εὑρεθείη πλὴν
μόνοις 'Ιουδαίοις, δηλοῖ δ', ὡς ἂν εἴποι τις, ἐκ τῆς μεθερμηνευό-
μενος διαλέκτου δῶρον θεοῦ, "He (Theophrastus) says that the
Tyrian laws prohibit the use of foreign oaths, among which he
also counts the oath called "Korban". This oath will be found
in no other nation except the Jews, and, translated from the
Hebrew, it means something like 'God's gift'."

The prohibition of the oath "Korban" by the Tyrian laws
as a ξενικὸς ὅρκος could have sense only if it were a real oath,[118]
but not a private vow in ordinary speech.[119]

The Jewish populace swore in real earnest by "the Korban,"
as they swore "by the fig-picker,"[120] and in both cases the
Rabbis could not recognize the validity of such an oath. The
term הקרבן (τὸν κορβάν) was a distinct oath, and as such was

[111] Nedarim I. 2, 27611, ed. pr. and Cod. Vienna.
[112] Read: [ה[קרבן [ה[עולה.
[113] Cod. Vienna: שני which is equal to שני, שאיני.
[114] =בקרבן. See below n. 129.
[115] Ibid. 13a.
[116] Ibid. I. 3, 37a.
[117] Cont. Ap. I. 167.
[118] See E. Ziebarth, de iureiurando in iure graeco quaestiones, p. 15–16.
[119] Josephus speaks of an oath by the word "Korban". Halevy, Doroth
Harishonim I³, p. 314 seq. and his followers misunderstood the passage
totally.
[120] See above, p. 127.

null in the uncertain formulas,[121] because it converted them into
oaths, and an oath by the Korban is not valid.

But there were vague terms used in uncertain formulas
whose validity was contested by differences of opinions. The
Mishna[122] records: האומר קרבן ... ש א י נ [123] אוכל לך אסור, ר'
יהודה מתיר. הקרבן כקרבן קרבן שאוכל לך אסור, "If one says:
'Korban ... that I shall not eat anything of yours', he is forbidden. R. Juda permitted [him]. [If he says] 'the Korban' [or]
'as a Korban' [or] 'Korban' be that which I might eat of yours,
he is forbidden.''

The latter clause contains a distinct vow-formula,[124] and
therefore even R. Juda admits that the vow is valid regardless
of the introductory term. But the former clause contains an
uncertain formula,[125] and since it is the introductory term which
determines the character of the whole formula, R. Juda takes it
as a worthless oath, and as such it is not binding. TP ad loc.
explains the difference of opinion between R. Juda and the
sages as follows: כל עמא מודיי הקרבן מותר. כקרבן אסור. מה פליגין
קרבן. ר' יודה אומר האומר קרבן כאומר הקרבן והוא מותר. ורבנין אמרין
[האומר] קרבן כאומר כקרבן והוא אסור, "Everybody admits that if a
man introduced [an uncertain vow-formula] with 'the Korban'
(i. e. the distinct term of an oath), he is not bound; if he used
the word 'as a Korban' (i. e. the distinct term of a vow) he is
bound; the difference of opinion arises when a man said (in
uncertain vow-formulas) 'Korban'. R. Juda considers him as if
he said "the Korban" and decides that he is not bound, but the
sages consider him as if he said 'as a Korban' and rule that he
is bound.''

TP mentions here only the term "Korban"[126] which is equated
by the sages to "as a Korban," the typical vow-term. Their

[121] Like הקרבן שאיני אוכל לך. See above, p. 129.

[122] Nedarim I. 4.

[123] This is the reading of all the old editions of the Mishna (including
the Mishna in TP).

[124] שאוכל לך. See above, p. 129.

[125] שאיני. See ibidem.

[126] Implying also its specific names like עולה, מנחה etc., as listed in the
Mishna.

reason was probably that since the usual dedication term was
קרבן, we must treat even uncertain formulas like קרבן שאיני אוכל לך
as binding and make them legal vows by taking the word קרבן
as כקרבן. Only when the man used the distinct הקרבן "the
Korban" is he said to have sworn by the Korban and is not
bound.[127] But any other vague term which in the view of the
Rabbis is a worthless oath is not binding in uncertain formulas.

The Tosephta[128] teaches: ירושלים בירושלים היכל ירושלים לירושלים
להיכל בהיכל מזבח למזבח במזבח אימרא לאימרא באימרא . . . כולן
שאני אוכל לך אסור. לא אוכל לך מותר. חולין לחולין בחולין בין שאוכל לך ובין
שלא אוכל לך אסור, "If one says: Jerusalem, [or] by Jerusalem,[129] [or]
by Jerusalem,[130] the Temple . . . the altar . . . the ram, [or] by the
ram . . . in all these cases, [if he says]: whatever I might eat of
yours, he is forbidden; I shall not eat of yours, he is permitted.
[If he said] Hullin,[131] [or] by Hullin, [or] by Hullin he is forbidden, whether he said: 'what I might eat of yours', or 'I shall
not eat of yours'." All the terms mentioned in the first clauses
of the Tosephta were also current as oath-terms among the
people. The Jews used to swear by Jerusalem, by the Temple,
by the altar[132] and probably by the other objects enumerated in

---

[127] In distinct oath-formulas even the term קרבן is taken as an oath and
is not binding, see Mishna Nedarim II. 2 and commentaries ad loc.

[128] Nedarim I. 3 (ed. prin.).

[129] This is the meaning of לירושלים, and not "for Jerusalem," see my
article in the annual גנזי קדם, ed. Lewin vol. V, p. 181 seq., where many instances are quoted to show that in Palestine they used the prepositional
prefixes ל and ב indiscriminately (Comp. the relation between εἰς and ἐν
in the Greek Koine. See Moulton, Prolegomena, p. 63 and p. 234–235). TB
Yoma 84a (and parallel) relates that R. Johanan swore to a matron לאלהא
דישראל לא מגלינא, "By the God of Israel, I shall not reveal it." But he did
reveal it and offered the excuse that what he meant was that he would not
reveal it to the God of Israel (taking לאלהא in its simple meaning: to the
God), but he would reveal it to His people. However, the use of לאלהא instead of באלהא did not raise any suspicion in the eyes of the matron, because
it was quite normal to use both prepositions interchangeably. See Additional
Note below p. 142.

[130] With a ב, as it is in ed. pr. and Cod. Vienna. Ed. Zuckermandel
reads: כירושלים, which is probably an emendation after TB ibid., 13a.

[131] I. e. not consecrated, ordinary objects.

[132] See Strack and Billerbeck, "Kommentar" I, p. 333, 334–335.

our Baraitha. But what does אימרא, באימרא, "the ram", "by the ram" mean? Even the early Amoraim[133] disagreed widely in their explanation of כאימרא mentioned in the Mishna.[134]

In our opinion, אימרא also belongs to the category of the popular oaths; it is equal to the common Greek oath, τὸν κριόν,[135] for אימרא is the exact translation of κριός — ram. If then a man says כאימר,[136] "*as* a ram," which is a distinct vow-term he is bound, because we take it to mean the daily burnt-offering or something similar,[137] but if he says אימרא, באימרא we may take it either as a worthless oath or as a binding vow. The Tosephta, therefore, drew a distinction between a definite vow-formula (שאני אוכל לך) and a clear oath-formula (לא אוכל לך). In the former case everyone of the terms, such as "by Jerusalem," or "by the ram," etc. binds the man; since he used it in a distinct vow-formula we regard him as if he said: "*As* Jerusalem," or "*As* the ram"[138] etc. But if he used it in a definite oath-formula all these terms, taken at their face value, are declared worthless and the oath is not binding.[139] If however the man used the term "Hullin" he is bound anyway because one never swears by "Hullin" and we must perforce interpret it as introducing a binding vow.[140]

But the Tosephta has not determined the status of the common uncertain formula (שאיני אוכל לך) when it is introduced with any of these terms (such as: "by Jerusalem" or "by the ram" etc.). It is however certain that in this case these terms

---

[133] TP Nedarim I. 3, 37a; BR LVI. 9, 6072.

[134] Nedarim I. 3.

[135] See Starkie's notes to Aristopanes, Wasps 83, p. 124; P. Meinhardt, De forma et usu iuramentorum, p. 74. But, of course, it is also possible that the people, in their vulgar talk, termed the "Korban", ram, see TB Shabbath 32a (bottom).

[136] Mishna l. c.

[137] See note 133.

[138] Which are binding. See Mishna l. c.

[139] See Me'iri Nedarim 13a s. v. אמר בכלן in the name of יש מפרשים.

[140] See TB Nedarim 11b. The Babylonian Amoraim had a different tradition, but the reading as preserved in our Tosephta is in accord with the Palestinian Halacha.

are not binding.[141] The rule of the Palestinian Halacha was that
all the ordinary uncertain formulas introduced with terms such
as . . . (המזבח שאיני . . . ההיכל שאיני . . . ירושלים שאיני) (" 'By Jerusalem'
that I shall not . . . or 'by the Temple' that I shall not . . . or
'by the Altar' that I shall not . . .") etc. are not binding. A man
is bound by an oath only when it contains the word שבועה or
His name (or His attributes); an oath by any other holy object
does not bind the man. An exception was made only for the
word קרבן because people were in the habit of dedicating objects
to the Temple by using this word, and TP[142] concluded that
when a man says קרבן, "Korban", we take him to mean כקרבן
"As a Korban,"[143] and he is bound.

We have therefore no ground for doubting the statement
that according to the Pharisees *he who swears by the Temple is
not bound, but he who swears by its gold is bound; he who swears
by the Altar is not bound, but he who swears by the gift that is
upon it is bound.*[144] For when a person, in ordinary speech,
swears by the gold of the Temple or by the gift of the Altar
we regard him as if he said כקרבן. It seems to me that the Jews
used to vow and swear not only by "Korban", which comprises
sacrifices as well as the "gold (treasury) of the Temple,"[145] but
also by הון המקדש or זהב ההיכל which is equivalent to קרבן. And
only by assuming this proposition shall we be able to understand the very obscure passage in the so-called "Covenant of
Damascus:"[146] ולהנזר מהון הרשעה הטמא בנדר ובחרם ובהון המקדש.

----

[141] Whoever is familiar with the Mishnaic style will realize that by its
middle clause which rules that these terms are not binding in distinct oath-
formulas, the Tosephta did not exclude the common uncertain formulas; it
speaks of the distinct oath-formulas only for stylistic reasons, viz. to emphasize that even in this case the man is bound when he introduced them
with the term "Hullin".

[142] Nedarim I. 4, 37a.

[143] קרבן כאומר כקרבן, namely "the object is forbidden to me like a Korban."

[144] Matt. XXIII. 16: ὃς ἂν ὀμόσῃ ἐν τῷ ναῷ οὐδέν ἐστιν· ὃς δ'ἂν ὀμόσῃ
ἐν τῷ χρυσῷ τοῦ ναοῦ, ὀφείλει . . . ὃς ἐὰν ὀμόσῃ ἐν τῷ θυσιαστηρίῳ οὐδέν
ἐστιν· ὃς δ'ἂν ὀμόσῃ ἐν τῷ δώρῳ τῷ ἐπάνω αὐτοῦ, ὀφείλει.

[145] Joseph., Bella Jud. II. 9.4, 175: . . . τὸν ἱερὸν θησαυρόν, καλεῖται δὲ
κορβωνᾶς. See also Matt. XXVII. 6.

[146] Schechter, Documents of Jewish Sectaries I, p. 615.

Schechter[147] translated: "And to separate from the wealth of wickedness which is contaminated by a vow and a curse and *from* the wealth of the Sanctuary." Charles[148] translated: "And to hold aloof from the polluted wealth of wickedness under a vow and a curse and *from* the wealth of the Sanctuary." Both of them correct ובהון to ומהון, thus connecting הון המקדש with הון הרשעה. But there is no need to emend the text: נדר, חרם, and הון המקדש (=קרבן) are all of them terms of vows (and oaths), and the translation is: "And to separate from the polluted[149] wealth of wickedness[150] under a vow, curse and Korban."[151]

The scholars have misunderstood the part of the Rabbis in their struggle with the common people in matters of oaths. The Rabbis taught that only the word שבועה (or its substitutes) or the mention of His name (or His attributes) are binding in an oath. The swearing by all other objects, holy as they may be, is not valid.

[147] P. XXXVIII.   [148] Pseudep., p. 813.

[149] A play on Lev. XXII.2.

[150] Μαμωνᾶ τῆς ἀδικίας (Charles ibid., p. 809 n. 11). See also Strack and Billerbeck, Kommentar II, p. 220.

[151] This document abounds in good Hebrew words and expressions which occur in Rabbinic literature in greater number than all editors of it were aware of. So the word למשכים (p. 1019) in the sense of "the following morning" occurs not only in Mishna Bikkurim (III. 2), but also in Seder Olam (V, ed. A. Marx, p. 14. See variants ibid. and Prof. Marx's note in the German translation, p. 22).

We read further (p. 1011): אשר ... מדי מרעיל אל ירחץ איש במים צואים ומיעוטים מדי מרעיל אין בו די מרעיל. All the editors gave it a far-fetched interpretation. The correct translation is: "No man shall wash in filthy water or [in water] that is less than a "Mar'eil"... that does not contain [water of the quantity] of a Mar'eil." מרעיל is a good Hebrew word already found in Tosephta (Kelim, Baba Mezia, VII, 585₁₅, in Cod. Vienna): ארבעה סלים ש ב מ ר ח ל (Zuckermandel and ed. pr. read: שבמרחץ!). Koheleth Rabba (II.20, ed. pr.) mentions: מלא מרחילה, but the parallel Vayyikra Rabba (XXV.5) reads: מרעליה. This word is rendered in the parallel Tanhuma (Kedoshim 8, ed. Buber p. 76): סל גדול, "A big hamper" (See my remarks in Tosefeth Rishonim III, p. 53, n. 15). This סל גדול (=מרעיל) is, it seems to me, no other than a kind of the גדולים (or סואים (סונים), "big hampers," regarding which it is stated (Tosephta Kelim, Baba Mezia, V. 1, 583₂₁; Sifra, Shemini VI.7, ed. Weiss, 53a): קופות גדולות והסאין גדולים ... מחזיקין ארבעים לח, "Big baskets and big hampers ... which hold *forty* Seah of liquid," namely, the legal measure of a Mikwa (See Menahoth XII. 4 and elsewhere).

The people however did not listen to them. The large Jewish masses in their excessive piety did not discriminate between real oaths and spurious ones. They had the same reverence for all of them. We have already related the story[152] of the man who swore in the court by the life of the fig-picker and had his oath accepted by his opponent, although the latter could originally have demanded a really legal oath.

The oath by the life of the fig-picker, absurd as it was in the eyes of the Rabbis, was nevertheless serious in the opinion of the common people. Even in monetary disputes it seemed adequate to them to serve as surety for the truth.

We have a most instructive passage in confirmation of our statement, which was misunderstood by the commentaries and unnoticed by the scholars. TP[153] quotes a Baraitha of the House of Rab (III c.): מניין לנדרים שהן מותרין לך מן השמים ובני אדם נוהגין בהן באיסור שלא תהא נודר ומבטל, תלמוד לומר לא יחל דברו, שלא יעשה דבריו חולין. הוון בעיין מימר כגון הקרבן בשבועה. הא בשאר הדברים. כל הדברים לא. אתא מימר לך אפילו בשאר כל הדברים. "Whence [do we know] that one should not take and nullify those vows (or oaths) which Heaven has permitted to you, but which the people treat as forbidden? From the passage: *'He shall not profane his word'* (Num. XXX.3), one should not make his word 'hullin'.[154] They (i. e. the sages) had thought [that this rule applied only to vows and oaths] like *'the Korban' in an oath-formula*[155] [but the Baraitha] came to teach us [that this rule applies] to all other things as well."

When we compare this passage to the parallel sources[156] we realize how much more enlightening our passage is than its parallels. Here we are clearly told that the people[157] scrupulously

---

[152] Above p. 127.
[153] Nedarim II. 1, 37b.
[154] Profane, ordinary as opposed to holy.
[155] Which is worthless, see above p. 130.
[156] Tosephta Nedarim IV. 6, 279₂₂; TB ibid., 81b.
[157] בני אדם. In TB ibid. we have a general statement regarding the proper behavior in the presence of "others" (Comp. R. Hisda's explanation of אחרים in TB Pesahim 51a, top) who treat permitted thing as forbidden. Strack and Billerbeck, "Kommentar" to I Corinth. VIII. 9 seq., recorded no Talmudic parallels.

observed the vows and oaths which were not binding by the
Law. We have here explicit evidence that the oath "by the
Korban" (הקרבן בשבועה) was respected by the people despite the
unanimous opinion[158] that such an oath is worthless. Moreover,
the Palestinian Talmud adds that this rule applies to many
other similar oaths.

Now, there can be no doubt that oaths like "by the life of
the head"[159] or "by heaven and by earth"[160] were highly respected
by the people. The pious Jewish masses were even content with
such oaths when taken by their opponents in the courts.[161]

Thus, the opinion that an oath by the Altar or by the Temple
or by heaven,[162] by the earth, or by Jerusalem, or by the head[163]
is binding is neither more nor less than the opinion prevalent
among the Jewish unlearned masses (ובני אדם נוהגין בהן באיסור) in
defiance of the standards set up by the learned sages. However
certain Rabbis did not entirely disregard the feelings of the
populace. We have seen that the House of Rab respected
the belief of the masses and forbade to slight this kind of
oaths.[164]

Moreover Maimonides[165] decided: מי שנשבע בשמים ובארץ
ובשמש וכיוצא בהן אף על פי שאין כוונתו אלא למי שבראם אין זו
שבועה, "When a man swears by heaven, by earth, *by the sun* and
by similar objects his oath is null although he had in mind Him
Who created all these objects." The example of a Jew swearing
by the sun is very striking. As far as I know there is no direct
instance of such an oath in ancient Talmudic literature.[165a] Yet
Maimonides hardly invented this instance; he probably found
his statement in a Rabbinic source (which is now lost) and

[158] See above p. 131.
[159] Mishna Sanhedrin III. 2 and parallels.
[160] Ibid., Shebuoth IV. 13.
[161] See above p. 127. Comp. Mishna ibid.
[162] Matt. XXIII, 20–22.
[163] Ibid. V, 34–36.
[164] Comp. also Sifre I (153, ed. Horovitz, 200₃) and the reading of ms.
מדרש חכמים ibid. Perhaps the vague word הבטאה (utterance) designated
promissory utterances confirmed by popular oaths.
[165] Mishneh Tora, hilkoth Shebuoth XII. 3.
[165a] See however below.

combined the examples cited there with those of the Mishna,[166] as he usually does.

We likewise know that the oath by the sun, τὸν ἥλιον, was very popular with the Greeks.[167] Philo[168] recommends swearing by the *sun* and the stars, and it is thereupon likely that his recommendation is based on a usage in vogue among the Jewish masses.

This assumption will explain an obscure passage in TP[169] which reads: תני בר קפרא חרס, לא חספא הוא. אמר ר' זעירא לשון גבוה הוא. האומר לחרס ולא יזרח "Bar Kappara (III c.) included 'Heres' [among the binding substitutes of חרם]. Now, does not חרס [also] mean a potsherd? (why then is it binding?) R. Ze'ira said it is grandiloquent[170] speech[171] [as it is written]: *'That commandeth the sun and it shineth not'* " (Job IX.7).

Thus, R. Ze'ira took it for granted that the man who used the term חרס in an oath designated the sun by it, bearing in mind 'Him Who commandeth it'. According to the accepted law[172] such an oath is not valid, but Bar Kappara seems to have adopted the view of those sages who did not entirely reject the popular worthless oath.[173]

We can now summarize the conflict between the opinion of the majority of the learned Rabbis and the popular belief of the masses in the domain of oaths and vows. The people in their fear of the real oath began to swear not only by holy objects (like Jerusalem, the Temple, the Altar, the Korban etc.) but by all kinds of matter, beginning with the heaven, earth, sun etc. and ending with the absurd oaths like "by the fish-nets" and "by the life of the fig-picker,"[174] No sooner did the absurd ex-

---

[166] Shebuoth IV. 13.

[167] See Hirzel, der Eid p. 24 (note).

[168] See above p. 124.

[169] Nedarim I. 2. 37a (and parallel).

[170] This is the meaning of לשון גבוה here, as can be ascertained from TP Sanhedrin VII. 16, 25d. The usual interpretation of the passage does not change our general argument below.

[171] חרס was no longer used in the meaning of "sun".

[172] See Maimonides, quoted above p. 137.

[173] See above p. 137.

[174] See above p. 127 and p. 128.

pression become a fixed oath-term, than the people tended to use a substitute for it,[175] thus progressing from the stupid to the ridiculous. Some Rabbis were ready to make concessions to the excessive popular zeal,[176] but the majority, in their hatred of "foolish saints who wear out the world"[177] abode by the strict opinion of the law that all these popular oaths are null and worthless.

But the Jewish masses also invented all kinds of substitutes for such valid and binding terms as קרבן, נזיר, חרם, נדר, שבועה etc., in order to avoid, for one reason or another, the utterance of these terms. In such cases the Rabbis had to confirm a great part of the substitutes; here they had to accept the rule[178] that in matters of vows and oaths we follow the language of the people. From the large number of substitutes they had to choose and select only the proper and adequate ones, and they concluded:[179] לשונות שבידרו להן ראשונים אין רשות לבירייה להוסיף "No עליהן . . . לשונות שבידרו להן משניות אין רשות לבירייה להוסיף עליהן human being has the right to add more terms (substitutes) to those selected by the ancients . . . No human being has the right to add more terms to those selected by the Mishnayoth."

In conclusion we shall finish our chapter with the explanation of an obscure oath pronounced by a Gentile, as recorded in Talmudic literature. Sifre[180] and TB[181] have preserved a peculiar story about a man who succeeded in controlling his violent passion. According to it there was a certain man who had always been very observant regarding the wearing of fringes (ציצית). Once he learned of a very beautiful courtesan in the coastal cities (בכרכי הים) who received four hundred gold pieces for her favors; he at once sent her the sum and arrived at her house. When he disrobed, however, his fringes "slapped him in

---

[175] Tosephta Sanhedrin V. 1, 422₂₈. See above p. 128, n. 99.

[176] See above p. 137 and p. 138.

[177] See Mishna Sota III. 4.

[178] TP Nedarim VI. 1, 39c and parallels; TB ibid. 30b and parallels. (הלכו בנדרים אחר לשון בני אדם).

[179] TP Nazir I. 1, 51a. Comp. also TB ibid. 10a and above p. 17, n. 14.

[180] I, 115, ed. Horovitz, p. 128₁₇.

[181] Menahoth 44a.

the face"; he abandoned his purpose and sought to withdraw.
"By the *Gappa* (גפה) of Rome," she swore — I will not let you
go till you tell me what blemish you saw in me — etc.

Many interpretations were given to the courtesan's oath by
גפה של רומי.[182] Among others Loew[183] mentions Sachs' suggestion
that גפה is ἀγάπη, "Love of Rome"; he correctly rejects it,
remarking that this word still remains an unsolved riddle; this is
also the opinion of Horovitz.[184]

It seems quite certain to me that גפה דרומי really means
ἀγάπη of Rome, but refers not to some obscure love of Rome,
but to the famous goddess — Isis, who was called ἀγάπη. In an
invocation of Isis[185] we read:

> (col v, l. 94): ἐν Δώροις φιλίαν· ἐν Στρ[άτω]ν[ος
>   πύργῳ Ἑλλάδα, ἀγαθήν . . .
> (l. 104):   ἐν Πέρσαις λατείνην . . .
> (l. 109):   ἐν Ἰταλία ἀ[γά]πην θε
>   ῶν.

At Dora[186] [Isis was called] 'Affection', At Straton's
Tower[187]— 'Greek', 'Good'. . . In Persia — 'Latin', In Italy —
'Love of gods'."

Thus, we have contemporary evidence[188] that at the coast
cities of Palestine Isis was called "Affection" or "Greek", and
it is almost certain that the disciple of R. Hiyya[189] who studied
in Galilee visited a courtesan who lived in Caesarea which was
termed כרכי הים. The oath "By Isis"— ἡ παρὰ γυναιξὶ θεὸς
καλουμένη[190]— is only natural in the mouth of a courtesan,

---

[182] See Loew in Krauss' LW p. 182.
[183] Ibidem.
[184] Sifre ad loc., p. 129 n. 2.
[185] Oxyr. Pap. XI, 1380, p. 197.
[186] Tantura, in the vicinity of Caesarea.
[187] Caesarea.
[188] This invocation of Isis was written in the second century, approximately
the period of the occurrence of our story.
[189] Or R. Meir. See Horovitz ad loc.
[190] "Who is called goddess by women," as stated in the famous inscription of Jos, l. 15. See the facsimile in Deissmann's Light etc. between
p. 138–139.

especially when we remember that Isis took the place of Venus[191]
by whom[192] the courtesans had been previously swearing.[193]

The oath גפא דרומא is recorded once more in TB[194] in the
name of a Gentile. R. Juda the Patriarch[195] (III c.) com-
missioned R. Oshaia to debate with this Gentile. The latter,
who apparently was in a position to harm the Jews, was a
Roman official[196] who lived in the same place as R. Oshaia,[197]
the head of the school in Caesarea.[198] That a Roman, stationed
at a place in whose vicinity Isis was called φιλία, swore by the
ἐν 'Ιταλία ἀγάπην θεῶν is natural and understandable.

[191] See Daremberg et Saglio, Dictionnaire des Antiquités etc. III, 580b
and n. 18 ibidem.

[192] See E. Ziebarth, de iureiurando in iure graeco quaestiones, p. 15.

[193] We must record here that ms. מדרש חכמים reads in the Sifre ספינדא דרומי
(instead of גפא דרומי) which might mean: σπένδω by Rome. See the Latin
lexicons s. v. spondeo. But this reading has no support whatever in the mss.
of both TB and Sifre.

[194] Pesahim 87b.

[195] This is the only correct reading, see דקדוקי סופרים ad loc., p. 268 n.
200. This reading is also corroborated by Seder Eliyyahu Rabba (XI ed.
Friedmann, p. 54) which drew from a different source. The reading of the
editions and ms. Munich is erroneous, for R. Hanina would not call R. Oshaia
"a disciple", whereas the Patriarch, R. Juda the Second, by virtue of his
office may have permitted himself to term R. Oshaia "disciple" in order to
show the Gentile that even his pupil will be able to give him the right answer.

[196] The text of TB reads מינא which very often means Gentile, especially
in sources originating in Palestine (See Krauss LW I, p. XV, n. 2). Seder
Eliyyahu Rabba ibid. states clearly that the man who questioned R. Juda
the Patriarch was a הגמון, ἡγεμών, a general. Similarly, TB (Aboda Zara 6b)
records that a מין presented the same Rabbi Juda the Patriarch with money,
whereas the parallel story in TP (ibid. I. 1, 39b) mentions דוקינר (δουκηνάριος,
ducenarius) instead of מין. In both cases the מין was a heathen Roman official.

[197] Where the Patriarch often came on account of his office.

[198] TP Terumoth X. 3. 47a and elsewhere. Comp. also the reply of
Philippus to R. El'asha in Midrash Tehilim IX. 9, p. 86.

Additional Note (to p. 132, n. 129)

As for the action of R. Johanan he used here the so called σοφιστικὸς ὅρκος (comp. also Joseph. Bel. Jud. VI. 6.1) which was also practiced by the Greeks (See Hirzel, Der Eid, p. 44 seq.). In the Jewish courts the sophistic oath was done away with by a special declaration which warned the swearer that he is adjured not according to his own mind, but according to the will of the court and of God (See TP Sota VII. 1, 21b and parallels; TB Shebuoth 39a and parallels; comp. the anecdote related in Pesiktha Rabbathi, ed. Friedmann 113a and parallels; TB Nedarim 25a).

Grotius (de iure belli ac pacis II. 8, ed. Het. Tromp, p. 361) writes: It tamen hanc exceptionem habeat, nisi qui iurat sciat, aut probabiliter credat ab eo quicum negotium est verba aliter accipi. nam dictis ipsis testem adhibens Deum debet dicta facere verba, quomodo putat intelligi. Et hoc est quod idem ait Cicero: Quod ita iuratum est, ut mens *deferentis* conciperet fieri oportere, id servandum est. "This is so with the exception of the case in which you who swear, know or believe that he with whom you have to do takes your words otherwise: for in taking God to witness his words he ought to perform them as he supposes them to be understood. So Cicero" (We shall quote his actual words presently) "formulates that only an oath which has been sworn as the mind of the proposer (adjurer) thought that it ought to be performed is binding." (See the sources recorded in note 9 ibidem).

TB (Nedarim 28a) and the "Gemara" in the minor tract Kalla (ed. Koronel 3b, Higger 19232) recommend resorting to the sophistic oath in case of extreme emergency. But in Palestinian literature there is no trace of advice to such effect. Where the above-mentioned TB suggests a sophistic oath, TP (Nedarim III. 5, 38a) simply remarks: ר' ישמעאל אומר לא תשבעו בשמי לשקר נשבע את להרגין ולחרמין ולמוכסין, "R. Ishmael (I–II c.) said: [it is written] 'Ye shall not swear by My name falsely' (Lev. XIX.12), but you may swear to murderers, to robbers and to tax-gatherers" (who were put in the category of robbers by the Jews of Palestine. See Prof. L. Ginzberg מקומה של ההלכה בחכמת ישראל p. 11). In this case the attitude of the Palestinian scholars approximated that of the strict and honest Romans. According to Cicero (de officiis III XXIX 107) we can refuse a pirate the price fixed for ransom; with him (i. e. the pirate) we can have no promises, no oaths that are mutually binding (cum hoc nec fides debet nec iusiurandum esse commune). The same opinion is uttered by Brutus in his speech in the Capitol (Appian, civil wars, II. XIX. 139): "no faith, no oath will ever bind the Romans to the tyrant" (οὐδὲν πιστόν ἐστι Ῥωμαίοις πρὸς τύραννον οὐδ' εὔορκον).

We may therefore assume with certainty that the interpretation of the "Gemara" in the above-mentioned minor tract Kalla, according to which R. Akiba took a sophistic oath, is a later explanation, adapted to the Halacha of the Babylonian Talmud. In Palestine it was probably understood literally: R. Akiba swore only with his lips but not with his heart (היה ר' עקיבא נשבע בשפתיו ומבטל לו בלבו,) and in case of emergency such oaths were not binding as they were not when sworn to murderers and robbers.

Cicero (de officiis III. XXIX. 108) maintains: Quod enim ita iuratum est, ut mens conciperet fieri opportere, id servandum est: quod aliter, id si non fecerit, nullum est periurium. "An oath which has been sworn in such a manner that in the mind [of the swearer] there was an idea present that it ought to be performed, must be kept. But in the case of an oath, in which it is otherwise (i. e. in which the swearer did not think at the time he swore it that it ought to be performed), is not perjury to break it." (See H. A. Holden's notes in his edition p. 436, where he refers to Grotius who misunderstood the words of Cicero).

Even more explicit are Cicero's words when he says (ibid.): Non enim falsum iurare periurare est, sed, quod *ex animi tui sententia iuraris*, sicut verbis concipitur more nostro, id non facere periurium est, "Perjury does not consist in swearing falsely but in not fulfilling what you have sworn upon your conscience, as our law-formulas express it." (See A. Stickney's notes in his edition p. 337). Thereupon Cicero quotes the famous passage of Euripides (Hippol. 612): ἡ γλῶσσ᾽ ὀμώμοχ᾽, ἡ δὲ φρὴν ἀνώμοτος, "My tongue has sworn, but my heart is unsworn."

R. Akiba swore with his tongue but not with his heart, and according to the Jewish law prevailing in Palestine this oath was not binding when taken under duress.

GREEK AND LATIN PROVERBS
IN RABBINIC LITERATURE

We had occasion, in another connection,[1] to point out that Rabbinic literature contains Greek proverbs in the original language. This can be accepted as a well established fact. But the question arises whether some of the Aramaic proverbs of the Rabbis do not represent translations from the Greek[2] or Judaized adaptations of such adages.

TB[2a] records a few adages in the name of Bar Kappara,[3] and among them we read: קרנא קריא ברומי בשוקא[4] בר מזבין

[1] Above p. 38 nn. 51 and 51a.

[2] R. Eleazar, who quoted (see previous note) the proverb παρὰ βασιλέως ὁ νόμος ἄγραφος in the original, somehow elaborated it in Hebrew and said (see above p. 38): "When a human king issues a law, if he wishes he obeys it, otherwise [only] others obey it etc." Dio Cassius (LIII. 28) records that the Roman Senate accorded Augustus (24 B.C.E.) the rights of supremacy over both himself and the laws, so that he might obey those laws he wishes to observe and disregard those he does not wish to abide by (. . . αὐτοκράτωρ καὶ ἑαυτοῦ καὶ τῶν νόμων πάντα τε ὅσα βούλοιτο ποιοίη καὶ πάνθ' ὅσα ἀβουλοίη μὴ πράττοι). It is very probable that not only the Greek phrase was borrowed by R. Eleazar from a Greek source but its Hebrew elaboration as well originated in the same source. Martialis (liber spectac. XXIX) remarks: sed Caesar legi paruit ipse suae, "But Caesar obeyed his own law." Comp. also the Cambridge Ancient History XII, 352, 372 seq.

According to the tradition of another Rabbinic source (see above p. 38, n. 51) this phrase was used by Palestinian Rabbis (of the I–II c.) in their sermon at *Rome*. Only a few decades earlier the "lex de imperio Vespasiano" (year 69) was promulgated in the streets of Rome by means of a bronze tablet (C.I.L. VI. 930). It reads: legibus plebisque scitis imp[erator] Caesar Vespasianus solutus est. "The Emperor Caesar Vespasian is released from the laws and the decrees of the [Roman] people." (Comp. H. T. F. Duckworth, A commentary on the LIII book of Dio Cassius' Roman History, p. 75). The *Oriental* Rabbis who visited Rome understood the formula literally; they utilized this bronze tablet in their sermons and demonstrated the difference between an earthly king and the Lord of the world.

[2a] Berakoth 62b.

[3] Palestinian Rabbi of the II–III c.

[4] This word is found in ms. Coronel. See Rabbinovicz ad loc.

תאני, תאני דאבוך זבין. The commentaries disagree in their interpretation of the passage.[5] However, it is reasonable to assume that the Roman crier advertised some products in the market. In my opinion, we have to vocalize the last word of the proverb: זְבִין, buy. Accordingly, the translation is: "The horn (i. e. the *praeco*, herald) calls in the market of Rome: 'Son of a figseller, buy thy father's (i. e. home-grown) figs!' " There is no ground whatever for doubting the exactness of the information given in the Talmud,[6] but we do not know whence Bar Kappara drew his information. It is possible that he received a direct report from a Jew who had been to Rome and had heard the heralds say that they themselves are "figsellers", and their sons have to buy their own home-grown figs, not imported ones. Perhaps the adage heard by the Jew was something like "ficorum venditoris fili, paternas ficos eme." It is also possible that the Rabbis drew from a literary source which had something like "συκοπώλου υἱέ, τὰ πάτρια σῦκα ἀγόραζε".[7]

[5] See Rashi ad loc. and Otzar Hageonim I, 1, ed. Dr. B. M. Lewin, p. 139.

[6] Figs were widely cultivated in Italy. Even Syrian varieties were cultivated as far as the 1st century (See Plin., Hist. nat. XV. 21).

As for the information given in the Talmud it probably originated in a *forum pomarium* in Rome (In the list of the various markets in Rome by Daremberg et Saglio, III, 1739a, such a market is not recorded). TB Megilla 6b (according to Rabbinovicz ad loc., p. 20, n. 8) mentions also a *forum aviarium* (שוק מוכרי עופות) in Rome. On the various kinds of advertisements by the fruitmongers see Daremberg et Saglio ibid., figure 4921.

[7] In the name of Samuel (III c.) TB (Aboda Zara 11b) records another *proclamation* (by the public crier) *in Rome* on the occasion of the *Ludi Saeculares* (as already noticed by S. Rapoport in ערך מלין s. v. איד. Comp. also H. Blaufuss, Römische Feste etc., Nürnberg 1900, p. 31, n. 1): ומכריזין... דחמי חמי ודלא חמי לא חמי, "And they proclaim... 'Let him who will see it see it; he who will not see it now will never see it'." Here we have independent evidence confirming the exactness of the tradition in the Talmud. Suetonius (Claud. 21.2) remarks about these games: vox praeconis... invitantis more sollemni ad ludos, quos nec spectasset quisquam nex spectaturus esset. "The herald's proclamation... when he invited the people, in a solemn manner, to games which no one had ever seen or would ever see again." Likewise, Herodian, III. 8 (referred to by Blaufuss ibid.), in describing these games, observes: κήρυκες... καλοῦντες ἥκειν καὶ θεάσασθαι πάντας ἃ μήτε εἶδον μήτε ὄψονται, "Heralds... calling everybody to come

Here the Talmud states explicitly that the proverb originated in the markets of Rome. In this case, what we do not know is only whether the proverb which the Rabbis quote in Aramaic was translated from Greek or Latin, but sometimes the very assumption that the origin of a certain Rabbinic proverb is to be traced to the Romans is only a conjecture.

In Aboth (IV. 15) we read: ר' מתיה בן חרש אומר ... והוי זנב לאריות ולא ראש לשועלים "R. Mathia b. Heresh said . . . 'Be a tail to lions and not a head to foxes'." Z. Frankel[8] remarks: "This saying is very appropriate in the mouth of a Jewish sage who resided in Rome.[9] It seems that he sought to counteract the famous saying of Caesar: 'It is better to be the first man in a village than the second man in Rome'." I. H. Weiss[10] pointed to TP[11] in which a proverb to the contrary is quoted, and according to him TP likewise had in mind the saying of Caesar. Bacher dismisses Weiss' suggestion as "groundless".[12]

Since the reading in our editions of TP is corrupt, we shall quote the true reading of TP: מתלה[13] רב ממתניתא. מתניתא אמרה הוי זנב לאריות ולא ראש לשועלים. מתלא אמר הוי ראש לשועלים ולא זנב לאריות וכו' (read: ותנינן) דתנינן. "The proverb is greater (i. e. goes farther) than the Mishna; the Mishna teaches: 'Be a tail to lions and not a head to foxes', and the proverb says: 'Be a head to foxes and not a tail to lions'. And we [also] learned etc."

Now the question is whether we have here a genuine Jewish proverb opposed to the teaching of the Mishna, or a Jewish

and see what they have never seen and will never see." Comp. also Claudianus, de sexto consul. Honorii 390; Zos. II. 5.

The traces of Palestinian Aramaic in the statement of Samuel indicate that the information originated in Palestine, and the Greek words in the previous sentence of the passage betray a Greek (literary?) source.

[8] דרכי המשנה, p. 130.

[9] He was the head of a Talmudic Academy in Rome (II c.). See TB Sanhedrin 32b.

[10] דור דור ודורשיו II[6], p. 110.

[11] Sanhedrin IV. 10, 22b.

[12] AdT I, p. 381, n. 1. It may incidentally be noted that none of the above scholars took the trouble to give the source in which Caesar's saying is recorded. See below n. 17.

[13] This מתלא is the reading of יוחסין השלם, ed. Filipowski, p. 119a. Our editions read erroneously מייתי לה.

adaptation[14] of Caesar's saying. It seems to me that we have every reason to suppose that the Jews knew the Roman proverb in Greek.

TP[15] asks: "Is not the second grade of Pelusian linen superior to the first grade of Indian linen, [why then does the High-Priest put on garments of Indian linen instead of second grade of Pelusian linen]? ... Is not the second grade of the first class oil superior to the first grade of the second class oil, [why then does the Mishna consider them equal]?" The answers of TP in both cases are: משם מילה דשמעה פרוטי, "Because the thing bears the designation (fame) πρώτη — first [grade]."

Here the Rabbis explain that although in the case of oil for the Menora they regard the first grade of the lower class as equal to the second grade of the higher class, yet in the case of the garments of the High-Priest (where their external beauty and reputation are taken into consideration) they go so far as *to prefer* the inferior first grade of Indian linen to the superior second grade of Pelusian linen. The laws were justified by the only argument that the approved inferior items bear the name πρῶτος.[16] How close to the saying of Caesar!

The fact that the Rabbis abandoned the Hebrew ראשון mentioned in the quoted Mishna and employed the Greek πρῶτος (which was not used in Jewish Aramaic) indicates that they alluded to a known proverb in Greek which praised the πρῶτος

---

[14] On "lions and foxes" in Jewish proverbs see Bacher in JQR V (1893), p. 170 and the various collections of Talmudic proverbs s. v. ארי. There is, however, one proverb which escaped the notice of all the collectors, on account of the corrupt text of the editions. In Kohelet Rabba III. 7 (ed. Romm 9d) we read that R. Mana was asked by R. Abun (on the relation between the two Rabbis see TP Moed Katan III. 7, 83b, top) to say a "word of Tora." Thereupon the former remarked: הא מטה ענתה דאוריתא דמחשי מתעלייה למשתקה, which makes no sense whatever. But the first edition reads: הא מטת ענתה דאריתא דמחשי (read: למחשי) מתעלייא (read: ותעלייא) למשרקה (read: למשרקה). Midrash Haggadol (Lev., p. 193) reads even more clearly: ענתא דיהון אריותא שתקין ותעליא שרקין. The sense is now quite simple: "A time has come for the lions to keep silent and for the foxes to yell." Comp. also TP Yebamoth IX. 5, 10a (bottom).

[15] Yoma III. 6, 40d.

[16] TP uses the feminine πρώτη in agreement with the feminine מילה.

of a low rank above the δεύτερος of a high rank.[17] The aphorism:
"Be a head to foxes and not a tail to lions" seems therefore to
be a Jewish formulation of the foreign saying.

We may add one more example. TP[18] introduces an adage in
the name of R. Jannai (III c.): אין קטא קטא שיחור ואין אובד אובד
מרגלי. I have shown[19] that this reading which is corroborated by
many authorities cannot be changed and that קטא is the Aramaic
form of κτάομαι. The proverb has to be translated: "If he
gained, he gained a trifle (literally: a charcoal); if he lost, he
lost a gem."[19a] But it is hard to understand why a Greek word
(which never occurs anywhere else in Rabbinic literature)
intruded upon the Aramaic. Here again, we shall not go far
astray if we presume that we have an Aramaic translation (or
formulation) of a Greek proverb which began with the words:
εἰ κτᾷ ... "If thou gainest ..." The Jews cleverly Aramaized
and transformed it into אין קטא etc.

The immediately following saying of Resh Lakish seems to
illustrate the above adage. He said: [20]אלו זבנת גרמך ללודין הות
מזבין להון בדמין יקרין. והכא בדמין קלילין, "If you had sold yourself
to the lanistae, you would have commanded a high price, but
now [you have sold yourself] at a low price." Resh Lakish
observed that drinking of uncovered water[21] is an even greater
act of recklessness than selling oneself to the lanistae, for in the
latter case he at least receives a considerable sum of money,[22]

---

[17] The famous proverb of Caesar is worded by Plutarch (Caesar XI):
Ἐγὼ μὲν ἐβουλόμην παρὰ τούτοις εἶναι μᾶλλον π ρ ῶ τ ο ς ἢ παρὰ Ῥωμαίοις δ ε ύ τ ε ρ ο ς.

[18] Terumoth VIII. 5, 45d and parallel.

[19] Tarbiz, vol. V, p. 100.

[19a] A play on ἄνθρακες (comp. ἄνθρακες ὁ θησαυρός) and ἄνθραξ (ruby)?

[20] So Cod. Vat. and parallel in Aboda Zara. The editions have ללודין
which may be a corruption of ללודרין, ludarii, see Jastrow, s. v.

[21] Josep. (cont. Ap. I. 22, 164) calls it δίψια ὕδατα, "serpents' water"
(See Liddell and Scott s. v. διψάς II), i. e. uncovered water, which was
forbidden to the Jews (Mishna Terumoth VIII. 4 and elsewhere) for fear
that a serpent might have tasted it. All the translators of Josep. have misunderstood the passage. See my remark in הירושלמי כפשוטו I, p. 49 in the
name of my regretted friend B. Soliternik.

[22] According to the famous inscription in Corp. Inscr. Lat. II, 6278
(with comments by Hübner and Mommsen in Ephem. Epigr. VII, 1890,

whereas by drinking uncovered liquid he risks his life for a mouthful of fluid.

Perhaps the previous proverb was also applied to the ludarii, who sold their life for money, or, as Seneca[23] expresses himself: edunt ac bibunt, quae per sanguinem reddant, "They eat and drink that for which they pay with their blood." The "moral" of the adage was: If they gain, they gain money; if they lose, they lose their life. Thus, the two sayings complete and explain each other.

This method of inquiry into the reasons for the use by the Rabbis of foreign words not otherwise mentioned in Rabbinic literature may sometimes guide us to the original sources from which the Jewish sages have drawn their lore and thus help us solve certain difficulties frequently met with in Palestinian Rabbinic literature.

So, for instance, we read in Tanhuma:[24] מעשה בגר אחד שהיה מבצרה. אמר כשהייתי נכרי הייתי בע"ז עכשיו נעשיתי ישראל ואסור לי. מה עשה? חבש את חמורו והלך במדינה ולא שאל בע"ז, ונכנס במדינה והיה ה פ י נ ס ו ר שלה עומד בפתח המדינה עם שהוא נכנס ראה אותם מיד נתירא, ירד (read: נפל) מן החמור וברח החמור. ירדו אותו שהיו עומדין שם, והוא מתיירא מהם, וזקפו אותו וסמכין אותו. היו אומרים הזקן הזה נפל. מיד הוליכו אותו אצל חמורו ונכנס בשלום ויצא בשלום. The commentaries misunderstood the whole passage. It has already been pointed out by me[25] that the same story is found in TP[26] in a contracted form. There it is clearly stated that the incident happened near the customhouse; the man wanted to smuggle goods into the town without paying the customs.[27] The translation of the passage is therefore: "This is a story about a proselyte from Bostra. He said: 'When I was a heathen I used to consult the idols[28]; now

p. 385 seq.) the minimum price for a gladiator was fixed (beginning of the fourth quarter of the second century) at one thousand sesterces (see Mommsen ibid., p. 413).

[23] Epist. XXXVII. 2.   [24] Shoftim 10, 99a (Mantua 1563).

[25] Tarbiz, vol. II, p. 237 and הירושלמי כפשוטו I, p. 115.

[26] Shabbath VI. 9, 8d.

[27] On the Jewish attitude towards the right of the Romans to collect taxes in Palestine see above p. 142.

[28] I. e. the oracle. From TP l. c. we gather that he used to read the stars in order to know if the hour is auspicious for trade.

I have become a Jew and it is forbidden to me'. What did he
do? He saddled his ass, went to town without consulting the
oracle. When he was about to enter the city he saw its 'defensor'[29]
[and the custom-men] standing at the gate. He was immediately
frightened and fell from the ass[30] which ran away. The [officials]
who were present there hurried down,"— this undoubtedly
scared our man all the more — "lifted and supported him saying:
'The [poor] old man fell down'. They brought him to his ass,[31]
and he entered in peace and left in peace."

The story is quite understandable in itself, but far more
light is shed upon it if we compare it with a Greek story recorded by Zenobius:[32] Λεύκων γάρ τις γεωργὸς μέλιτος ἀσκοὺς
εἰς φορμοὺς ἐμβαλὼν, ἐκόμιζεν ᾿Αθήναζε. Κριθὰς οὖν τοῖς
φορμοῖς ἐμβαλὼν, ὡς ὑπὲρ κριθῶν ὀλίγον εἰσπραχθησόμενος
τέλος, ἐκόμιζε. Τοῦ δ᾿ ὄνου πεσόντος, οἱ τελῶναι βοηθῆσαι
βουλόμενοι, ἔμαθον ὅτι μέλι ἐστὶ, καὶ ἀπηνέγκαντο αὐτὸ ὡς
ἀτελώνητον. "A certain peasant named Leucos filled leather-
bags with honey, put it into baskets (for carrying corn) and
carried it to Athens. He brought it after having poured barley
into the baskets, for only a small tariff was levied on barley.
But the ass fell and when the tax-collectors wanted to help
[the peasant] they discovered that it was honey and confiscated
it as smuggled (untaxed) goods." Here the ass ruined the
peasant; when it fell and when the custom-house officials wanted
to help him they discovered the honey. The Rabbis told a
similar story; but in it the proselyte who had faith in God was
saved by his ass. It kicked him down near the city gate just at
the time when he noticed the custom-officers and was seized
with fright. The latter hurried to help him, had sympathy for
him (attributing his fright to the shock of the fall) and brought

[29] The text reads הפינסור which makes no sense. But we know that the
Spanish scribes used to enclose the י within the ד, so that די could be read ה
and vice versa (See Levita, חשבי s. v. משקט). We can therefore read דיפינסור
(instead of הפינסור), δηφήνσορ, defensor.

[30] The version in TP l. c. tells that the ass kicked him down.

[31] Which was already within the city together with the goods.

[32] I. 74. Corpus paroem. graec., ed. Leutsch, Gotingae 1851, p. 26.

him to his ass (which was already within the city-bounds) and
forgot to search it.

The story was very famous in Greece, as the proverb (recorded by Zenob. ibid.) shows. They used to say: Ἄλλα μὲν
Λεύκων λέγει, ἄλλα δὲ Λεύκωνος ὄνος φέρει, "What Leucon
says and what Leucon's ass carries are two different things."
It has already been noted[33] that the episode was really taken
from the comedies of Leucon[34] which were acted in the theatres
of Athens.

We have seen that the Rabbis probably knew the story, but
the question is whether they took it directly from a Greek
source or from a collection of Oriental fables, which may also
have served as the source of the Greeks.

One word may possibly solve our question. It was pointed
out[35] that Nahmanides[36] quoted from TP: חד גיור הוה אסטרולוגוס
וכו' [37]שבקית למדינת] . . . [והוה מתעסק בהדין לסוטה] חד זמן . . . [שבקית למדינת]. "A proselyte had formerly been an astrologer [and he dealt in stuff for
veils]. Once . . . [She left the city[38]] etc." It is very amazing
that the words which we bracketed are found only in the quotation by Nahmanides,[39] whereas our editions,[40] the Geniza fragment[41] and Sefer Hasidim[42] show no trace of it. It cannot be a
later interpolation, for there is no reason for such an addition.
The good Palestinian Aramaic also argues against the suspicion
of an interpolation. Shall we suppose that the phrase was
accidentally omitted in all mss., originating in at least three
different countries? This is very improbable. It is more plausible

[33] See the editor's notes.
[34] V–IV c. B.C.E.
[35] ירושלמי כפשוטו I, p. 114–115.
[36] A Spanish Rabbi of the XIII c.
[37] Me'iri reads: שבקה ועלת למדינתא.
[38] According to this version the proselyte was saved from the export-tax.
Bostra (in Arabia), having been an important transit center for Oriental
wares, had probably an export-tax. Comp. the Tariff of Palmyra in Cooke's
North-Semitic Inscriptions, p. 316 seq.
[39] Me'iri is dependent on the latter, as usual.
[40] First edition printed in Italy and based on four mss.
[41] Egypt.
[42] Germany. See the reading in ירושלמי כפשוטו ibid.

to suppose that this is a case of a deliberate omission. The scribes sometimes omitted what they did not understand, especially foreign words.[43] Since Nahmanides is the only authority[44] who records this addition, the suggestion that the word לסוטה be slightly emended is quite warranted. We have only to transpose the letters and read מליטה.[45] Since מליטה, on the one hand, never occurs in Rabbinic literature and לסוטה, on the other, is very frequent in TP,[46] it is no wonder that the scribes misread or misspelt לסוטה for מליטה. Other scribes deliberately omitted the entire phrase because it was unintelligible. If our conjecture is true, then the Rabbis stated that the proselyte *dealt in honey* (μέλι, μέλιτος), exactly as the peasant does in the story of Leucon. The use of the Greek word — a hapaxlegomenon in Talmudic literature — testifies in favor of a Greek source.

The probability that the Rabbis and the heathen writers often drew from earlier Oriental fables and proverbs independently of one another may be illustrated by the following comparisons, which are very important both for the study of the history of Rabbinic sources and that of classic literature.

We read in the Satyricon of Petronius (I c.) 31: vinum dominicum ministratoris gratia est. It was already noticed by the early editors of the Cena Trimalchionis that we have a proverb here. Dr. Zielinski[47] pointed to Aristoph. (Eq. 1205): τοῦ παραϑέντος ἡ χάρις ("The favor is his who served it"), and he surmised the existence of a proverb which read something like: δεσπόσυνος (δεσποτικὸς) οἶνος, τοῦ παραϑέντος δ'ἡ χάρις ("The wine is the master's, the favor the butler's"), which Petronius also quoted.

Here again Rabbinic literature comes to the aid of the classics. The proverb in full is quoted by Raba (IV c.) in TB:[48]

[43] See my remarks in Tosefeth Rishonim I, p. 212 (bottom) and IV, p. 181. The Greek sentences from Midrash Shir Hashirim quoted above p. 45 and Introduction n. 30 are missing in Cod. Francf. (as I am informed by Prof. M. Kaplan). Comp. also אות אמת ad loc.

[44] See above, n. 39.

[45] ס and מ, ו and י are often interchangeable in mss.

[46] Even the combination בהדין (וההן) לסוטה occurs twice in TP, see Jastrow s. v. לסוטה.

[47] Philologus LXIV, p. 20.   [48] Baba Kamma 92b.

חמרא למריה טיבותא לשקייה, which Rashi explains to mean: "The wine is the master's, the thanks [belong] to the butler." Tosaphoth[49] interpret it to mean: "The wine is the master's, the favor[50] the butler's," i. e. it is in the butler's power to serve either good or cheap wine. A Midrash is quoted by Tosaphoth in support of their opinion. The context in Petronius (where the butler is indebted to the guests for their intervention in his favor and therefore promises them good wine) agrees better with the connotation given by Tosaphoth.

Again, we read in the Satyricon 38: sociorum olla male fervet, "The pot of a company cooks badly." Bacher[51] has already shown that this proverb is identical with the adage in TB:[52] קידרא דבי שותפי לא חמימא ולא קרירא, "A pot of a company is neither hot nor cold."

Further we read (ibid. 45): qui asinum non potest, stratum caedit, "He who cannot beat his donkey beats the saddle." Midrash Tanhuma[53] quotes a proverb (משל) in the name of R. Hiyya[54] (a Babylonian Rabbi who immigrated to Palestine): מי שאינו יכול להכות את החמור מכה את האוכף, word for word as we find in the Satyricon.

Finally, it should be mentioned that the famous story of the Ephesian Widow related in the Satyricon (111) was most probably known to the Rabbis,[55] as already noted by many scholars.[56]

The fact that in the Satyricon — a comparatively small book — we find a story and three proverbs which were known to the Babylonian Rabbis is very instructive. It is very

[49] Ad loc. s. v. חמרא.

[50] טיבותא like χάρις has the meaning of either thanks or favor. Comp. also דקדוקי סופרים ad loc., p. 221, n. 2.

[51] JQR V (1893), p. 169.

[52] Erubin 3a; Baba Bathra 24b.

[53] פקודי sect. 4.

[54] Bar Abba (III–IV c.). See Tanhuma, ed. Buber ibid., p. 129 and Shemoth Rabba LI, 5 where, however, the proverb is missing.

[55] TB Kiddushin 80b, see Tosaphoth ibid., s. v. כי.

[56] Dukes, Lebrecht and Landsberger; see Steinschneider, Hebraeische Bibliographie XII, p. 78 (Comp. also Isr. Letterbode XII, p. 81). Krauss (Hebrew periodical הגרן IV, p. 27) wrote an article on that subject, but he overlooked that a number of scholars anticipated him.

unlikely that the Babylonian Rabbis were acquainted with the work of Petronius; it is almost certain that both drew from a common oriental source, a fact quite important for the source-history of the Satyricon.

As stated above, it is often impossible to prove the dependence of Rabbinic proverbs on those of the Greeks or vice versa. In matters of popular common sense human minds often react and formulate the reaction in the same way and in the same manner in different countries and among different nations. Yet, the comparative study of these sources of popular wisdom often contributes to the investigation of both Rabbinic and Greek literature.

H. Lewy published a valuable article[57] on "Parallelen zu antiken Sprichwörtern und Apophtegmen" in which a number of Jewish parallels (from the Bible, the Apocrypha and the Talmud) to some Greek adages were cited.[58] We shall not repeat the instances quoted by him, but shall only correct him in two places.

He quotes:[59] δρυὸς πεσούσης πᾶς ἀνὴρ ξυλεύεται,[60] "When the oak falls all chop wood," or as the Latin proverb[61] says: Arbore deiecta ligna quivis colligit. Lewy adduces ad hoc Midrash Eka Rabba:[62] רבנן דתמן אמרי כד יפול תורא מחרפין סכינוי, ורבנן דהכא אמרי כד נפל תורא סגין טבחוי "The Babylonian Rabbis[63] say: 'When the ox falls [all] sharpen their knives'.[64] The Palestinian Rabbis say: 'When the ox falls his slaughterers are numerous'."

The proverb of the Palestinian Sages approaches the above adage, but the saying of the Babylonian Rabbis finds an even

---

[57] Philologus LVIII (1899), p. 77 seq.

[58] I see now that he already anticipated me in the parallel mentioned above p. 124 n. 74.

[59] P. 84, No. 25 (from Prov. Bodl. 354).

[60] See Menan., Monost. 123. Comp. R. Altenkirch, Archiv für slavische Philologie, vol. XXX (Berlin 1909), p. 344.

[61] Publ. Syrus 58.

[62] I. 7. Lewy translates according to the erroneous reading of the ordinary editions. We substitute for it the correct text, ed. Buber, p. 71.

[63] Literally: "The Rabbis of there ... The Rabbis of here."

[64] See TB Shabbath 32a.

closer parallel. In K. Krumbacher's publication[65] we read: ἔπεσε βοῦς καὶ πάντες τὰ ξίφη αὐτῶν ἦραν, "The ox has fallen, and all draw their swords."

Even more striking is the Neo-Greek parallel in the collection published by N. G. Politis:[66] ἀφότις ἐξέπεσεν ὁ βοῦς, ἠκόνισαν ὅλοι τὰς μαχαίρας αὐτῶν, "After the ox has fallen all sharpen their knives." But the application of this proverb to Adam's sin[67] suggests a Jewish origin.[68]

Lewy[69] quotes from ps. Diogenian (VI. 92): ξύλον ἀγκύλον οὐδέποτ' ὀρθόν· ὅτι δυσχερὲς ἐκ φαύλων ἀγαθοὺς ἀπεργάσασθαι, "There is no straightening of a crooked stick, for it is difficult to produce good from bad." Lewy was not able to find a satisfactory Jewish equivalent.

However, a good parallel is available in Sifre[70] where the difficulty of straightening a crooked stick is described. Another Greek proverb supplements the above adage: τὸ σκαμβὸν ξύλον τὸ πῦρ ἰθύνει,[71] "[Only] the fire straightens a crooked stick." The passage from the Sifre, as quoted by the Greek[72] Rabbi, Tobia ben Eliezer (XI c.), in his Midrash[73] reads: דור עקש ופתלתול. עקמנים אתם אין אתם מתכוונין אלא באור. משל לעץ מעוקם, נתנו לאומן שיכוונו, נתנו במכוון ולא נתייושר, הכהו במעצד ולא נתיישר, עשאוהו קליפין והשליכוהו לאור וכו'. " 'They are a perversed and crooked generation'.[74] [Moses said to the Jews]: 'You are tricksters, you cannot be straightened except by fire. [You are] like a crooked stick[75] which was given to the artisan for the purpose of straightening it. He placed it in a vise and it was not straightened; he

---

[65] Moskauer Sammlung mittelgriechischen Sprichwörter, Sitzungsberichte der k. bayer. Akademie der Wissensch., 1900, p. 403, No. 31.

[66] παροιμίαι I (Athens 1899), p. 29, πʹ.

[67] See ibid.

[68] Comp. the adages in TB Shabbath 32a and Rashi ibid., s. v. מחטרא.

[69] Philologus ibid., p. 82, No. 17.

[70] Deut., sect. 308, ed. Finkelstein, p. 348.

[71] Politis (see above n. 66), p. 110, No. 2332. Comp. also Altenkirch (see above n. 60), p. 356.

[72] See Buber, Introduction to Midrash Lekah-Tob 11a.

[73] To Deuter. XXXII. 5, ed. Romm 56a.

[74] Deut. XXXII. 5.

[75] עץ, ξύλον. Sifre reads מקל.

hewed it with an adze and it was not straightened, [then] it
was chopped into chips and thrown into the fire etc.' " The
version in our editions of the Sifre is slightly different, but the
Greek Rabbi changed it somewhat and cleverly adjusted it to
the Greek proverb, with which the Greek Jews were probably
acquainted. The whole passage is, therefore, a skilful elaboration of a popular proverb.

We shall not indulge here in a detailed comparison between
Greek proverbs and those found in Rabbinic literature. We
have only to point out that the comparison between these two
sources[76] may be very beneficial to either of them or to both at
the same time. We shall quote a few examples.

TB[77] quotes a popular proverb: ממרי רשוותך פרי אפרע. The
usual interpretation is: "From your debtor[78] take payment even
in bran." However, a fragment of a Geonic commentary[79] explains the adage to mean: "If your debtor is poor take from
him even a little bran," i. e. accept payment *in small install-
ments*. At first sight this explanation seems difficult.[80] But the
anonymous Gaon, it seems to me, is undoubtedly right. The
context of the Talmud shows that the discussion concerns *a bad
debtor* (who either has no means or does not want to pay), and
a *popular* advice is cited which recommends that a creditor
should take whatever a bad debtor offers him, be it bad in
quality or small in quantity.

The Greek proverb[81] says: ἀπὸ κακοῦ δανειστοῦ κᾶν σακκίον
ἀχύρου, "From a bad creditor take even a small bag of bran."

---

[76] Even the mediaeval Greek collections very often contain ancient
material. It is, of course, possible that some of the later proverbs are borrowed
from Jewish sources.

[77] Baba Kamma 46b and parallels.

[78] Lit. "the owner of your loan," in Hebrew: בעל חוב. Whereas the older
literary use of both בעל חוב and מרי רשו (See Targum Onk. Deut. XV, 2 and
ps.-Jonathan I Sam. XXII.2) is in the sense of "creditor", the popular usage
of this word is in the sense of "debtor". The Greek δανειστής has the same
double meaning. Our Hebrew dictionaries designate the use of בעל חוב in
the sense of debtor as modern!

[79] Published by Prof. Louis Ginzberg in his Genizah Studies II, p. 160.

[80] See Ginzberg's remarks ibid. p. 156.

[81] Max. Plan. No. 80.

It is literally the same proverb as in the Talmud, and its meaning agrees with the interpretation given by the Gaon.

Again, we read in BR:[82] בשוק סמייה צווחין לעוירא סגי נהורא
ולזעירא בירבי, "In the market place of the blind they call the
one-eyed man 'rich of light' and the small man 'great'." This
reading is very difficult, for סגי נהור was employed by the Jews
as a euphemism for blind, and it makes no sense here. It is also
hard to understand what the connection is between the small
man and the market place of the blind. Theodor[83] remarks that
in the majority of mss. the words סגי נהורא ולזעירא are missing,[84]
and the reading is therefore: בשוק סמייה צווחין לעוירא בירבי,
"In the market place of the blind they call the one-eyed man
'great'."

The very popular Greek proverb[85] says: εἰς τῶν τυφλῶν τῇ
χώρᾳ μονόφθαλμος βασιλεύει, "In the land of the blind the one-
eyed is a king,"[86] which is approximately the same as the proverb in our Midrash, according to the reading of the majority
of Codd.

Again, we read in Mekiltha:[87] ר' יוסי אומר לא מקומו של אדם
מכבדו אלא הוא מכבד את מקומו. In TB[88] we read (in the second
half of the saying): אלא א ד ם מכבד את מקומו. "R. Jose (II c.)
said: It is not the place which honors the man but the man
who honors his place." R. Juda b. Barzilai of Barcelona (XII c.)
remarks:[89] ואית דגרסי את עצמו, "And some read: [It is the man
who honors] himself."[90]

---

[82] XXX. 9, 275₁₂.

[83] In his notes ad loc.

[84] The word זעירא is an easy corruption of עוירא, and סגי נהורא was interpolated by association with TP Pe'a V, 5, 19a; Kethuboth I. 1, 25a (bottom).

[85] Βενίξελος I., παροιμίαι δημώδεις, No. 106.

[86] Comp. O. Crusius, Rheinisches Museum für Philologie, 1887, p. 423;
Altenkirch (see above n. 60), p. 344. Comp. also Liddell and Scott s. v.
γλαμυρός.

[87] Jethro, Bahodesh III, ed. Horovitz, p. 213₆; ed. Lauterbach II, p.
214 (bottom).

[88] Taanith 21b. According to the editions, Cod. Monac. and R. Hananel.

[89] Commentary on Sefer Yezira, p. 49.

[90] Malter (in his edition of Taanith, p. 87₂₂) does not record any such
reading.

The Greek proverb[91] says: οὐχ ὁ τόπος τὸν ἄνδρα, ἀλλ' ὁ ἀνὴρ αὐτὸν ἔντιμον ποιεῖ. It is word for word the same proverb as we find it in TB, in our editions.

Again, we read in Mekiltha:[92] שכל המקבל פני חבירו כאלו מקבל פני שכינה, "When one welcomes his friend, it is as if he welcomed the Lord." The reading is not sure. The reading חברים in the sense of scholars was preferred by me.[93] The Greek proverb[94] says: εἶδες τὸν φίλον σου, εἶδες τὸν θεόν σου, "When you have met your friend, you have met your Lord." In this case the Greek proverb helps to establish the correct Jewish text (II c.), and the Jewish source explains the Greek.[95]

Sometimes the Jewish proverb needs no explanation, but it confirms one of the readings of the Greek proverb. The Greek adage[96] says: ἡ κοιλία βαστάζει τὰ πόνατα,[97] but Cod. Vat.[98] reads: τὰ γόνατα, namely "The stomach carries the feet." H. Lewy[99] correctly compares it with BR:[100] כרסה טענא רגליא, the same as the proverb in Cod. Vat.[101]

The comparative study of the Jewish and Greek proverbs will sometimes help us to trace the date of the proverb. TB[102] quotes in the name of R. Akiba (II c.): אם בקשת ליחנק התלה באילן גדול, "If you wish to strangle yourself, hang yourself on a big tree." Mr. Taviow[103] concludes that R. Akiba himself was

[91] Apost. XIII, 62 (Corp. paroem., p. 592). Lewy, Philol. LVIII, p. 86 also compared this proverb with the Talmud.

[92] Jethro, Amalek I, ed. Horovitz, p. 196, ed. Lauterbach II, p. 178.

[93] הירושלמי כפשוטו I, p. 291.

[94] Max. Plan. 33.

[95] Crusius (see above n. 86), p. 402, and Kurtz, Philologus IL (1890), p. 459, misunderstood the meaning of the proverb. Comp. also Genes. XXXIII. 10.

[96] Max. Plan. 182.

[97] Kurtz suggested to read: πάντα.

[98] Crusius (see above n. 86), p. 414.

[99] Philolgus LVIII, p. 80, No. 9.

[100] LXX. 8, 805ȝ.

[101] Comp. also Kurtz, Philologus IL (1890), p. 446; Krumbacher, Sitzungsberichte der k. bayer. Akademie der Wiss., 1893, p. 254.

[102] Pesahim 112a.

[103] Introduction to his אוצר המשלים והפתגמים, Berlin תרפ״ב, p. 17.

the author of this saying. However, Lewy[104] correctly pointed to Aristophan.[105] καὶ κατορθώσασι γὰρ εὔλογον· κἄν τι σφαλῆτ', ἐξ ἀξίου γοῦν τοῦ ξύλου, ἤ τι καὶ πάσχητε, πάσχειν τοῖς σοφοῖς δοκήσετε, "For if you succeed you will be praised; if you fall, you will seem in the judgment of the wise to suffer death — if suffer you must — falling from a worthy tree." The scholiast explains it παρὰ τὴν παροιμίαν "ἀπὸ καλοῦ ξύλου κἄν ἀπάγξασθαι,"[106] "If you must hang yourself better pick a good tree." This is an exact duplicate of the proverb used by R. Akiba. The adage seems to be very old, and certainly, R. Akiba was not the author of it; he only quoted popular wisdom.

This method of study can be especially beneficial for the tracing of the date of the aphorisms contained in the Greek mediaeval collections which include both ancient and later material. So, Plan. 223: πᾶσα ἀρχὴ δύσκολος, "Every beginning is difficult." Kurtz[107] traces the proverb to Nilus (V c.) who says:[108] χαλεπαὶ γὰρ αἱ ἀρχαὶ παντὸς ἔργου, "For the beginning of every undertaking is difficult." However, the adage is already quoted in a Tannaitic text of the second century. Mekiltha[109] quotes: שכל התחלות קשות, "For all beginnings are difficult."

Again, we read in the Moscow Collection of Greek proverbs:[110] ὁ δηχθεὶς ὑπὸ ὄφεως καὶ τὸ σχοινίον φοβεῖται, "One who has been bitten by a snake is afraid even of a rope." Here also the Rabbinic literature offers an early parallel. We read in the Midrash:[111] אמר ר' יהושע בן לוי מתלא אמר מאן דנכתיה חיויא חבלא מדחיל ליה, "R. Joshua b. Levi (III c.) said: The proverb declares, 'One who has been bitten by a snake is terrified even at [the sight of] a rope'" (literally: the rope terrifies him).

[104] Philolog. LVIII, p. 85, No. 26.
[105] Ranae 736.
[106] Publ. Syrus, 976: vel strangulari pulcro de ligno iuvat.
[107] Philologus (1890), p. 464.
[108] Peristeria V. Migne PG, 948c.
[109] Jethro, Bahodesh II, ed. Horovitz, 208⁷, Lauterbach II, 203³⁸.
[110] Sitzungsberichte etc. (see above, n. 65), p. 414, No. 119.
[111] Koheleth Rabba VII. 1, ed. Romm 18b and parallel in Midrash Samuel XXIII, ed. Buber, p. 115 (top). Comp. also Shir Hashirim Rabba I. 2, ed. Romm 4d.

Many more parallels can be quoted, but, I trust, sufficient material has been adduced to show how variously and many-sidedly beneficial a comparative study in the field of popular wisdom can be for both the Jewish and the non-Jewish litera-ture.[112] Whether for the purpose of elucidating the text, or of establishing the correct reading, or of tracing the authorship[113] and the date, such a comparative study will often produce good results.

[112] It is especially a matter of regret that the collectors of Jewish proverbs contained in mediaeval Hebrew sources did not engage in such a comparative study. It is certain that the latter embody numerous non-Jewish adages which they merely translated. And here the source of the translation is particularly interesting. We shall quote two examples. Taviow (see above n. 103), p. 31 suspects the proverb (See Hyman, אוצר דברי חכמים ופתגמיהם, p. 275) טורא בטורא לא פגע איניש באיניש פגע ("Two mountains do not meet, two men may") of being a mere translation from the Russian. But it is found both in Greek (Apost. XIII. 2, p. 270: ὄρος ὄρει οὐ μίγγυται, ἄνθρωπος δ'ἀν-θρώπῳ) and in Arabic (See Altenkirch, Aruch für slav. Philol. XXX, p. 345).

Likewise, the late Prof. I. Davidson quotes (Essays and Studies in memory of L. R. Miller, p. מ'ו, No. 485) from עומר השכחה (commentary on Proverbs): אם המספר פתי יהי השומע חכם וערום, "If the narrator is a fool let the hearer be wise and clever." However, the source (Me'iri ad Prov. I.4) from which the latter has drawn introduces it as an *Arabic* proverb. The Arabic original is found in Martini's Pugio Fidei (ed. Karpzov, p. 534) who states: "Dicunt Arabes in proverbio suo: אדא כאן אלמחדת אחמק יכון אלמסתמע עקאל, Cum fuerit stultus narrator verborum, sit auditor sapiens." Cod. Majoric. of Pugio Fidei quotes also the Hebrew: ואם יהיה המגיד פתי יהיה השומע חכם.

[113] We read in Aboth V (end): בן הא הא אומר לפום צערה אגרה, "Ben He-He said: 'According to the toil is the reward'." The identity of Ben He-He is not established. Comp. the commentary on Sefer Yezira by R. Juda b. Barzilai of Barcelona, p. 7–8; Tosaphoth Hagiga 9b s. v. בר. The reading בר הי הי in TB is not sure. A Geonic responsum (published in the Weekly המגיד XV, p. 294) reads: בר תנחן (See my note in קרית ספר XIII, p. 186). The adage itself is attributed by Aboth deR. Nathan (A XII, p. 55; B XXVII, p. 56) to Hillel the Elder who heard it from Palestinian ass-drivers.

The ancient Samaritan writer Marqah (143a. Ed. Heidenheim p. 64; comp. Introduction ibid. XIV) quotes: בן עדן לפם די (read: בן) וכן אמר דן עבדתה הוא אגרה, "And so said Ben Ben Eden: 'According to the toil is the reward'." This is found word for word in "Joshua's Prayer" (Cowley, Sama-ritan Liturgy I, p. 4, bottom). See also H. Baneth, Des samaritaners Marqah an die 22 Buchstaben, p. 13. Thus, the saying attributed to the mysterious Ben He-he was a popular adage current in Palestine, and various sages were credited with it.

MISUNDERSTOOD EXPRESSIONS AND WORDS

A more intensive study of Haggadic literature will convince us that the Rabbis were in close touch with the actual life in Palestine; that they thoroughly understood the needs and desires of the people and that they handled their task in masterly fashion. A large part of the Haggadic literature consists of sermons or fragments of sermons which are incorporated in the texts of the Midrashim. The sermon is a special literary genre which has its individual peculiarities and has to be investigated accordingly. The Jewish audience did not remain indifferent to the contents of the sermon. They very often reacted immediately and keenly and gave varied expression to their feelings.

In BR[1] we read: כד דרשה ר' אבהו גחך צבורא, "When R. Abbahu preached thus, the audience laughed" (in disapproval). Again we find:[2] רבי היה יושב ודורש נתנמנם הציבור "Rabbi was preaching, and his audience began to doze." Consequently it was very natural for the preachers to make every effort to appeal to the taste of the public and to speak to them in their language. It of course, important to inquire whether the sermon was preached before a rural or before an urban audience. Was the audience made up of intelligent academicians, or did it consist of unlearned craftsmen, petty tradesmen, vendors in market places, who formed the bulk of the population of the oriental towns — or was the sermon preached before the simple-minded unsophisticated peasants of the small settlements?

The comments on the Biblical verses, regarding both style and contents, varied according to the audience the preacher had before him. We find, for instance, in Vayyikra Rabba:[3] ושבו העבים אחר הגשם, ר' לוי אמר תרתי חדא לחבריא וחדא לבוריא. חדא לחבריא. בא לבכות זלגו עיניו דמעות. חדא לבוריא. בא להטיל מים הגללים מקדמין אותו. " 'And the clouds return after the rain' (Eccl. XII.2), R. Levi

---

[1] XXVIII. 3, 261₃.
[2] Shir Hashirim Rabba I. 15.
[3] XVIII. 1 (and parallels).

161

interpreted it in two ways: one for the fellow-academicians and
one for the uneducated. When he addressed the former [he
interpreted the verse to mean that] no sooner does he (i. e. the
aged man) begin to cry than his tears flow. To the latter [he
interpreted it to mean that] before he begins to pass water he
casts his excrements." The preacher's approach to his two
audiences speaks for itself.

Sometimes the preachers probably used expressions and
words familiar only in the locality where the sermons were
delivered. They employed figurative language which was well
known to the people in their time and which appealed to the
hearers but are meaningless to us. We shall quote here a few
instances of figurative, popular and seemingly local expressions.

פני שביעית

In Sifre[4] we read: משל למה הדבר דומה לשתי נשים שהיו לוקות
בבית דין אחת לוקה על שקלקלה ואחת לוקה על שגנבה[5] פני שביעית. זו
שגנבה[5] פני שביעית אומרת בבקשה מכם הודיעו סורחני שלא יהיו העומדים
סבורים לומר כשם שזו קלקלה אף זו קלקלה. תלו לה הפנים בצוארה והיה
הכרוז מכריז לפניה, על הפנים זו לוקה. "This case may be compared
to the case of two women who were about to be flogged in
court; one for having commited adultery, the other for having
gathered (or eaten) unripe figs grown during the Sabbatical
year.[6] Thereupon the woman who had gathered (or eaten) the
unripe figs said: 'I beg of you make my offence public lest the
bystanders think that just as the other woman has commited
adultery so have I'. They suspended unripe figs from her neck,
and the public crier kept on announcing before her: 'This woman
is being flogged for unripe figs'."[7] The frequent association of

---

[4] I, 137, ed. Horovitz, p. 183 20.

[5] (שארתה=שלקטה) שגבבה? , see Aruch s. v. אר II; BR XLVI (beginning)
458 and Theodor's notes ad loc. Ms. London reads here: שאכלה.

[6] See Mishna Shebiith IV. 7.

[7] See also TB Yoma 86b, Bemidbar Rabba XIX. 12. In the other Midrashim (VayR. XXXI. 4, Debarim Rabba II. 6, ibid. ed. Lieberman p. 50) the
parable is transformed by the later Haggadists. Comp. also Sifre ואתחנן
(beginning); I agree with Prof. Finkelstein that at this point the parable is a
later interpolation. See his arguments ad loc.

these two sins (adultery and the gathering or the eating of unripe figs) is quite strange.

Moreover, in TB[8] we read: תנא דבי ר' ישמעאל ראויה היתה לדוד בת שבע בת אליעם אלא שאכלה פגה "The school of R. Ishmael taught: Bath Sheba, the daughter of Eliam, was predestined for David [from the six days of creation] but he enjoyed her as an 'unripe fig'." The expression is quite clear: it means that he enjoyed her before the proper time,[9] before it was licit.[10] It is therefore quite certain that the Rabbis used here a figurative expression, implying by פגי שביעית the favors of an unmarried woman or even the connubium of the betrothed with her own bridegroom before they were fully married.[11]

This accounts for the emphasis of the Midrash[12] on the fact that the woman who ate unripe figs[13] was a בת טובים, "a daughter of good family."[14] When the sinner committed a sexual offence it reflected upon the family, and therefore her noble descent was stressed by the Rabbis.

The regular procedure was to exhibit the sinner adorned with objects which reminded him of the character of his sin.[15] The unripe figs were taken in our case as a symbol of premature enjoyment.

Our conjecture will explain a very obscure passage in the Palestinian Talmud:[16] מהו שיהו נאמנין לומר יוצאין היו ללקט בפני שביעית ושמענו פלוני ממלל על פלונית אשתו. אשה פלונית ממללת על בניה

---

[8] Sanhedrin 107a.

[9] See also BR IL. 9, 509s and Theodor's notes.

[10] R. Solomon Luria in his notes to TB Sanhedrin ad loc. remarks that some books read: שאכלה פגי שביעית (See דקדוקי סופרים ad loc., p. 335, n. 60) and offers a forced explanation of the passage, although he associated the expression with that of our Midrash.

[11] See TP Pesahim X. 1, 37b, Kiddushin III. 10, 64b and parallels. In our case the fruit may be picked (in the Sabbatical year) when it is ripe.

[12] VayR XXXI. 4 and parallels.

[13] The reading of the mss. See Debarim Rabba, ed. Lieberman, p. 50, n. 1.

[14] Ms. London adds: ובת נגיסים, "And of noble descent."

[15] See Ziegler, Königsgleichnisse, p. 121. We can add Tanhuma, Cod. De Rossi (quoted by Buber, Introduction to Tanhuma, p. 157): משל לגנב שנתפס תולין הגנוב על כתיפו. כך בתאנה סרחו ובתאנה נתכסו.

[16] Kethuboth II. 10, 26d.

"Are they[17] believed when they say: 'we were going out to
gather unripe figs of the Sabbatical year', or: 'we heard that
man gossiping about his wife' (i. e. of her bad behavior), or:
'[we heard] that woman gossiping about her children'." Thus,
we have here once more the same association of unripe figs[18]
with gossip about bad behavior of a woman. Besides, the question regarding their veracity concerning their witnessing of their
gathering of unripe figs during the Sabbatical year has no sense
whatever.

Following our conjecture it is most probable that "unripe
figs of the Sabbatical year" allude to a woman who prematurely
enjoyed the favors of her bridegroom (or something similar).
According to an old custom they used to symbolize the woman's
bad behavior by suspending unripe figs from her neck. In
order to make the punishment public, figs were probably also
distributed among children, just as, in the case of a man marry-
ing a woman who was not worthy of him (or of his family),
they used to perform a similar practice.[19] The question raised
in this passage is whether grown up men are believed when they
say they remember having participated in such a ceremony as
minors, as they are believed in case of an unsuitable marriage.[20]

ב ן   א ש ת ו

R. Abraham ibn Da'ud (XII c.) informs us:[21] אספסינוס וטיטוס
חורגו הנקרא בנו "Vespasian and his step-son Titus who was called
his son." This is very curious: Where did the author find that
Titus was the stepson of Vespasian? It seems that the author
drew his information from the words of the Sifre:[22] טיטוס הרשע
בן אשתו של אספסיינוס "Titus the wicked, the son of Vespasian's
wife."[23] The Rabbis, of course, did not intend to infer that

[17] I. e. adults witnessing facts they saw when they were minors.
[18] Of the Sabbatical year, which are forbidden.
[19] TP ibid. and parallels.
[20] See TP ibidem.
[21] ספר הקבלה, ed. Neubauer, p. 50.
[22] Deut., sec. 328, ed. Finkelstein, p. 378[14].
[23] The same is found word for word in Aboth deR. Nathan, ed. Schechter
p. 151; ibid., vers. II, ch. VII, p. 20.

Titus was Vespasian's step-son. They rather coined this con-
temptuous expression out of hatred for the destroyers of the
Temple and the mass-murderers of the Jewish people. They
were allegedly only sure that he was the son of his mother, but
they were not certain of his father. Moreover, Cod. Halberstam
of Aboth deR. Nathan vers. II[24] reads: בן אחותו של אספסיינוס,
"The son of Vespasian's sister."[25] It is very probable that they
sought to express even deeper contempt for Titus by making
his mother an "'Αδελφή'' of her husband[26] and suggesting that
she was not beyond adultery.[27]

It is the author of the ספר הקבלה who did not sense the
sarcasm of the expression and took it literally.

(ק פ ץ   ע ל י ו   ה ד ב ר   (ה ד י ב ר

The so-called Yelamdenu Midrashim employ the expression
קפץ עליו הדבר, — "The 'davar' jumped upon him" — very
frequently.

In Tanhuma[28] we find: מיד קפץ עליו הדבר[29]; the same expression
is found in Debarim Rabba,[30] in a Geniza fragment[31] and in
Pesiktha Rabbathi.[32] Ibid.[32a]: קפץ הדיבור על אברהם[33]; Bemidbar

[24] See Schechter's note, ibid., p. 20, n. 12.

[25] See also Midrash Tehilim CXXI, ed. Buber, p. 506 n. 9; Lieberman,
Debarim Rabba, p. 21, n. 10.

[26] Deissmann (Light etc., p. 167 n. 4) suggests that the marriage of
brothers and sisters in Egypt was customary not only in the royal family
but also among the common people.

[27] I do not exclude the possibility of an error. The original בר אחתיה may
have been wrongly copied by a scribe as בר אחתיה, and then translated into
Hebrew as בן אחותו. See also BR, p. 742₆ and the variants ibidem.

[28] וירא sec. 18, ed. Mantua 11c.

[29] In Buber's edition sec. 42, p. 109 the word הדבר has been omitted.

[30] Ed. Lieberman, p. 27 (bottom).

[31] Published by Prof. L. Ginzberg in his Genizah Studies I, p. 39₂₆ (In this
source the reading is הדיבר).

[32] III, ed. Friedmann, 12a (הדיבור).

[32a] 10a.

[33] The parallel in Tanhuma ויצא 21, ed. Buber, p. 159: נתייחד עליו הדיבור.

Rabba[34] has קפץ הדיבור על משה. What does the expression קפץ
הדבר על mean? Prof. Ginzberg[35] compares it to קפץ עליו אלהים,[36]
"God jumped upon him." Yet, the expression needs further
investigation. It seems that we have here a remnant of theological terminology with a definite meaning. הדבר,[37] it seems to
me, designates prophecy.[38] The same meaning is implied in
"dominus verbi,"[39] "The lord of the word," i. e. the lord of
prophecy.[40]

On the other hand, the word קפץ (i. e. the "jumping" of
prophecy) may mark a certain type of revelation in counterpart
to נתייחד.[41] In Midrash Samuel[42] we read: קפץ הדבר על עלי ודבר[43]
עם שמואל, "The דבר jumped on Eli and spoke to Samuel." This
may imply something like an echo rebounding[44] from Eli which
was carried back to Samuel.[45]

Another word of similar meaning deserves notice at this
point. After stating that no woman (with the exception of
Sara) received direct divine inspiration TP[46] explains God's

[34] IV. 7 and IX. 14.

[35] Ibid., p. 29.

[36] Shemoth Rabba XVIII. 1 and the Geniza fragment, ed. Ginzberg
ibid. p. 224₁₈. See also Mann, the Bible as read etc., p. פ.א.

[37] This is the correct reading, see my note in Debarim Rabba 27₁₀ (and
the sources referred to ibid.).

[38] See Jer. XVIII.18 and comp. the LXX to II Chr. IX.29. It has nothing
to do with the Stoic and Neo-Platonic term λόγος. Comp. also the Crit.
Intern. Commen. on the Apocal. I. 2. 9. pp. 7 and 21.

[39] Assumptio Mosis XI. 16.

[40] Marqah in his ספר פליאתה 195a (ed. Heidenheim, p. 95) calls Moses
מלך נביותא. In Seder Olam XXX, ed. Neubauer, p. 66 (Cod. Opp.) Moses is
termed אבי הנבואה. Comp. also Mekiltha, beginning, and Horovitz' notes
ad loc.; ibid. 9 and 197₁₃.

[41] See Bacher, Terminologie, s. v. יחד.

[42] IX, ed. Buber, p. 25.

[43] So Redak ad I Sam. III.4. The editions have: הדבור אל.

[44] The Greek equivalent of קפץ — ἅλλομαι — is also used in connection
with sound. So Plato, Phaedrus 255c: καὶ οἷον πνεῦμα ἤ τις ἠχὼ ἀπὸ λείων
τε καὶ στερεῶν ἁλλομένη ... "And as a wind or an echo rebounding from
smooth and solid bodies"...

[45] Rashi (I Sam. III.4) reads indeed: וקפץ הקול ד ר ך ע ל י לשמואל.

[46] Sota VII. 1, 21b.

words to Rebecca[47] by calling them: הדיבור נפלה[48] לה. This
degree of prophecy seems to be near to that designated by
קפץ הדבר על.

צור

In Vayyikra Rabba[49] we are told: מה עשה עמד ונעל בתי כנסיות
ובתי מדרשות הדא דכתיב צור תעודה חתום תורה בלמודי. רב הונא בשם ר'
אלעזר אמר למה נקרא שמו אחז שאחז בתי כנסיות ובתי מדרשות. "What did
he (i. e. king Ahaz) do? He arose and closed the synagogues and
the houses of study. This is [indicated by] what is written:
'Bind up the testimony, seal up instruction among my disciples'
(Is. VIII.16). R. Huna said in the name of R. Eleazar: Why
was he called Ahaz? — Because he closed the synagogues and
houses of study."[50] The commentaries misunderstood the pur-
port of the play of words. אחז means to keep, to seize and to
close; צור also has all these meanings. The dictionaries and
commentaries seem to have ignored these meanings of צור.

TP[51] relates: בר קפרא אשכח חד עיזקא. צר חד טלי ארמאי הוה
פרי בתריה "Bar Kappara found a ring, he seized a Gentile[52] boy,
he ran after him"[53] etc.

Again Vayyikra Rabba[54] has the expression: קם תפסיה, but
the genuine reading is:[55] קם צ ר י ה, "He went and seized him."
The same phrase is found in Eka Rabba:[56] קם וצריי ה. We
may also refer to the difficult passage in the same Midrash:[57]

---

[47] Gen. XXV.23.

[48] Cod. Vat. reads: נפלא, see my על הירושלמי, p. 71 n. 83. דבר is also explained to mean an angel, see Yalkut I, 765; Buber, Tanhuma בלק, p. 141,
n. ק"נ and Judaica, Festschrift zu Herman Cohens etc., p. 320; TB Hagiga 14a.
See also BR LII.5, 5451 where חצי דבר is mentioned.

[49] XI. 7.

[50] See also TP Sanhedrin X. 2, 28b; BR XLII. 3, p. 4022 (and parallels
noted ibid.), Tanhuma שמיני sec. 9.

[51] Aboda Zara IV. 4, 49a.

[52] See above p. 86 n. 130.

[53] The boy escaped at first.   [54] IX. 3.

[55] So Cod. Vat. and Yalkut Hamakiri Ps. L, 279. Cod. Oxf. reads: קם
בריה, an obvious error for קם צריה.

[56] I. 3 (ed. pr. Ed. Romm 14b: וצריה; ed. Buber, p. 63: וצדייה.

[57] V. 12, ed. Buber 157.

אפיטרופא הוה עליל לקרתא וצייר על שורי קרתא ותלי להון. The words
וצייר על שורי קרתא are meaningless. All editions (except Buber's)
read instead: נסיב טבי דקרתא. It is therefore most likely that the
true reading is: וצייר (ע)לטובי קרתא. The translation will accordingly be: "When the [Roman] Procurator used to enter a town
he would seize its best men (ἄριστοι) and hang them." In
Pesiktha deR. Kahana[58] we find: צייר אומנתהון דאבהתך, "Stick
(=תפוס) to the profession of thy ancestors." Again we read:[59]
מה אתה מיצור חבלא בתרין ראשין. In all the parallel sources the reading is: מה אתה תופש חבלא etc., thus מיצר=תופש.[60] WayR[60a] has
the expression: צור הדין קניא, which is equal to תפוש הדין קניא.

צור may also mean to close. TP[61] reads: כאינש דצייר פומהון
דשהדייא דלא ישהדון[61a], "Like a man who closes the mouth of the
witnesses that they should not testify." This verb was also
employed as a technical term: צור כנישתא, "Close the synagogue."
We find in TP:[62] איזיל צור כנישתא עלוי, "Go and close the synagogue on him" (until justice will be done to thee), as correctly
interpreted by our mediaeval authorities.[63] אחז like צור (and like
the Aramaic אחד) also means to close.[63a] Seder Eliyyahu Rabba[64]

[58] 93a.   [59] Ibid. 125b.

[60] In TP Ma'asroth (III. 10, 51a) we read: צור דוקניתך which means:
"stick to thy [question regarding] דוקני." The Palestinian ספר המעשים (Tarbiz
I, fasc. 1, p. 100) records: וציירא היא ... והיא צייירא ... הויא צייירא. The reading
in מעשה הגאונים is (See Tarbiz ibid.): ושמאלה הויא צ י י ר ה ע ר ק י ה which is
parallel to TP Yebamoth XII. 1, 12c: ותופסתן בשמאל "And she seizes
[the laces] with the left hand." Comp. also פיוטי יני ed. Zulay, p. 45 and
above p. 112.

[60a] VI. 3 (and parallel).

[61] Shebuoth VI. 7, 37a.

[61a] In an old Aramaic inscription (Cooke, North-Sem. Inscr., p. 189)
we read: מן מלן (=לא אתאחז) פמי לאתאחז, "My mouth was not closed
from words." אחז corresponds here to צור in TP. Comp. n. 63[a].

[62] Pe'a I. 1, 15d (and parallels).

[63] Rashba, Responsa, IV. 56; Sefer Hasidim, ed. Mekize Nirdamim p.
411 (top); Kaftor Wapherah XLIV, ed. Lunz, p. 584. See Ratner ad loc.,
p. 10.

[63a] See Krauss MGWJ vol. LXXV (1931), p. 192. He referred also to
the passage of our Midrash. Comp. also the Hebrew אוחזי עינים and our note
below. See also above n. 61[a].

[64] VII, ed. Friedmann VIII, p. 40. Comp. the Introduction ibid., p. 123
(bottom). He also referred to our passage.

has: אחזו עליהן את המים כדי שלא יטבלו "They closed up the water [places] on them that they should not immerse."[65]

We can now understand that the Haggada associated the name אחז with its synonym צור, interpreting the verse צור תעודה to mean: close the synagogue, as in the phrase צור כנישתא.

In the Onomastica Sacra[66] we read: Ἄχαζ κατάσχετος.[67] The Papyrus Onomasticon Sacrum[68] records: IAXAZ IAWKPA-TOC,[69] which shows that the interpretation of this name was quite popular.[70]

א י ת ב . . .

We read in BR:[71] אמר ליה עד כדון אית ביה. יש לאל ידי וגו'. אמר לית היא מיניה. All the commentaries were at a loss to explain this passage. But it is really very simple. אית בי is a common locution for אית בחיילי,[72] "It is in my power," I am able. So TP:[73] עד אתר פלן אית בי צפר "I can whistle." Vayyikra Rabba:[74] א י ת ב י, מהלך באתר פלן לא א י ת ב י מהלך "I can go to this point but cannot go beyond this point." Ibid.:[75] ולית בי משבק לה, "And I cannot divorce her." Ibid.:[76] אית בך מחמי לה לי, "Can you show it to me." Eka Rabba:[77] שור דנור[78] אית בי מקפלה . . . אית בי מקפלה

---

[65] See also Ps. LXXVII.5.

[66] 20136, ed. Lagarde, Gottingae 1870.

[67] See also ibid. 18045, 18743.

[68] Deissmann, Die Septuaginta-Papyri, Heidelberg 1905, p. 89, l. 18.

[69] See the editor's remarks ibid., p. 92. We may note here that the verse of Luc. (XXIV. 16) "οἱ δὲ ὀφθαλμοὶ αὐτῶν ἐκρατοῦντο" is translated by the Peshitta: הוי ועיניהון א ח י ד י ן, whereas the Palestinian Syriac translation (The Palestinian Syriac Lectionary, London 1899, p. 5) is: ועיניהון הוו צ י ד י ן (=Aramaic צירין). Comp. Schulthess, lexicon, s. v. צוד No. 6; Margoliouth, The Journal of the Royal As. Society, 1896, p. 680 n. 1; Jastrow, s. v. צוד II.

[70] On the interpretation of the Hebrew names in general see Deissmann ibid. p. 86 seq. Comp. BR XLII. 5, p. 4097 (and parallels) and elsewhere.

[71] LXXIV. 8, p. 8657.

[72] Comp. מתנות כהונה ad loc.

[73] Hagiga II. 2, 78a. See the parallel Sanhedrin, 23c.

[74] XVIII. 1. In mss. Vat. and Brit. Mus.

[75] XXXIV. 14 (twice).

[76] Ibid. 16.

[77] II. 2, ed. Buber, p. 110.

[78] מקף לה=.

שור דמיא ... אית בי מקפלה שור דברזל, "I can surround it (i. e.
Jerusalem) with a wall of fire ... I can surround it with a wall
of water ... I can surround it with a wall of iron." Pesiktha
deR. Kahana:[79] ואית בך מתני לי, "Can you teach me."

The same expression was also used by the Samaritans. We
read in ספר פליאתה דמרקה 5b:[80] איד לי מפק לך אטר "I can bring a
stick forth for thee." Hildesheimer translated it correctly but
hesitatingly.[81] Marqah himself used the same expression in his
מימרא on the death of Moses:[82] מה בי אעבד ... מה בי אעבד, "What
can I do ... what can I do." There can therefore be no doubt
of the meaning of the expression.

The passage in BR should accordingly be translated: "He
(Laban) said to him (Jacob) that so far he (Laban) has the
power, [as it is said]: '*It is in the power of my hand* [*to do you
hurt*]'.[83] 'That indeed does not depend on him' he (Jacob)
retorted."

It is probable that we have here a fragment of an Aramaic
translation of this verse, which read: אית בי עביד עמכון בישא.

ק ק ב א

In Aboth deR. Nathan[84] we find the expression קומקומוס של
חמין,[85] "A kettle of boiling water." The spelling קומקום (or קומקוס)
is also usual in Rabbinic literature,[86] and it designates a kettle
for water. But version II of Aboth deR. Nathan[87] reads
קבקביות, whereas Cod. Parma[88] reads: קקביות, without mentioning חמין.

Jewish scholars[89] made repeated efforts to explain the word,
but no unanimous opinion has been reached. However, it

---

[79] 93a.

[80] Ed. Heidenheim, p. 4; ed. Hildesheimer, p. 33.

[81] See his note, p. 32, n. 41.

[82] Ed. Munk, p. 24.

[83] Gen. XXXI.29.

[84] X, ed. Schechter, p. 43.

[85] In the parallel TP Pesahim VI. 1, 33a and TB Menahoth 109b: קומקום.

[86] See Jastrow s. v. קומקום.   [88] See ibid., p. 169.

[87] Ibid. XX, p. 43.

[89] See Ginzberg in Festschrift Schwarz, p. 338 and Epstein in פירוש
הגאונים to Seder Taharoth, p. 47 n. 11; ibid., p. 167–168.

seems to me that the original reading in Aboth deR. Nathan, version II, was: קקביו' (or קבקיו'), which the copyists completed it into קקביות, whereas the real resolution of the abbreviation should be: קקביון (or קבקיון). It seems that the people distinguished the קומקום from the קקביון. The former was mostly used for boiling water,[90] the latter was a simple jar. We have explicit testimony bearing on the use of this word by the Jews in Tiberias in the IV century. Epiphanius, relating the miracles performed in Tiberias by a Jewish convert, remarks:[91] "καὶ ὕδωρ κελεύσας ἐνεχθῆναι ἐν ἀγγείῳ,[92] ἐν καψάκη[93] φημί (κακκούβιον δὲ τοῦτο οἱ ἐπιχώριοι καλοῦσι)." "And having ordered to bring water in a vessel, i. e. a cruse (the natives call it 'cacoubion')." Thus, we see that a jar for water was called in Tiberias קקביון.

Another passage in TP will confirm our opinion. We read in Mishna Aboda Zara:[94] . . . המוצא כלים ועליהם צורת חמה צורת לבנה שעל המכובדים אסורין שעל המבוזין מותרין, "If one finds objects upon which the figure of the sun or of the moon is engraved . . . if the objects are ornamental[95] they are forbidden, if common they are allowed." Thereupon TP[96] records: ר' חייה בר ווא הווה ליה קווקין והוות טיכי דרומי צירה בגווה אתה שאל לרבנין[97] אמרין מיכיון שהמיים צפין על גבה דבר שלבזיון הוא. והן קיתונה מיכיון שאת משקיעו במים דבר שלבזיון הוא. "R. Hyya bar Abba (fl. in Tiberias in III–IV c.) had a קווקין wherein the Fortune of Rome was portrayed. He came to ask the Rabbis.[98] They said, since the water flows on it (i. e. on the Fortune of Rome) it is regarded a common object and [therefore] that pitcher, since it is dipped in water,[98a] is

---

[90] See Mishna Kelim III. 7; XIV. 1; XXV. 8 and elsewhere.

[91] Panarion haer. XXX. 12, ed. Holl, p. 348.

[92] The Septuagint translates with this word the Hebrew כלי, נבל, vessel, skin.

[93] The Septuagint renders with it the Hebrew צפחת, cruse (in I Kings XIX.6), whereas the Peshitta has there: קוקתא.

[94] III. 3.   [95] See Tosephta ibid. 468⁴.

[96] Ad loc., 42d. I quote from the Geniza fragments published by Prof. Epstein in Tarbiz III, p. 19.

[97] Ed. pr. reads: לר' יוחנן.

[98] I. e. whether the קווקין is to be considered ornamental or common.

[98a] Comp. TB Aboda Zara 43b.

considered a common object." We see that the Rabbis called
the קיתון—קווקין. Thus קווקין is the same as קבקין,⁹⁹ קקבין or קבבין
or קקבין, a pitcher.¹⁰⁰

In a Vth or VIth c. inventory of the village of Ibion in Egypt
we find:¹⁰¹ λέβης χαλκ(οῦς) α, κοκκούμ(ιον) χαλκ(οῦν) α, "One
bronze basin, one bronze flagon." The editor correctly remarks¹⁰²
that the basin was for handwashing in the church. The "co-
coumion" probably served a similar purpose. We find the same
two objects quoted together in a marriage document of the
XI c.:¹⁰³ כבבין בזהוב א' וקומקום לבטין בזהוב א', A "cacabin" of the
value of one gold coin and a "coumcoum", a small basin of the
value of one gold coin." The Mishna¹⁰⁴ quotes כבכב¹⁰⁵ and¹⁰⁶ טפי
together. It is very likely that we have here the κακκάβιον
(or κακκούβιον) and the λέβης; טפיח (or טפי) would be the
Hebrew translation of λέβης, if the latter is a derivative of
λείβω.¹⁰⁷ The use of טפיח in the sense of this Greek noun is
explicitly implied in Tosephta Berakoth¹⁰⁸ and TB Yoma.¹⁰⁹ We
conclude that קבבין, קבקין, קווקין, כבכב, כפכף or קקבין, קקוביון,
ככבין are one and the same vessel used for water.

הבו בלכון

The importance of the so-called Palestinian Syriac texts for
the understanding of Palestinian Rabbinic literature has been
frequently emphasized by me.¹¹⁰ An exhaustive study of the
relation between the Palestinian Syriac vocabulary and that of

---

⁹⁹ κακκάβιν (See above p. 57 n. 185). See Sophocles s. v. κακκάβιον.
Comp. Sachs, Beitraege II, 49.

¹⁰⁰ Comp. Tosephta Aboda Zara 468₅, TB ibid. 43b.

¹⁰¹ Grenfell and Hunt, New Class. Fragm., Greek Papyri, ser. II, p. 161,
No. CXI, l. 22 seq.

¹⁰² P. 162.

¹⁰³ Mann, the Jews in Egypt II, p. 94₁₅.   ¹⁰⁴ Kelim II. 3.

¹⁰⁵ In פירוש הגאונים ad loc., ed. Epstein, p. 10: כפכף. Comp. also my Tosefeth Rishonim III, p. 7, n. 38.

¹⁰⁶ Ibid. טפיח.

¹⁰⁷ So in the earlier editions of Liddell and Scott's lexicon.

¹⁰⁸ IV, p. 9₂₀.

¹⁰⁹ 30a. See רש"י ibid., s. v. ומחזיר.

¹¹⁰ Tarbiz VI, 234, ibid. VIII, 367 and elsewhere.

the Rabbinic Palestinian literature would be a significant contribution. True, we possess only part of the Palestinian Rabbinic literature and only a very meager portion of Palestinian
Syriac texts and the time has not yet come to speak with certainty of the relation between the vocabularies of the two
dialects. However we can state that in the extant literature
certain words and expressions occur in one to the exclusion of
the other, while others are used frequently in one and very
rarely in the other.

If, therefore, a Rabbi employs an expression which occurs
seldom in Palestinian Rabbinic literature but is quite common
in Palestinian Syriac, we may assume that he taught or preached
in a locality where this vernacular was spoken. We shall quote
a few instances. In TP[111] we find: א ב ו ה מאיר 'ר לון אמר
הוא ביש נש בר ,מיניה כו ן ל. "R. Meir said to them: 'Beware
of him, he is a wicked man'." The translation of the words הובא
מיניה לכון is derived from the context which lends itself to no
other interpretation. But the expression is not found again in
the Palestinian Talmud. Moreover, Cod. Leyden vocalizes the
word (הוֹבָּא), a practice usually resorted to when the scribe is
responsible for a correction.

We find a similar expression in the Palestinian Syriac
Lectionary:[112] דגליא נביא מן בלכון הבו — προσέχετε ἀπὸ τῶν
ψευδοπροφητῶν — "Beware of false prophets." Ibid.:[113] בלכון הבו
נשא בני מן — προσέχετε δὲ ἀπὸ τῶν ἀνϑρώπων — "Beware of
men." Ibid.:[114] ספריא מן בלכון האבו — βλέπετε ἀπὸ τῶν γραμ-
ματέων — "Beware of the Scribes." Ibid.:[115] אנש יהי דלא בלכון הבו
—βλέπετε μή τις — "Beware that none."

The same expression was current in Samaritan. Marqah[116]
says: תהי ולא בלך בלך הב, "Beware lest you." Ibid. 152b:[117] לא בלך הב.

---

[111] Rosh Hashana III. 9, 59a. Comp. TB Yoma 83b and Tanhuma בראשית,
Buber p. 22 (quoted below).

[112] P. 65 (London 1899).

[113] P. 290.

[114] P. 250.

[115] P. 13 (London 1897).

[116] פליאתה ספר 135a.b, ed. Heidenheim p. 59, ed. Rettig p. 49. The expression is repeated four times in succession.

[117] Heidenheim, p. 69.

Ibid. 173a:[118] הב בלך תילף, "Beware lest you learn." The expression probably occurred in other passages but was misread by the editor. For example, ibid. 33a:[119] הר[ז] דלם תזבח which Hildesheimer[120] read correctly הב בלך תזבח, "Beware lest you sacrifice."

D. Rettig[121] explained the word בל to mean "Sinn, Aufmerksamkeit" (mind, attention), like the Arabic بال, and compared it to שם בל לשיזבותיה (Dan. VI.15), *"He put his mind to saving him."* בל also occurs in the Aramaic version of the Story of Ahikar:[122] [זי], תאתא על בלך, "[Which] comes into thy mind."

There can therefore be no doubt that הב בלך in Palestinian Aramaic and in Palestinian Syriac[123] is just the same as הב דעתך in Aramaic and תן דעתך in Hebrew, meaning: "Beware!" So we read in TP:[124] הב דעתך דאית תמן מן אינון[125] פסולייא דלא תפגע בהון, "Beware lest you come in contact there with such among them as are disqualified [for intermarriage]." Again we find in TP:[125a] הב דעתך דאת חד ואנן תרי, "Beware! for you are one and we are two." Likewise we read in BR:[126] תנו דעתכם שלא [יהא] ערל נוגע, "Beware lest an uncircumcised person touch" etc.

Now it is certain that the original reading of TP Rosh Hashana was: ה[ב]ו באלכון מיניה (instead of הובא לכון[126a]), "Beware of him."

This is confirmed by Tanhuma Bereshith[127] which reads in the same story: הזהרו עצמיכם ממנו...הזהרו ע צמי כ ם[127a] מכידור זה, "Beware of him, beware of this Kiddor."

---

[118] Ibid., p. 81.

[119] Ibid., p. 22.

[120] ספר פליאתה למרקה, p. 57.

[121] Memar Marqa, p. 74, n. 50.

[122] Ed. Cowley, Aramaic Papyri of the Vth century B.C.E., p. 215 97.

[123] Schulthess did not record בל in his lexicon.

[124] Kiddushin III. 14, 64d.

[125] Read: אילין.

[125a] Sanhedrin VI. 6 (end), 23c.

[126] C. 2, 12844.

[126a] Perhaps we have to read: הובאלכון (in one word), a contraction of הבו באלכון.

[127] Ed. Buber, p. 22, overlooked by Theodor, BR 409 7.

[127a] So Yalkut Is. 313 and Yalkut Hamakiri ibid., p. 119.

Although the translation (by Midrash Tanhuma) of הבו באלכון מיניה into the Hebrew הזהרו עצמיכם ממנו is perfectly correct it is possible that our phrase is a contraction of הבו באלכון [למידחל] מיניה, "Put your mind to fearing him." Thus we read in the Hebrew "original" of Sirach[128] (XII.11): תן לבך להתירא ממנו and in the Syriac: הב לבך למדחל מנה "Put thy mind to fearing him."

We shall now understand a very difficult passage in VayR.:[128a] האביון. אהן מסכינא הב הונך מינה, " 'Ha'ebyon' ('the needy one'; Deut. XV.7), that poor, poor man! [Playing on the word 'Ha'ebyon' people say[128b]]: 'Beware of him'."

Thus, the expressions: הב הונך, הב בלך, הב דעתך, הב לבך are identical and mean: "Beware".

בר יומו. בר שעתיה.

In Midrash Haggadol[129] we read: ולא נראה לו בן יומו. Schechter suggests that בן יומו be corrected to בעצמו. This suggestion cannot be accepted, since we have the same reading in the source from which the author of the Midrash Haggadol drew the passage.[129a] Moreover, the expression בן יומו occurs also in BR,[130] in Shemoth Rabba[130a] and in Targum (=Peshitta) to Prov. XII.16 (שטיא בר יומיה מודע רוגזיה) in the sense of "in the same day."[131] In Palestinian Syriac the similar expression בר שעתה, בר שעתהון, which means ipsā horā, statim (in the same hour, immediately), occurs very frequently.[132]

---

[128] I am indebted to Prof. H. L. Ginsberg for calling my attention to this verse.

[128a] XXXIV. 9, referred to by יפה מראה ad loc.

[128b] Ha'ebyon =hab hon, הב הונך, which is equivalent to הב דעתך. See Jastrow, Brockelmann and Schulthess s. v. הון.

[129] Genes., ed. Schechter, p. 688.

[129a] The source was quoted from a Geniza ms. in my מדרשי תימן, p. 4.

[130] LIX. 11, 638₁; ibid. LXVIII. 8, 776₄.

[130a] XXI. 3 (end).

[131] This expression has, of course, nothing to do with בן יומו and בת יומה which mean "one day old" (or: "used the same day").

[132] See Schulthess, lexicon, p. 212, s. v. שעא. Add H. Duensing, Christlich-palaestinisch-aramaeische Texte und Fragmente, p. 20, col. b, l. 10: בר שעתה מסר רוחה.

The phrase is also found in Rabbinic Aramaic:[133] כספל הזה
שהוא מתמלא ב י ן שעתו ומתפנה ב י ן שעתו. But ed. pr. reads:
ב ן שעתו ... שעתו ב ן שעתו. The authentic translation therefore is:
"Like a bowl which is filled instantly and emptied at once."

פסקל שוה

In an old Midrash-fragment[134] we read: בעיתה ניזיל ונפסקליה
שווה ... ואם מפסקל את אותו מיד. The editor remarks that the word
פסקל is not found in the dictionaries, and according to the context it has the meaning of "chastising", "flogging". But this
word occurs frequently in Samaritan and in Palestinian Syriac,[135]
and it has the same meaning as פסק, to agree, to fix a price, to
cut off, to subscribe to charity etc.

There is no doubt that this word occurs also in the Palestinian Talmud. In TP[136] we find: אזלון לגביה ופסקלוניה[137]
עמיה במאה דינר ... בעו מייתון[138] ליה בפסיקוליה[139] אחרייא, "They went
to him and *agreed upon* one hundred denars . . . they wanted to
give him according to the last offer."

Again we read in TP:[140] כגון ההן סיפסלא דמעוניא, "Like the
סיפסלא of the Maoneans."[141] The word סיפסלא makes here no
sense whatever: But it is quite certain to me that we have to
read פסיקולא = פסיקא, "subscription for charity."[142]

As for the word שוה we may note that the dictionaries of
Rabbinic literature do not list for it the sense of "directly",

[133] Bemidbar Rabba X. 4.

[134] Published by Mann, The Bible as read etc., p. ק'א. See on this fragment above p. 63, n. 226.

[135] See Nöldeke in ZdMG XXII, p. 520; Schwally, Idioticon, pp. 75–76
and 124; Schulthess, lexicon, p. 160 s. v. פסקל.

[136] Pe'a I. 1, 15c, according to the reading of Cod. Leyden.

[137] The letters "לוניה" are crossed in the ms.

[138] Read with the parallels: מיתן.

[139] Read: כפסיקוליה.

[140] Megilla III. 2, 74a.

[141] Maon, a town in Galilee, near Tiberias.

[142] See Jastrow, s. v. פסיקא.

'immediately''. But it is very frequent in Palestinian Syriac,[143] and it translates the Greek εὐθέως, at once, directly.[144]

Yet we have every reason to believe that this word did occur more than once (in the sense of "immediately") in Palestinian Rabbinic literature. In the poem אקדמות (composed by R. Meir ben Isaac Ha-hazan, XI c.) we read: יקבלון דין מן דין שׁ ו י דלא בששתא, "They receive [sanction] from one another directly and without delay." Although the phrase as a whole was coined by R. Meir himself, it is most likely that he borrowed the word שׁוי from an earlier, Palestinian poet (a regular practice with the Paytanim).

Thus, we see that the use of שׁוי (שׁוה) in the sense of "immediately" was not foreign to Rabbinic Palestinian Aramaic. The sentence in our Midrash-fragment should accordingly be translated: "Do you want me to go and *settle with him* immediately . . . if you *settle with him* at once."

ט ר ס

We sometimes come across words which occur equally seldom in both Rabbinic Palestinian Aramaic and Palestinian Syriac. In such cases the use of the word in one of the dialects helps to clarify the meaning in the other.

We read in Vayyikra Rabba:[145] פשפשון בההיא שעתא לכל[146] אלפיא, "They then searched all the ships." But Aruch[147] quotes this passage: ט ר ס ו ן בשוקא . . . ס״א פשפשון. The dictionaries concluded that טרס has the same meaning as פשפש, to search. It seems that this word has fared ill at the hands of the copyists. So we read in TP:[148] דנפקין ו ס ח ר י ן ארבע וחמש קורײן, but Cod. Vat.

---

[143] See Schwally, Idioticon, p. 93, and Schulthess, lexicon, p. 202, s. v. שׁוא.

[144] Dr. A. Halkin called my attention to Hildesheimer (ספר פליאתה למרקה, p. 13) who points out that שׁוי was used in this sense in Samaritan. Comp. Marqah 3b, 7a (ed. Heidenheim pp. 2 and 5, ed. Hildesheimer pp. 37, bottom, and 39, top). Add idem 39a (ed. Heidenheim, p. 26).

[145] XXXVII. 2.

[146] Ms. Oxf. reads: כל.

[147] s. v. טרס.

[148] Maasroth, II. 3, 49d.

reads:[149] דנפקין וטרסין etc. This was also the original reading of Cod. Leyden, but was subsequently altered into וסחרין. In TP the meaning of טרס is clear; it is equal to וחזרין, "to go round."[150] The translation of the passage should be: "Who go out and make the circuit of four or five villages."

Likewise we read in the Palestinian Syriac translation[151] of Lev. VIII.24: על מדבחא טרס, "*Upon the altar round about.*"[152]

Ibid.[153] ואטרסה ה סיאג. The Greek reads: καὶ φραγμὸν αὐτῷ περιέθηκεν, "And he surrounded it with a hedge."

Ibid.[154] [דאתון] טרסין ימא ויבשא. The Greek reads: ὅτι περιά- γετε τὴν θάλασσαν καὶ τὴν ξηράν, "For yea compass sea and land."[155]

Ibid.[156] אתון טרסין במדעכון מן דן דקרא יתכון. The Greek reads: μετατίθεστε[157] ἀπὸ τοῦ καλέσαντος ὑμᾶς, "Ye turn away from him who called you."

It is very noteworthy that we find this word only in the Palestinian Syriac of the Cod. Climaci, the oldest ms. of this dialect.[158] In the younger mss. of the Palestinain Syriac texts we read in the respective places:[159] וחגל יתה סיאג and [160] דאתון חגלין ימא ויבשא. Thus, the word was used only in a certain locality of Palestine.

---

[149] This reading is not recorded in שרידי הירושלמי, p. 368.

[150] As a matter of fact the altered reading "וסחרין" is a good translation of וטרסין. See on the meaning of סחר the remarks of Prof. Louis Ginzberg in MGWJ vol. LXXVIII, p. 26. His correction of למיחסדה (VayR V.8) into למסחרה is certain. This is the reading of Codd. Vat. and Brit. Mus. See also Dalman, Aramäische Dialektproben (Leipzig 1927), p. 24.

[151] Horae Semiticae VIII (ed. Lewis, Cambridge 1909), p. 4.

[152] See Horae Semiticae IX, Cambridge 1912, p. 34.

[153] P. 44.

[154] P. 48.

[155] Comp. VayR l. c. (according to the reading of the Aruch): טרסון בההיא שעתא לכל אלפיא ולכל מדינתא, "They then compassed all the ships and all the country."

[156] P. 144.

[157] See on μετατίθημι (in med. or pass.) in the Internat. Crit. Comm. on the Epistle to the Galatians ad loc., p. 19–20.

[158] Comp. Introduction ibid. (above n. 152), p. XIII.

[159] Palestinian Syriac Lectionary, London 1899, p. 154.

[160] Ibid., p. 159.

ארההומי

Sometimes it is difficult to account for the strange form of
a word which occurs only once in Rabbinic literature. In a
Nabataean inscription[161] of the year 94 we find the expression
במנין ארהומיא, "By the reckoning of the Romans." אלהומיא
(instead of רומיא, להומיא) occurs also in Syriac.[162] No dictionary
records such a spelling of the word in Aramaic or in Christian
Syriac.

Yet, it seems to me, this form can be recognized in an old
Jewish Midrash, in Shir Hashirim Zuta, end.[163] The passage
refers to important historic facts, and, as far as I know, due
attention has not been devoted to it by historians.[164] We shall
copy the whole passage from Cod. New York[165] and collate it
with Buber's and Schechter's editions,[166] occasionally substituting their better readings for those of N.[167]

ד"א ברח דודי. אימתי, יום שכרתו[168] ברית עם ארחומו,[169] והעלו שני
טלאים אחד לצפון המזבח לשם ארחומו,[170] ואחד לדרום המזבח לשם
אנשי[171] ירושלם ... ד"א ברח דודי. בימי מנחם והלל, שנפלה מחלוקת ביניהם,
ויצא מנחם, הוא ושמנה מאות תלמידים עמו, מלובשים ב(ס)תרקי[172] זהב, ובא

---

[161] Cooke, North-Semitic Inscriptions, p. 249.

[162] See Cooke ibid., p. 250.

[163] This Midrash was simultaneously published by Buber (Berlin 1894)
and by Schechter (JQR VI, p. 673 seq.) from the same manuscript (Parma,
de Rossi 541).

[164] The only exception is W. Jawitz, תולדות ישראל V (Krakau 1904), p.
196 seq., who tried to explain it. However he relied upon Buber's erroneous
text and ventured to correct it by forced emendations.

[165] In the Jewish Theological Seminary (I learned of the existence of this
manuscript from Prof. Alexander Marx). Schechter quoted (separate reprint
p. 96) this passage from Cod. Parma (de Rossi 626 which contains fragments
of it). Its readings are very similar to those of Cod. New York.

[166] =P. We shall follow Schechter in designating the fragments in Cod.
de Rossi 626 by F.

[167] =Cod. New York.

[168] P שכריתי.

[169] So P. N ברית ארח ארחמך. F ברית ארח ארחמך.

[170] So P. NF ארחמו.

[171] P om.

[172] P סריקונין של. See note 187.

חנין[173] בן מטרון ובעטן[174] בן יהודה[175] אחיו של מנחם והרגו. ועלה אלעזר
והתלמידים עמו והכה את אלחנן,[176] וחתכו מנות מנות.[177] אותה שעה שלחו אנשי
אורחמו והושיבו קסתרא על ירושלם, והיו מטמאין כל הנשים שהיו בתוכה,[178]
ועלה אלעזר והתלמידים עמו ו ה ב א ו[179] את[180] אנשי קסתרא. מיד[181] נפלה
קטטה ומחלוקת[182] בירושלם. על אותה שעה הוא אומר: ברח דודי.

The mysterious word ארחומו[183] is no other than ארהומי, Rome,
the same form as in the Nabataean inscription.[184] The whole
passage deals with certain events relating to the Jews and
Romans. The translation should therefore be: "Another interpretation. *'Flee my beloved'* (Song of Sol. VIII.14), when did it
happen? In the day when they made a covenant with Rome,[185]
and sacrificed two lambs, one at the Northern end of the altar,
for Rome, and one at the Southern end of the altar for the
people of Jerusalem ... Another interpretation. *'Flee my
beloved'*, when did it happen? In the time of Menahem and
Hillel, when a dissension arose between them, and Menahem
left together with eight hundred students[186] who were dressed in

[173] F om. חנן P.

[174] P ובעינן!

[175] So P. Read ב ו יהודה. NF ביהודה. This may be a mere contraction
of בו יהודה, see my remarks in Tarbiz V, p. 106, bottom.

[176] P om. והכה את אלחנן.

[177] P מניות מניות.

[178] So P according to Schechter. NF מיד שלח ארחימו והושיב קסתרא בירושלים
והיו מטמאין כל האנשים והנשים שבתוכה.

[179] F והביאו. P והכו.

[180] P כל.

[181] P באותה שעה.

[182] P om. ו קטטה.

[183] See Schechter ad loc., p. 96 and Jawitz (referred to above n. 164),
p. 198.

[184] Probably influenced by Syriac; רהומי for Ῥώμη.

[185] The Rabbis (See TB Aboda Zara 8b) saw the beginning of the Jewish
subjection to Rome in the "covenant" (See I Macc. VIII.23 seq.) between
the Hasmoneans and the latter.

[186] Comp. TP Hagiga II. 2, 77d; TB ibid. 16b. Jewish scholars (see, for
instance, J. Derenbourg, Essai etc., p. 464) have already observed that the
facts bear on Menahem ben Juda (Jos. Bel. Jud. II. 17. 8) and not on Menahem the colleague of Hillel.

golden scale armor[187]; Hanin ben Matron[188] came,[189] and Juda the brother of Menahem kicked him to death.[190] Eleazar and the students arose and killed Elhanan and cut him to pieces. At that time the Romans went and encamped in Jerusalem where they defiled all the women. Eleazar and the students arose and brought the soldiers down[191] from the camp; thereupon dissensions and quarrels broke out in Jerusalem. [It is in reference] to this hour that the verse says: '*Flee my beloved*'."

The Rabbis felt that the first words of the last verse of the Song of Songs could be applied to different sins committed by the Jews during the Second Commonwealth, on account of which the Divine Presence had to depart from its Sanctuary. In the opinion of some of the Rabbis, the conclusion of the treaty between the Jews and the Romans marked the first stage in the gradual departure of the *Shekina* from Jerusalem.[192] In the opinion of others, two grave offenses (committed during the latest phase of the Jewish tragedy) were responsible for it: two important leaders of the community were assassinated, and a grievous wrong was perpetrated against the Roman soldiers in Jerusalem.

For stylistic reasons the author of the Midrash recounts the assassination of the two leaders as one event, although the

[187] NF read בסתרקי which can hardly fit our story (See Prof. Geiger's observations in Krauss' Additamenta to the Aruch Compl., p. צ'ח). The scribe probably substituted the common בסתרקי for the rare בתרקי. TP ibid. reads תירקי, θωράκια (Comp. Jos. Bel. Jud. II. 17. 9, 144). The reading of P: סריקונין (the Aramaic plural of סריקון, σηρικόν), silk dresses, originated in the Babylonian tradition, see TB Hagiga 16b and Rabbinovicz ad loc., p. 65, n. 10. Comp. also Jos. ibid. VII. 5. 4, 126.

[188] Probably a nickname. Μέτριος, "The Moderate"? Comp. בן הרצחן, "The Murderer," in Mishna Sota IX. 9; ב ר א קטולה in TP ibid. (according to the Yerushalmi Fragments, ed. Ginzberg 22114; Cod. Vat. in Lieberman's על הירושלמי, p. 82); υἱὸς καθλᾶ in Jos. (Bel. Jud. IV. 4. 2 in the variants by Niese). The connection between the Mishna in Sota and Jos. was already observed by several scholars. Comp. note 195 (below).

[189] To negociate?

[190] Comp. the expression in TP Taanith IV. 4, 68d, bottom. For the reading here see above, n. 175.

[191] According to P: killed.   [192] See above n. 185.

betrayal of the Roman garrison occurred between the first and the second murders.[193]

According to our Midrash, the two murdered leaders bore almost the same name, which approximated the form Anan (Hanan). The first was murdered by the brother of Menahem, the second was cut to pieces by Eleazar and the *students*. Jos.[194] describes the murder of the high-priest Ananias ('Ανανίας) by Menahem and his men. This Ananias[195] belonged to the peace-party, but was not altogether wanting in Jewish loyalties.[196] It is not to be wondered at that the Rabbis condemned this assassination as an ugly crime.

The second victim, it seems to me, is no other than Ananus the high-priest (son of Ananus). According to Josephus,[197] Ananus was murdered by the Idumeans, who were originally summoned by Eleazar the son of Simeon.[198] In an old Tannaitic source, a part of which was recently discovered in its original form,[199] we read: היו תלמידים אדומים לבית שמי באותה שעה,

---

[193] The author may have also drawn from different chronicles.

[194] Bel. Jud. II. 17. 9, 441 seq.

[195] =νεδεβαίον. TB (Pesahim 57a and parallel) calls him יוחנן בן נדבאי. Derenbourg's emendation of נרבאי into נדבאי (Essai etc., p. 233, n. 2) is now well attested (See Rabbinowicz ad loc., p. 169 and n. 3 ibid.). According to Schürer (Geschichte etc. II⁴, p. 272), the man was notorious for his avarice(?)· Josephus (Antiq. XX. 9. 2, 205) qualifies him as χρημάτων ποριστικός, "Past-master in making money." Perhaps he was ironically nicknamed Ben Nadbai — The Generous — for his avarice. TB (Pesahim ibid.) tells us that he was surnamed בן פינקאי, "The Glutton," on account of his daily excessive indulgence in food and drink. The nickname Μέτριος (πρὸς τὰς ἡδονάς, πρὸς τὴν καθ' ἡμέραν δίαιταν), "The Moderate," would be biting irony. Comp. also Lonzano's remark (to TP Joma V. 2, 42b) in Azulai's ככר לאדן, fol. 162b.

It is also possible that בן מטרון means τῶν μετρίων, "Of the moderate men," in the political sense. See Jos. Bel. Jud. II. 17. 10, 455 and elsewhere.

[196] See Jos. Antiq. XX. 6. 2, 131.

[197] Bel. Jud. IV. 5. 2.

[198] Ibid. 4. 1, 225, 228.

[199] Sifre Zuta, ed. Epstein, Tarbiz I, fasc. 1, p. 70 17.

"At that time there were *Idumean* students among the Sham-maites." The editor[200] correctly surmised that *"that time"* refers to the period immediately before the destruction of the Second Temple. Our text corroborates his conjectures.

The תלמידים were the Idumeans mentioned by Josephus and in Sifre Zuta; they were led by Eleazar.[201] Josephus[202] relates that Ananias was barbarously murdered by the Idumeans and that his body was cast away without burial (καὶ ἀτάφους ῥῖψαι). He concludes:[203] "I should not mistake if I said that the death of Ananus was the beginning of the destruction of the city, and that from this very day may be dated the overthrow of her wall, and the ruin of her affairs etc." The Rabbis were exactly of the same opinion: when Eleazar and the students (= תלמידים אדומים) murdered Ananus and cut his body to pieces, the Divine Presence had to flee from Jerusalem.

The Rabbis recorded another crime committed between the two assassinations. The Roman soldiers under the command of Florus were guilty of a terrible slaughter in Jerusalem.[204] According-ing to the Mishna (Kethuboth II. 9) all the women in Jeru-salem were once regarded as probable victims of rape [by the soldiers]. I. Halevy[205] correctly surmised that the Mishna referred to this outrage, and our Midrash supports his view. Subsequently the Roman soldiers who were left in the camp agreed to capitulate on condition that their lives be spared. Eleazar (the son of Ananias) and his men swore to this effect, but later broke their oath and killed them all (but their leader). In this abominable violation of the oath the Jews saw the pre-lude to destruction.[206]

---

[200] Ibid., p. 52–53.

[201] It is possible that the Rabbis had in mind not Eleazar the son of Simeon, but Eleazar the son Ananias (אלעזר בן חנניה) who was appointed general to Idumea (Jos. Bel. Jud. II. 20. 2).

[202] Ibid. IV. 5. 2, 316.

[203] Ibid. 318.

[204] Ibid. II. 15. 5.

[205] דורות הראשונים I, vol. V, 7, n. 9.

[206] Jos. ibid. 17. 10, 454 seq.

The Rabbis were of the same opinion. Even after all the abominations committed by the Roman soldiers, Eleazar had no right to have them brought down[207] and killed, after having solemnly pledged their safety under oath. At that hour the Divine Presence had to depart from Jerusalem.

The text hitherto considered very confused becomes clear with the aid of the preceding exposition.

---

[207] והביאו. Jos. ibid. 451 expresses himself: κατῆγεν τοὺς στρατιώτας ὁ Μετίλιος, "[After the oath] Metilius (the Roman officer) brought down the soldiers." In P it is clearly stated: והכו, "And they killed." The reading of NF seems, however, to be more original.

APPENDIX

X and Θ

The phrase חתיכה ופסיפס[1] mentioned in the Sifre has been identified by some scholars[2] with חתוכין ופספס quoted in Midrash Eka Rabba.[3] However, on a closer examination of the text and context of the Midrash we must decidedly abandon this identification, for the expression in the latter has nothing to do with the terms mentioned in the former.

The Midrash explains that תו (Taw) in Ezekiel IX.4[4] is: חתוכין ופספס[5]. Mussafia[6] records the more correct reading: כתיטא בפספס, "Like the Θ (theta) in a ψῆφος" (vote or decree). He[7] also suggested that the Rabbis interpreted the word תו to be the last letter of the Hebrew alphabet, whose sound is equivalent to the Greek Θ.[8] This letter served as an abbreviation of θάνατος — death — in the capital sentences of the Gentile courts. Yet, not all the dictionaries have accepted this explanation.

However, it seems to me, that Mussafia is undoubtedly right. The Midrash says explicitly that the angel who put the mark served also as a quaestor[9]; in other words, it is the quaestor

[1] See above p. 74.

[2] Hoffmann, Midrash Tannaim, p. 7, n. 50; Finkelstein ad loc. 218.

[3] II. 1. See ed. Buber, p. 98, n. 36.

[4] והתוית תו על מצחות האנשים, "And set a mark on the foreheads of the men" etc.

[5] Aruch reads: התיבה פספסן. Ed. Buber התורה פספס.

[6] S. v. פסליון.

[7] Ibidem.

[8] See above p. 48 n. 111.

[9] Ed. Buber and Aruch read קייסטור, Yalkut: קריסטור which are obvious mistakes for קויסטור. There is no ground whatever for changing the reading into סקריפטור, scriptor. The Midrash took the word סופר as γραμματεύς which designated various high officials. See Deissmann, Bible Studies, p. 110 seq.

who put the ϑ on the foreheads of the men. We find an exact
parallel in the Epigrams of Martialis (VII. 37): Nosti morti-
ferum quaestoris, Castrice, signum? Est operae pretium discere
theta novum. "Do you know, Castricus, *the quaestor's*[10] *death-
bringing mark?* It is very important to know this new [kind of]
theta."

The Rabbis followed an old tradition which explained the
תו in Ezekiel as referring to the last letter of the Hebrew al-
phabet. Aquila and Theodotion rendered it: $\tau\grave{o}$ $\theta a\tilde{v}$, designating the Hebrew letter Taw. TB[11] records the explicit opinion of
Rab (III c.) that the letter תו stands for death (תמות), and there
can, therefore, be no doubt that the Midrash Eka Rabba
recorded the same opinion and expressed it by comparing the
Hebrew Taw (ת) to the Theta (ϑ) in a $\psi\tilde{\eta}\varphi os$ (vote or decree).
It is thus absolutely certain that the Rabbis interpreted תו as
ϑ (nigrum theta — $\vartheta\acute{a}\nu a\tau os$).

This will shed new light on the difficult sayings of Rabbinic
sages of the III c. TB (ibid.) records: אמר רב תיו תחיה; תיו
תמות. ושמואל אמר תיו[12] תמה זכות אבות. ור' יוחנן אמר תיו[12] תחון זכות
אבות. "Rab said Taw [stands for] תחיה — thou shalt live; Taw
[stands for] תמות — thou shalt die. Samuel said Taw [stands
for] תמה — ended —, the merit of the Patriarchs is at an end
(i. e. exhausted). R. Johanan said Taw [stands for] תחון — confer mercy —, the merit of the Patriarchs will confer mercy."
Only the statement of Samuel is understandable, for since Taw
is a radical of the root תמם, the word תו can reasonably be
treated as an abbreviation of תמה,[13] the Taw in תחון, תמות, תחיה,
however, is a preformative, a prefix which can be added to
any verb, and the word in Ezekiel can hardly be regarded as a
definite indication of any of these three words. We, therefore,
have to presume that the letter Taw in itself conveyed the idea
of life, death, mercy or end, and that TB merely paraphrased

[10] See L. Friedlaender's note in his edition, Leipzig 1886, p. 493. The
helpfulness of Rabbinic literature for the understanding of Latin classics is
illustrated here again.

[11] Shabbath 55a.

[12] So Cod. Monac.

[13] On the correct meaning of Samuel's saying see below, n. 26.

the original utterances of the previously quoted Rabbis. This suggestion is confirmed by other sources.[14]

An early Christian Church Father, Tertullian, asserted[15] that the תו of Ezekiel was the sign of the cross. He probably was not the inventor of this idea but found it in the various "books of testimonies" current among the Christians. Origen, a contemporary of the quoted Rabbis, is more explicit. He states[16] about our Taw: πυνθανομένων δὲ τῶν Ἑβραίων εἴ τι πάτριον περὶ τοῦ Θαῦ ἔχοιεν λέγειν μάθημα, ταῦτα ἠκούσαμεν· τινὸς μὲν φάσκοντος, ὅτι τὸ Θαῦ ἐν τοῖς παρ' Ἑβραίοις κβ' στοιχείοις ἐστὶ τὸ τελευταῖον ὡς πρὸς τὴν παρ' αὐτοῖς τάξιν γραμμάτων. Τὸ τελευταῖον οὖν εἴληπται στοιχεῖον εἰς παράστασιν τῆς τελειότητος τῶν διὰ τὴν ἐν αὐτοῖς ἀρετὴν στεναζόντων καὶ ὀδυνωμένων ἐπὶ τοῖς ἁμαρτανομένοις ἐν τῷ λαῷ, καὶ συμπασχόντων τοῖς παρανομοῦσι. Δεύτερος δὲ ἔλεγε σύμβολον εἶναι τὸ Θαῦ τῶν τὸν νόμον τετηρηκότων· ἐπείπερ ὁ νόμος παρ' Ἑβραίοις Θωρὰ καλεῖται, καὶ τὸ πρῶτον αὐτοῦ στοιχεῖόν ἐστι τὸ Θαῦ· καὶ σύμβολον εἶναι τῶν κατὰ τὸν νόμον βεβιωκότων. Τρίτος δέ τις φάσκων, τῶν καὶ εἰς τὸν Χριστὸν πεπιστευκότων, ἔλεγε τὰ ἀρχαῖα στοιχεῖα ἐμφερὲς ἔχειν τὸ Θαῦ τῷ τοῦ σταυροῦ χαρακτῆρι, καὶ προφητεύεσθαι περὶ τοῦ γενομένου ἐν Χριστιανοῖς ἐπὶ τοῦ μετώπου σημείου. "Upon inquiring of the Jews whether they can relate [to me] any traditional teaching regarding the Taw, I heard the following. One of them said that in the order of the Hebrew letters the Taw is the last of the twenty two consonantal sounds. The last consonant is therefore taken as proof of the perfection[17] of those who, because of their virtue, moan and groan[17a] over the sinners among the

---

[14] The Mystical idea that the Taw mentioned in Ezekiel denotes either life (for the righteous) or death (for the wicked) was probably alluded to in the Psalms of Solomon XV.8–10 (See the International Critical Commentary on the Apocalypse VII.4, p. 194).

[15] Adv. Marcionem (written in the beginning of the III c.) III. 22, Migne PL II, 353a.

[16] Selecta in Ezechielem, Migne PG XIII, 800d.

[17] The Hebrew תם, שלם, has a double meaning, denoting both finished, ended, complete and perfect. The Jew transmitted a true Jewish tradition, see below n. 19 and n. 26.

[17a] The Jew followed the translation of הנאנחים והנאנקים by the Septuagint.

people and *suffer together with*[18] the transgressors. Another said that the Taw symbolizes the observers of the Law. Since the Law, which is called Tora by the Jews, begins [its name] with the consonant Taw, it is a symbol of those who live according to the Law.[19] A third [Jew], one of those who believe in Christ, said the form of the Taw in the old [Hebrew] script resembles the cross,[20] and it predicts the mark which is to be placed on the foreheads of the Christians."

We can assume with the utmost certainty that, like the first two Jews, the Jewish Christian transmitted a genuine Jewish idea which he applied to the Christians. The question, however, is what symbol did the Jews see in the Taw of the ancient script — X?

Deissmann[21] called attention to the X found in documents of the first century, which served as a mark of cancelling a debt.[22] He concludes:[23] "We have learned from the new texts that it was generally customary to cancel a bond (or other document) by crossing it out with the Greek cross-letter Chi (X) . . . The subject is perhaps not without some bearing on the origin of later allegorical and mystical trifling with the cross-letter Chi among the Christians." Thus, we have very early[23a] evidence to the effect that the X served as a mark of cancellation of bonds, a mark of freedom; at the same time we have first-century evidence[24] that the ϑ was used as a mark of death.

---

[18] See Migne PL XXV, 88, n. *a*. I would rather translate συμπασχόντων *"who commiserate."* TB (Shabbath 55a) records the same opinion: הללו צדיקים גמורים . . . היה בידם למחות ולא מיחו, "Those (moaners and groaners) are completely righteous [but nevertheless suffer because] they could have protested but did not."

[19] TB ibid. records: אמר ר' שמואל בר נחמני אלו בני אדם שקיימו את התורה כולה מאלף ועד תו, "R. Samuel b. Nahmani (III c.) said [the Taw denotes] those people who fulfilled the Tora from Alef to Taw" (i. e. from the beginning to the end). Midrash Eka Rabba II.1. (ed. Buber 98, bottom) records the same opinion in the name of R. Juda (II c.).

[20] X. See JE I, p. 449. Migne (referred to above n. 18), n. *b*. Comp. the International Crit. Comment. on Ez. ad loc., p. 106, and J. C. James, The Language of Palestine, p. 211–12.

[21] Light, p. 334.   [22] See figure 50, ibid., p. 268.
[23] Ibid., p. 333.   [23a] See below p. 193.
[24] Martialis (see above) and Persius, see below n. 38.

Since the Hebrew letter Taw, in the ancient script, was almost identical in form with X (Chi) and in sound with Θ (Theta), the Rabbis, being well acquainted with both marks, interpreted the Taw to stand for either life (freedom, mercy) or death. The mark X was inscribed on the foreheads of the righteous, the mark Θ was put on those of the wicked. TB preserved only a paraphrase of the statements of the Rabbis who originally maintained that the Taw indicated either life (חיים, תחיה) or mercy (תחון,[25] חנינה) or death or end[26] (תמה).

Perhaps we shall now be able to establish the correct reading in the passage of Eka Rabba (II.1): ורב אמר אות[27] שנתנה בכל צד (ורבנין אמרי)[28] תיהי תיהי ותיהי תיהי. The correct reading (of the last four words) should possibly be: תיו כי ותיו תיטה. "And Rab said [the Taw] is a letter which can be read in any position[29]— Taw is X and Taw is Θ.[30]

---

[25] R. Johanan preferred to see the symbol of mercy, grace (תחון, חנינה), in the X because he wanted to connect the exegesis of his own name with the idea of future salvation. Onomastica sacra (Lagarde, p. 170₉₇) explains the meaning of יוחנן (I Chron. III.15): Ιωαννης ἀοράτου χάρις, "Johanan [means] grace of God" (See Deissmann, Papyrus Onomasticon sacrum, p. 90, n. 10). R. Johanan, accordingly, saw an allusion to his name in the sign of salvation. This was a regular practice (probably based upon the belief that the characters and future lots of individuals somehow depend on their respective names. See above p. 169 n. 70 and n. 111) among the ancient Rabbis. See, for instance, TB Sanhedrin 98b.

[26] Samuel did not take the Taw (ת) as an abbreviation of תמה (is ended) but as a symbol. It is the last letter of the Hebrew alphabet, and it can accordingly be treated as the symbol of "end"—"the merit the Patriarchs is at an end," see above n. 13. Comp. also n. 17.

[27] Ed. pr. reads: עד, but ed. Buber, p. 99, top, reads: אותו, an obvious mistake for אות.

[28] An obvious dittography from the previous line.

[29] I. e. both as a letter (the symbol represents X whether it stands upright or is laid on its side) and as an abbreviation.

[30] It is noteworthy that according to a Yemenite source (Midrash Haggadol Gen., p. 12) the letter Taw was the mark God put on Cain's hand to serve him as a protection mark. The other Rabbinic sources (See Rabbi M. M. Kasher's Torah Shelemah II, p. שׁ"ל, nss. 116–119) do not mention that the mark of Cain was a Taw. It is possible that the original allusion to the Taw, X, was dropped after the Christians began to interpret this mark in their own way. And it is again a Yemenite source which has pre-

TB Shabbath (55a) records another interpretation of the
verse in Ezekiel: אמר ליה הקב"ה לגבריאל לך ורשום על מצחן של צדיקים
תיו של דיו שלא ישלטו בהם מלאכי חבלה ועל מצחם של רשעים תיו של דם
כדי שישלטו בהם מלאכי חבלה. "The Holy One, blessed be He, said
to Gabriel: 'Go and set a Taw of ink upon the foreheads of the
righteous that the destroying angels may have no power over
them, and a Taw of blood upon the foreheads of the wicked
that the destroying angels may have power over them'." The
Talmudic commentaries ad loc. did not account for these two
respective colours.[31] The Rabbinic commentaries on Ezekiel[32]
allude to the sign with the blood of the Paschal lamb, which
is a mark of salvation. Then we should expect to find the reverse of our reading in TB, namely that the blood was the mark
of salvation and the ink the mark of doom.

Although the reading in TB is well attested,[33] a remnant of
a different tradition has been preserved. We read in Tanhuma:[34]
תיו של דיו כדי שלא ישלטו בהם מלאכי חבלה וימותו מיד[35], "The
Taw of ink was [was set on the righteous] in order that the
destroying angels may have no power [to torture] them *and they
will die immediately*." This reading indicates the trace of a
tradition which connected the Taw of ink with death.

The Hebraeus which preserved many Rabbinic traditions[36]
translates וקסת הספר (Ezek. ibid. 2): μέλαν καὶ κάλαμος γραφέως,
"Ink and the scribe's reed-pen."[37] Thus there was a widely
spread tradition about the ink (μέλαν) used for the mark.
Perhaps this is only another form of the previous interpretation.

---

served an ancient uncensored Rabbinic tradition (See the conclusions in my
lecture on the Yemenite Midrashim — מדרשי תימן — p. 39).

[31] See Tosaphoth ad loc. s. v. ועל.

[32] R. Eliezer of Beaugency. Comp. Redak who combined it with the
tradition in TB.

[33] See Rabbinovicz ad loc. Comp. also Tanhuma Mishpatim 7, Tazria,
ed. Buber, p. 41.

[34] Tazria sec. 9.

[35] The last two words are found only in ed. Mantua (and the later
editions) which is based upon four mss. They are missing in the first edition.

[36] See above p. 53, n. 142.

[37] See Field ad loc., p. 790, n. 10.

Instead of תיו, Taw, Θ, Theta, some Rabbis worded it
תיו של דיו, ink-mark, black-mark, which was equal to μέλαν
ϑῆτα.[38] The ink-mark had served as a sign of death, whereas
the blood-mark (reminiscent of the blood of the Paschal
lamb) had served a sign of salvation.

However, since the early Christian Church Fathers[39] had
already connected the mark of Ezekiel with the blood of the
Paschal lamb in the Christian sense, and since the blood-mark
was monopolized by the Christians as the symbol of salvation,
it is not surprising that the Jewish teaching was reversed: the
sign of blood became the sign of doom.

It is noteworthy that the mediaeval Rabbinic sources knew
of the nigrum Theta. R. Bahya in his commentary on the
Pentateuch[40] records: שרמזו במדרש דורשי רשומות כי לשון טיטא סימן
הריגה בין האומות, "It is alluded in the Midrash of 'interpreters of
signs'[41] that the Theta (ט!) is a mark of death (execution)
among the Gentiles." Prof. L. Ginzberg[42] has justly expressed
his doubts as to the existence of this Midrash. It is very likely
that the Spanish Jews got their information through the very
popular work in the middle ages of Isidore of Seville (VII c.).
He writes:[43] Θ, quae mortem significat. Nam iudices eamdem
litteram theta apponebant ad eorum nomina quos supplicio
afficiebant etc. "Θ which signifies death. For the judges put
this very letter next to the names of those whom they sentenced
to death."[44] Isidore, of course, did not fail to repeat[45] the Christian interpretation of the תו mentioned in the previously quoted
verse of Ezekiel.[46]

---

[38] Persius, Sat. IV. 13: et potis es *nigrum* vitio praefigere theta. "Would
you be able to put the black Theta to vice," i. e. to condemn vice.

[39] Cyprian, ad Demertianum XXII, Migne PL IV, 580b; idem, Testim.
adv. Jud. II.22, ibid. 745a.

[40] Jethro, ed. Venice 1546, fol. 98a.

[41] Those who interpret the Law symbolically; see Lauterbach, JQR N.S.
I, p. 329.

[42] Legends of the Jews VI, p. 60, n. 308.

[43] Orig. I. 3. 8. Migne PL LXXXII, 76b.

[44] Isidore copied the old scholiast of Persius (see above, n. 38) almost
verbatim.

[45] Orig. ibid. 9.   [46] See Migne ibid. n. *m*.

ADDITIONS AND CORRECTIONS

P. 11. It is also possible that the topic of the passage is the right of marriage not between Romans and peregrini but between Romans and Syrians as such (privilegium odiosum).

The Gnomon of the Idios Logos § 52 (ʹΡωμαίοις ἐξὸν Αἰγυπ-τίαν γ[ῆμαι]) suggests that in Egypt marriage between Romans and natives was not licit prior to this decree. However this decree is much earlier than the passage in Pesiktha deR. Kahana. See A. Segré, Note sullo status civitatis dei soldati peregrini etc., in Rendiconti della Pont. Accad. Romana di Arch., XVII, ch. 5. Our passage requires further investigation.

P. 43, n. 76. The principle that the property of the debtors and not their persons may be seized is already emphasized in the Hellenistic law (around 260 B.C.E.) in Syria and *Palestine*. See the forthcoming article by A. Segré "Free Persons in Bondage" (The author has kindly sent me the manuscript of the article).

P. 104, n. 62. See now the long article by L. Wallach in the Journal of Biblical Literature LX (December 1941), p. 403 ff. The ugly practice of putting out the lights for licentious purposes (Comp. also A. Halkin, Moslem Schisms and Sects, p. 90 and n. 1 ibid.) has of course nothing to do with the passage of our Midrash.

P. 118. The change of one single letter in our text would remove all difficulties. If we read לחיי instead of בחיי the passage would assume quite a different meaning. The Rabbis, in commenting on the verse (Num. XXX.3) נדר לה׳ ("A vow *to* God"), remarked that the formula of a vow is followed by a ל, whereas the formula of an oath is followed by a ב.[1] Thus, they explained that the characteristic of a vow is like vowing *for* the life (votum pro salute, ob salutem; εὐχὴ ὑπὲρ σωτηρίας) of the king[2] etc. The Jews followed the general practice; they also

---

[1] See Nahmanides ad loc. who also quoted our passage from the Sifre.

[2] A good summary of the material bearing on the *vota* for the king is now available in the Yale Classical Studies, 1940 (The Feriale Duranum, p. 52–66).

made *vota* for the safety of the king.[3] Evidence of a contemporary[4] Jewish vow for the safety of Septimius Severus and his family has been preserved in Palestine.[5] The inscription begins with ὑπὲρ σωτηρίας etc. and finishes with [ἐξ] εὐχῆς Ἰουδαίων. The Jews who happened to witness the annual ceremonies (on the third of January), when both vows for the welfare of the king and oaths of loyalty to him[6] were pronounced, could not help being impressed by them. Although both the *vota* and the *iuramenta* were expressions of loyalty, the difference between them was quite obvious. The Rabbis drew the same distinction between the force of vows and that of oaths in the religious sense.

The passage in the Sifre should accordingly be translated: "What is the difference between vows and oaths? The former is like vowing *for* the life of the king, the latter is like swearing *by* the king himself, and although there is no [Scriptural] proof for it, there is an allusion to it: *'God liveth! And as thy soul liveth,*[7] *I will not leave thee'* "[8] (II Kings IV.30).

Although this explanation makes good sense of the text, I suggest it hesitatingly since it requires an emendation (even a very slight one) of an old Tannaitic text, the readings of which are well attested. Any assumption that we have here a case of the frequent indiscrimination between ב and ל (See above p. 132, n. 129) has to be abandoned, since the whole basis of the Rabbinic interpretation lies here in the distinction between the ל (לה׳) and the ב (בה׳).

P. 188. On the X as a mark of cancellation in the documents of debts (κεχιασμένοι εἰς ἀκύρωσιν) see A. Segrè, Bull. Ist. Dir. Rom. XXIV, 1925, p. 67 ff. This practice is thus much earlier than the I c. C.E.

---

[3] See Ezra VI.10. Comp. Schürer II[4], 360 ff.

[4] The final redaction of our text is either at the end of the II c. or the beginning of the III.

[5] Klein, CI No. 11, p. 81.

[6] See The Feriale Duranum ibid., p. 65–66.

[7] Observe the different vocalization of חי and וחי in our verse and comp. ps.-Jonathan ad loc. See also Horovitz's note in the Sifre ad loc.

[8] The first was a preliminary εὐχή in the form of praise (God liveth [for ever]), the second was an oath by the life of the prophet.

KEY TO ABBREVIATIONS

AdPA	Die Agada der palästinischen Amoräer, von W. Bacher.
AdT	Die Agada der Tannaiten.
b.	ben (the son).
Blaufuss	Römische Feste und Feiertage nach den Traktaten über fremden Dienst.
BK	Baba Kamma.
BR	Bereshith Rabba, quoted by chapter and page, ed. Theodor and Albeck.
Brockelmann	Lexicon Syriacum 1928.
CI	Jüdisch-palästinisches Corpus Inscriptionum, von S. Klein.
CIJ	Corpus Inscriptionum Judaicarum by P. J. B. Frey.
CIL	Corpus Inscriptionum Latinarum.
Daremberg et Saglio	Dictionnaire des Antiquités Grecques et Romaines.
De Vogüé	Syrie Centrale, Inscriptions Sémitiques.
Deissmann	Light from the Ancient East, 1927.
Durham	The Vocabulary of Menander considered in its relation to the koine.
Jastrow	A Dictionary of the Targumim, the Talmud Babli and Yerushalmi etc.
JQR	The Jewish Quarterly Review.
JE	The Jewish Encyclopedia.
Kommentar	Kommentar zum Neuen Testament aus Talmud und Midrasch, von Strack und Billerbeck.
Liddell and Scott	A Greek-English Lexicon 1937.
LW	Griechische und lateinische Lehnwörter im Talmud, Midrasch und Targum, von S. Krauss, Teil II, 1899.
LW I	Idem I, 1898.

Mann	The Bible as Read and Preached in the Old Synagogue, 1940.
MGWJ	Monatsschrift für Geschichte und Wissenschaft des Judentums.
Moulton, Prolegomena	A Grammar of New Testament Greek, 1906.
Ott	Beiträge zur Kenntniss des griechischen Eides, Leipzig, 1896.
Payne Smith	Thesaurus Syriacus.
PG	Patrologia Graeca.
PL	Patrologia Latina.
Preisigke	Wörterbuch der griechischen Papyrusurkunden, Berlin, 1925.
R.	Rabbi.
Rabbinovicz	Variae lectiones in Mischnam et in Talmud Babylonicum vol. I–XVI.
Ratner	אהבת ציון וירושלים, vol. I–XII.
REJ	Revue des Études Juives.
Schulthess	Lexicon Syropalaestinum, Berlin, 1903.
Stephanus	Thesaurus Graecae Linguae, London, 1816–1825.
Swete	An Introduction to the Old Testament in Greek, Cambridge, 1902.
TB	Babylonian Talmud.
TP	Palestinian Talmud, quoted by treatise, chapter, folio and column of ed. Venice.
VayR	Vayyikra Rabba.
WdJ	Wissenschaft des Judentums.
ZdMG	Zeitschrift der deutschen morgenländischen Gesellschaft.

בן נדבאי	182[195]	אבא טיס	57 ff.
בן פינקאי	182[195]	אגרפוס	see פרא
(בסיליאוס) בסיליום	see פרא	אונגדוי	26
בעל חוב	156[78]	אוליאוס	see סנדריאוס
בר שעתיה, בר יומו	175 ff.	אונומוס	see פרא
ברא קטולה	181[188]	אונטיס	55
ברור	51[122]	אורקומסיות	7
בריכסון	see קורי	אזמרגדין	57 ff.
ברירין	52	אילופוסה	25
ברר	51	איספטליא	61, 62
		איפופי	120
גפה של רומי	140	איפרסן	52[136]
גרי אומות העולם	84	אית ב . . .	169 ff.
גרי הארץ	83	אנדרטין	9
		אנטיגרפון	55[163]
דבר (prophecy)	166	אנטילרות	13
דבר (angel)	167[48]	אנטלר	12, 13, 14
דולוס	8	אנקלסיא	9
דחיין	49[113]	אספטיה	61
דיאתימון	26[76]	אספטילי (see איספטליא)	61
דייקינתין	57 ff.	אספטלין	see ספאטאלון
		אספליאות	8
הבו בלכון, הב בלך	172 ff.	אפטרופא	13[88]
הב הונך	175	אפילון	53 ff.
הון	see הב הונך	אפיקטחין	96
הימונויות	48	ארנון	8
הימיסיון	57 ff.	ארהומי	179, 180
הצדא	55	ארכסטס	33
		אראמי	86[130]
זיטא איפטה איטה אוכטו	22	בא	see יבוא עלי
זכור לטוב	70[23]	בבוליא	32[21]
זקף	41[60]	בדה	17[14]
		בייה	see כורוסתי
חליטר	28	בכל	120
חליץ	62, 62[255]	בל	see הב בלך
חלק טוב	72 ff.	בלספימיסון	52
חלק רע	73	בן אשתו	164 ff.
חשבון יפה	74	בן מטרון	182[195]
חתיכה ופסיפוס	74		

מטברטי ולא מקנוניא · 385_{1}a
טלמסן למנע בסמה דמטרונה · 39, 40, 42, 43
טפיח · 172
טרס · 177 ff.

ר and י · 1014_{8}, 1279_{8}
יבוא עלי · 121 ff.
יראי שמים · 77 ff.

כבל · 119
כוחלין · 57 ff.
כורוסתי בייה · 44
כך מכך, כך וכך · 123
כסא דפושרין · 113
כפכף · 172
כרכרינין · 57 ff.

לשון גבוה · 138_{170}
לשון חכמה · 22, 23

מטרונה · see טלמסן
מין · 141_{196}
מליטה · 152
מצוה · 71_{32}
מקטייא · see קייטא
מרנליטוס · 57 ff.
מרעיל · 135_{151}
משכים · 135_{151}
משכן · 41_{60}

נאמן · 75 ff.
נדר (=oath) · 117 ff.
נוח נפש · 70
נחתומר · 28
נקיטי · see קיטא

סבתא · 22, 224_{0}
סחר · 178_{150}
סמה · 437_{6}
סנדריאוס אם אוליאוס · 50, 51
סנפירינון · 57 ff.
ספאטאלון · 60 ff.
ספינדא · 141_{193}

עיצומין · 4

פני פילאי קקום כאמי · 44, 45
פני שביעית · 162 ff.
פטרון · 64

פילאי · see פני פילאי
פילומה · 93 ff.
פינסור · 150_{29}
פיספיסאי פיסיאו · 59
פיפי · 120_{38}
פיקופסלום · 63_{226}
פנדקקא, פנטקקה · 31
פנים · see ראיית
פסיפוס · 74, 75, 185
פסיפיסטס · 74_{65}
פסיקולא · 176
פסקל · 176 ff.
פרא בסיליוס אונומוס אנגרפוס · 37–38, 385_{1}, 144_{2}
פראלוקין · 57 ff.
פרוטונמיא · 9
פרוטי · 147
פרוסטטיה · 63
פרק טוב · 73 ff.

צדיק · 69, 70
צור · 169_{69}
צור · 167 ff.
צור כנישתא · 168–169

קאנוסין · 48
קבל · 119
קבלי · 120_{36}
קבקא · see קקבא
קדח · 111
קדשים · 49
קוויקין · see קקבא
קונטא · 26
קורדימא · 93, 94
קורי פלי בריכסון · 34, 35–36
קטא · 141
קטיסון · 48
קיומא · 65
קייטא · 128_{99}
קייץ · 127 ff.
קיליוון · 8
קינינין מכללה · 63_{0}
קירומא · 94, 95, 96
קנוניא · see טברטי
קפץ עליו הדבר · 165 ff.
קקבא, קקביון · 170 ff.

בין זכאי בין חייב לשבועה לא

תיעול 124_{74}

בר מזבן תאני תאני דאבוך זבין 144–145

בשוק סמייה צווחין לעיירא סני נהורא

ולעיירא בירבי 157

דחמי חמי ודלא חמי לא חמי 145_7

המקבל פני חברו כאילו מקבל פני

שכינה 158

חמרא למריה טיבותא לשקייה 152–153

תורא בטורא לא פגע איניש

באיניש פגע 160_{112}

כד יפול תורא מחרפין סכינוי 154

כל התחלות קשות 159

כפה סייח את המנורה 104_{62}

כרסה טענא רגליא 158

לא מקומו של אדם מכבדו אלא אדם

מכבד את מקומו 157

לפום צערא אגרה 160_{113}

מאן דנכתיה חיויא חבלא מדחיל ליה 159

מטת ענתה דאריתא למחשי ותעלייא

למשרקא 147_{14}

מי שאינו יכול להכות את החמור מכה

את האוכף 153

ממרי רשוותך פרי אפרע 156

קידרא דבי שותפי לא חמימא ולא

קרירא 153

פרא בסיליאוס נומוס

אנרפוס 37–38, 385_1, 144_2

תהא מטבריטי ולא מקנוניא 385_{1a}

תנין דאינין תנין 343_2

קקום″כאמי   פני פילאי see

קרבן (=oath)   130 ff.

קרומטסין   57 ff.

קרטיסים   9, 10

ראיית פנים 52_{130}, 105_{66}

רויון   49

רחים מצוותא   71, 72

רחים עמא   71

שדרגנין   שרדנגין see

שוה   177

שומפוין   57 ff.

שחק (נשתחק) 70_{20}

שטר 101_{48}

שרדגנין   57 ff.

תיו של דיו   191

תיטא   185 ff.

תרקי 181_{187}

PROVERBS

אין עץ מעוקם מתכוון אלא באור   155

אין קטא קטא שיחור ואין אובד אובד

מרנלי   148

אם בקשת ליחנק התלה באילן

גדול   158 ff.

אם המספר פתי יהי השומע חכם

וערום 160_{112}

INDEX II

ἀγάπη   140–141

'Αλύπις Τιβεριεύς   25

ἀμέθυστος   58

ἀνδριάντιον   9

ἀπορέω, ἠπόρησε 52_{136}

-άριος   28

ἀσφάλειαι   8

ἀχάτης   58

*βαβούλια¹ 322_1

βηρύλιον   58

ἐβλασφήμησε   52

γεώρας 83_{115}

διεθέμην 267_6

δόλος   8

¹ The words marked with an asterisk are omitted by Liddell and Scott (in the last edition) and Sophocles.

ἔγκλησις 9
*ἐντελλάριος 13
*ἐντολάριος 13
ἐπὶ τῶν ἔργων 9
ἐπιλλῶν 54, 55
*ἐπιτροπή 1388

*ζανδρεία 51124

ϑ=ʊ 48111
ϑ=ח 186
ϑ—nigrum theta 186 ff., 191
ϑεωρητής 3851a
ϑωράκια 181187

ἴασπις 58
ιν=ιον 9, 157185
ἰσοπολιτεία 62221

κάθισαν 48
*κακέσχατος 46, 47
κακκάβιον 172
*κακκούβιον 171
καρχηδόνιος 57, 58
κήρωμα 95, 96
κράτησις 9 ff.
κτάομαι 148
κυνηγός 3851a

μαργαρίτης 58
μέλι 152
μέτριος? 181188, 182195

*ὀλημερίδιον 85125
ὁμόνοια 48
ὄντως 55
ὀρκωμόσια (τά) 7, 738
ὀρχηστής 33

παλαιὰ πόρνη 50
παντόκακος 31
παράλευκον 58
πεντήκοντα altered to ὀγδοήκοντα 26

πήλωμα 94, 95
πιπι 12038
προστατεία 63
πρώτη 147
πρωτογάμια 9
*πυκιψελλός 63226

σαπφείρινον 58
σαρδονύχιον 57, 58
σμάραγδος 58
σπατάλη 61, 62
σπάταλος, σπαταλῶν 61, 62
σπένδω 141193
συντόμως 7997

τοπάζιον 57, 58

ὑάκινθος 57, 58

χ 188 ff., 194
χαρίζεσθαι βία 44
*χρῶμα θαλάσσιον² 58
ψηφιστής 74, 7465
ψῆφος 74, 75, 185 ff.

PHRASES AND PROVERBS

ἀνδρεία (ζανδρεία) ὡς ὁ ἥλιος 51
ζῇ τὰ ἑπτὰ [μᾶλλον] ἢ τὰ ὀκτώ 23
κῦρι πολὺ βρέξον 34, 35, 36
μωρῷ καὶ βασιλεῖ νόμος
ἄγραφος 3851
παγὶ παλαιὰ κακέσχατε 45
παρὰ βασιλέως ὁ νόμος
ἄγραφος 38, 1442
πιήσω σοι ὅπως ποίησας 59
τὰ σῦκα σῦκα λέγειν 3432
ἐτόλμησε τοῦ ματρώνης σώματος
ἅψασθαι 39, 40, 42, 43

See also Index V s. v. Greek proverbs.

² Name of a precious stone.

INDEX III

BIBLE

Gen. IX.27   18
Gen. XII.17   39
Gen. XV.13   61
Exod. IV.24   60
Exod. XII.48   79₉₇
Exod. XX.7   35
Exod. XXVIII.17–20   56, 57
Lev. XIX.12   142
Lev. XIX.20   20
Lev. XIX.26   98
Num. XXX.3   136
Deut. IV.35   113
Deut. XVIII.13   97
Deut. XXXI.16   59
Joshua I.8   16
I Sam. XXV.6   65
I Kings V.10   98
I Kings XXI.13   52
Is. III.12   49
Is. XLIII.17   7₃₀
Is. XLIV.5   83
Is. XLVII.1   46
Is. LIV.15   80
Jer. X.2   99
Ezek. IX.4   185 ff.
Ezek. XVI.59   59
Ezek. XXIII.42   48 ff. 50
Ps. X.3   52
Ps. XXII.24   82
Ps. XLV.3   18
Ps. L.20   89
Ps. CIV.32   53
Prov. X.7   69
Job IX.7   138
Song of Sol. VI.10   52
Song of Sol. VIII.14   180 ff.
Eccl. I.8   23
Eccl. XII.2   161 ff.

Esth. III.14   55₁₆₃
Dan. III.14   55
Dan. VIII.13   19

SEPTUAGINT

Exod. XXVIII.17–20   57, 58
II Kings VI.20   33
III Kings XXI.13   52₁₃₇
Ps. CIV.32   54
Song of Sol. VI.10   50
Job I.11 (II.5)   52₁₃₇
Sirach XXIII.10   34
Sirach XXXVIII.17   104₆₁
Esth. III.14   55₁₆₃
Tobit VI.12   51₁₂₃
Ezek. XVI.59   60
Ezek. XXIII.42   48, 49
Dan. III.14   55
IV Mac. X.15   125₇₇
Ps. of Solomon III.16   80₁₀₁

APOCALYPTIC WRITINGS

IV Ezra X.1   104
Sibyllina III.227   98₁₇

RABBINIC WRITINGS[3]
MISHNA

Shabbath XXII.6   93, 96
Nedarim I.3   133
Nedarim II.5   128
Aboda Zara I.3   9
Aboth IV.15   146
Aboth V.23   160
Aboth VI.1   69 ff.
Aboth VI.6   71, 72
Nidda VII.3   102₅₁

[3] Only passages explained or paralleled are listed in this Index.

TOSEPHTA

Shebiith 6130[4]	101
Nedarim 2761$_{11}$	130
Nedarim 2761$_{12}$	132
Sanhedrin 4222$_{8}$	128$_{99}$, 139
Sanhedrin 4231	127, 138
Sanhedrin 4251$_{7}$	73
Shebuoth 4462$_{4}$	182$_{3}$
Shebuoth 4483$_{1}$	122
Shebuoth 450$_{6}$	119, 120$_{36}$
Aboda Zara 460$_{27}$	9
Aboda Zara 464$_{12}$	34
Hullin 503$_{22}$	224$_{0}$
Kellim 585$_{15}$	135$_{151}$

MEKILTHA

7[5]	99
196	158
208	159
213	157
226	126
SIFRA 90b[6]	98

SIFRE I

115[7]	140
131	104$_{62}$
153	118, 193
153	137$_{164}$

SIFRE II

13	74
308	155
311	15$_{2}$
328	164
Sifre Zuta, Hukkath	182 ff.
Sifre Zuta, Phineas	74
Midrash Tannaim 139	41$_{60}$

PALESTINIAN TALMUD

Berakoth IV, 7d	73
Berakoth IX, 13a	64
Berakoth IX, 13b	100$_{31}$
Berakoth IX, 13c	53
Pe'a I, 15c	24
Shebiith IV, 35a	86
Shebiith IV, 35b	101
Terumoth I, 40c	25
Terumoth V, 43d	5$_{20}$
Terumoth VIII, 45c	72
Terumoth VIII, 45d	148
Terumoth VIII, 46a	126$_{91}$
Terumoth X, 47b	89$_{139}$
Maaser Sheni I, 52d	5
Bikkurim III, 65d	22
Shabbath VI, 8d	100$_{32}$, 151 ff.
Shabbath XX, 17d	111
Yoma III, 40d	147
Rosh Hashana I, 57a	37 ff., 144$_{2}$
Rosh Hashana III, 59a	173
Taanith I, 64a	31 ff.
Megilla I, 71c	17
Megilla I, 72b	78
Megilla III, 74a	176
Megilla III, 74a	78
Megilla III, 74a	22
Kethuboth I, 24d	110$_{105}$
Kethuboth II, 26d	163
Kethuboth VII, 31d	39 ff.
Nedarim I, 37a	138
Nedarim II, 37b	136
Nedarim III, 38a	44
Nedarim III, 38a	142
Nedarim IX, 41c	123$_{70}$
Nedarim XI, 42c	120$_{38,\,39}$
Gittin I, 43b	89$_{139}$
Gittin V, 47b	4
Nazir VIII, 57a	110
Kiddushin I, 59a	19–20
Baba Bathra II, 13c	85

---

[4] P. 61, line 30, ed. Zuckermandel.
[5] P. 7, ed. Horovitz.   [6] Fol. 90b, ed. Weiss.
[7] פיסקא קט"ו.

Baba Bathra VIII, 16c   26[76]
Baba Bathra X, 17c   26
Baba Bathra X, 17c   4[15]
Sanhedrin I, 19c   73
Sanhedrin II, 19d   12
Sanhedrin II, 20b   65
Sanhedrin II, 20b   33
Sanhedrin IV, 22b   146
Sanhedrin VI, 25d   112
Sanhedrin X, 28a   51
Sanhedrin X, 28b   167
Shebuoth III, 34d   33
Shebuoth VI, 37b   124[74]
Aboda Zara I, 39c   10
Aboda Zara III, 42d   171

BABYLONIAN TALMUD

Berakoth 33a   35
Berakoth 62b   144 ff.
Shabbath 32a   154
Shabbath 55a   186 ff., 190
Shabbath 67a   109[96]
Shabbath 67a   111[110]
Shabbath 67a   103
Shabbath 156a   99
Erubin 3a   153
Pesahim 87b   141[195]
Pesahim 110a   111
Pesahim 112a   158
Pesahim 113b   97
Yoma 84a   132[139], 142
Taanith 16a, 16b   73
Taanith 21b   157
Megilla 6a   66
Yebamoth 24b   80
Kethuboth 85a   37[47]
Nedarim 28a   142
Kiddushin 80b   153
Sota 49b   20
Baba Kamma 46b   156
Baba Kamma 92b   153
Baba Mezia 29b   112
Baba Bathra 60b   105–106

Sanhedrin 107a   163
Shebuoth 35a   119
Aboda Zara 8b   10
Aboda Zara 11b   145[7]
Menahoth 44a   140

MINOR TRACTS

Aboth deR. Nathan VII   165
Aboth deR. Nathan XXVIII   75[68]
Aboth deR. Nathan XXXVI   83
Semahoth I   76
Kalla II   142, 143
Kalla IV   74

MIDRASHIM

BR 127[8]   22
BR 198   19
BR 275   157
BR 385   41
BR 388   40[58]
BR 389   40
BR 440   61
BR 690   8[40]
BR 699   105[71]
BR 805   158
BR 818   103
BR 865   169
BR 1156   40[58]

Shemoth Rabba XII   11
Shemoth Rabba XV   50 ff.
Shemoth Rabba XXX   38[51], 144[2]
Shemoth Rabba XXXVIII   56 ff.
VayR III   82
VayR VI   124[14]
VayR VI   7
VayR XI   167
VayR XXV   8[39]
VayR XXX   55
VayR XXX   47 ff.
VayR XXXIV   175
VayR XXXIV   63[225]
VayR XXXV   37[49]

[8] P. 127, ed. Theodor and Albeck.

Debarim Rabba V — 63
Debarim Rabba VII — 8
Debarim Rabba (ed. Lieberman), p. 36 — 71[32]
Debarim Rabba (ed. Lieberman), p. 70 — 53[141]
Esther Rabba III — 49
Esther Rabba III — 55[163]
Esther Rabba IV — 17
Shir Rabba I — 79[97]
Shir Rabba II — 124[77]
Shir Rabba II — 6[30]
Shir Rabba II — 61
Shir Rabba III — 44 ff.
Shir Rabba VII — 106 ff.
Shir Rabba VII — 108[85]
Shir Rabba VIII — 53–54
Eka Rabba I — 154
Eka Rabba II — 185 ff., 189
Koheleth Rabba III — 147[14]
Koheleth Rabba VII — 159
Koheleth Rabba XI — 20[32]
Koheleth Rabba XII — 51[127]

Eka Zuta — 104 ff.
Shir Zuta — 179 ff.
Midrash Abkir — 112
Midrash Samuel IX — 166
Pesiktha deR. Kahana 79b — 126[91]
Pesiktha deR. Kahana 104b — 10
Pesiktha deR. Kahana 119b — 105[67]
Pesiktha deR. Kahana 131a — 59
Pesiktha Rabbathi XXI — 89[138]
Pesiktha Rabbathi XXII — 34[32]
Tanhuma Lek leka 5 — 43[76]
Tanhuma Pekudei 4 — 153
Tanhuma Tazria 9 — 190
Tanhuma Shoftim 10 — 149 ff.
Tanhuma Shoftim 10 — 99
Tanhuma Buber I, p. 126 — 105[71]
Tanhuma Buber II, p. 22 — 84[7]
Tanhuma Buber II, p. 27 — 102[51]
Yelamdenu — 51, 52, 60, 63[226], 176 ff.
Midrash Tehilim I — 106[75], 109[97]
Seder Eliyyahu Zuta (Geniza) — 113–114

INDEX IV

Ancient and Mediaeval non Rabbinic Sources

ACTS XXIII.12 — 119[27]
Aelianus — 126[91]
Aesopus — 126[91]
Ahikar — 174
Alcaeus — 23
Amphis Comicus — 45
Antoninus, M. Aurelius — 36
Apocalypse — 46, 56
Apostolius — 158[91], 160[112]
Appianus — 142
Aquila — 17, 18, 18[23], 19, 20, 43[75], 49, 50, 53, 54, 100[32]
Aristophanes — 29[3], 125[82], 125[83], 128, 152, 159
Aristoteles — 101[42]
Athenaeus — 45[88], 66

BARDESAN — 62, 99, 100[31]
Bar Hebraeus — 110[104]
Basilius — 83[115]
Ps. Ben Sira — 71[29]
Ben Sira, Hebrew "original" — 175
CASSIUS, DIO — 106[6], 98[19], 144[2]
Catalogus Codicum Astrologorum Graecorum — 74[63]
Celsus — 85 ff.
Charisius — 94
Cicero — 142, 143
Claudianus — 146[7]
Cleomedes — 29
Covenant of Damascus — 51[122], 134, 135[151]
Cyprian — 19[139]

DAMAGETUS 73

EPIPHANIUS 100$_{32}$, 171
Epistle to the Hebrews 64
Eugarius 120$_{38}$
Euripides 126$_{91}$, 143
Eusebius 2, 62, 99$_{30}$

GREEK ANTHOLOGY 23$_{50}$, 66$_{246}$, 73, 125$_{81}$

HEBRAEUS 53, 53$_{142}$, 55$_{161}$, 190
Herodian 117$_{3}$, 145$_{7}$
Hesychius 73$_{8}$, 32$_{21}$
Hieronymus see Jerome
Homer 55
Horace 38$_{51}$

INCANTATIONS:
Aramaic Incantation Texts
from Nippur 119$_{27}$
Archiv Orientální 111, 112
Ephemeris für semitische
Epigraphic 112$_{117}$
Inscriptions Mandaïtes 15$_{3}$

Inscriptions:
Beth She'arim Inscriptions 69, 72
CI (Klein) 127$_{5}$; 69, 70
CIJ (Frey) 25, 69, 72
CIL 95$_{7}$, 144$_{2}$, 148$_{22}$
Ephemeris Epigraphica 148$_{22}$
Epigraphische Miscellen 69$_{6}$
Inschriften der jüdischen
Katakombe etc. 69$_{8}$,
North-Semitic Inscriptions 71, 151, 168, 179

Irenaeus 234$_{9}$
Isidore of Seville 191

JEIUNATOR Joaness 12
Jerome 18, 19
Josephus 53, 56, 65, 98, 129, 130, 134, 142, 148, 180, 182 ff.
Justin Martyr 87 ff.
Justinian 42
Juvenal 79$_{94}$

LEGES saeculares 138$_{8}$
Leucon 151
Libanius 75
Lucianus 45, 93$_{7}$

MARQAH 160$_{113}$, 166$_{40}$, 170, 173, 177$_{144}$
Martialis 144$_{2}$, 186
Martini R. 84$_{120}$, 160$_{112}$
Matt. V. 33 117$_{17}$
Matt. V. 34, 36 137$_{163}$
Matt. XXIII.16 134
Matt. XXIII.20, 22 137$_{162}$
Matt. XXVII.6 129$_{107}$, 134$_{145}$
Menander 45, 46, 134$_{145}$

NILUS 159

ORIBASIUS 96, 96$_{9}$
Origen 85, 108$_{89}$, 187

PALESTINIAN Syriac Texts:
Christlich-palästinisch-aramäische
Texte und Fragmente 175$_{132}$
Christlich-Palästinische Frag-
mente aus der Omajjaden-
Moschee zu Damaskus 64$_{232}$
Horae Semiticae 86$_{130}$, 96$_{8}$, 178
Palestinian Syriac Lectionary 173

Papyri:
Aramaic Papyri 174$_{122}$
Catalogue du Musée du Caire 138$_{9}$
Fayûm Towns and their Papyri 106$_{3}$
Grenfell and Hunt, New Classical
Fragments 172$_{101}$
Griechische Urkunden der Pap.
zu Leipzig 139$_{1}$
Oxyrhynchi 41$_{6}$, 41$_{7}$, 100$_{31}$, 122$_{57}$, 140
Papyrus Onomasticon
Sacrum 169, 189$_{25}$
Tebtunis Papyri 122$_{57}$

Persius 191$_{38}$, 191$_{44}$
Petronius 152 ff.
Philo Judaeus 65$_{235}$, 116, 117$_{18}$, 124, 125, 138

Philostratus 93$_{7}$, 126	Suidas 128$_{99}$
Planudes Maximus 124$_{74}$, 156$_{81}$	Symmachus 55$_{161}$
158$_{94}$, 159	
Plato 166$_{44}$	TERTULLIAN 104$_{62}$, 118, 187
Plinius 101$_{42}$, 145$_{6}$	Theodoretus 35
Plutarch 58$_{196}$, 95, 102, 107, 126$_{91}$,	Theodotion 53
148$_{17}$	Theophrastus 101$_{42}$
Porphyrio 38$_{51}$	
Publilius Syrus 154$_{61}$, 159$_{106}$	VALERIUS Maximus 42, 437$_{6}$
SAMARITAN Liturgy 160$_{113}$	XENOPHON 40$_{57}$
Scriptores Historiae Augustae 11$_{13}$	
Seneca 96, 149	ZENOBIUS 150, 151
Suetonius 145$_{7}$	Zosimus 146$_{7}$

INDEX V

ABBAHU R. 21 ff.	Calf, golden see Golden Calf
ἀδελφή 165	caprification 101 ff.
adjurations 108	charms 100 ff.
ἄδολος 84$_{6}$	Christians, relations to 87 ff.
adulteration of wares 5, 8	
Akiba R. 18 ff.	DANCER, contempt for 33
alterations (fraudulent) in documents 27	divinatio naturalis 101$_{39}$
Amorites, practices of 101	δίψια ὕδατα 148$_{21}$
Ananias 182 ff.	Domna, Julia 11
animals, love for man 126$_{91}$	Dora 140
Antoninus 78 ff.	
astrology 79 ff.	ELEAZAR, son of Ananias 183 ff.
astrology has no power over Jews 99 ff.	Eleazar R., b. Pedath 37 ff.
athletes 96	Eleazar, son of Simeon 182
Augustus 10	Eliezer R., b. Hyrkanos 16 ff.
	ἐντολή 71$_{32}$
BARBARIAN, translation of the Bible by 17$_{15}$	εὐμοίρει 72
Ben ben Eden 160$_{113}$	εὔμοιρος 72, 74
Ben He-He 160$_{113}$	
Beth She'arim 72	FIGS, unripe 163
"binding" of brides 110	φιλέντολος 72
Bostra 149, 150	φιλόλαος 72
	five, a round number 31$_{18}$
CAESAREA VII, 21, 26, 30, 33$_{24}$, 140	footprints, in magic 114
Cain, the mark of 190$_{30}$	
	GAIUS 89
	Gamaliel R. 20, 126
	Gentiles, relations to 89
	Golden Calf, creation of 113 ff.

Greek, academy in Palestine   1, 20
Greek, Babylonian Rabbis did
   not know   26
Greek documents   26
Greek epigrammatic style   66
Greek, R. Hiyya and Simeon b.
   Abba did not know   24–25
Greek inscriptions in Jaffa   30 ff.
Greek Jargon   27
Greek, the language into which
   the Bible can be perfectly
   translated   17
Greek, law quoted in   42
Greek of the middle classes   27
Greek poetry   21
Greek play of words   22 ff.
Greek prayers for rain   35 ff.
Greek proverbs   see proverbs
Greek, quotations in   42 ff.
Greek, Rab did not know   26
Greek of the Rabbis   27 ff.
Greek, recommended by R.
   Juda the Patriarch   21
Greek sermons translated into
   Aramaic   2
Greek, Shema read in   30
Greek of the Synagogue   29 ff.
Greek, teaching to daughters   24
Greek, teaching to sons   16
Greek translations of the Bible 48 ff.
Greek translations of the Breast-
   plate-stones   56 ff.
Greek wisdom   1, 16[10]

HADRIAN   16
Hanin b. Matron (or Metron)   181
heathen   77 ff., 86
High Priest   65
Hiyya R., b. Abba   24 ff.

Ἱκανὴ μερίς   73
incantations   15[3], 109, 111 ff.
inflation   5
Isis   140, 141

JAFFA   30
Johanan R.   24, 89, 99

Jonathan R. (b. Eleazar)   85
Joshua R.   16 ff.

Κακὰ μερίς   73
Koiné, Jonic elements in   48[111]
Koiné, poetic elements in   63[226]
Koiné, spoken by the Rabbis   47

LAMPS, turned over   104 ff.
languages, number of   15[3]
law, quoted in Greek   42
law, on the fool and the king   38
law, operation of, in Egypt and
   and Palestine   4
legal terms   7 ff., 44
lentils, served at weddings   105[71]
lions and foxes   147[14]
love-charms   109, 110, 112
Lucius of Susitha   89
ludarii   148
ludi saeculares   145[7]

MAGIC   100 ff.
marriage between Romans and
   provincials   11, 192
Menahem   180, 182
mine, despised   33
mole, blood of   102

NAMES, interpretation of   169[70], 189[25]

OATHS and incantation terminology   120
oaths and vows   115 ff.
oaths by the almond   127
oaths by the cabbage   127
oaths by the caper-plant   127
oaths by the fig-picker, figs   127,
   128[99]
oaths by the fishing nets   128
oaths by the dog, goose   125
oaths by the King   118
oaths by the Korban   130, 134 ff.
oaths by the life of the King 118, 193
oaths by the ram   133
oaths by the sun   137

oaths, substitutes and
  handles of 116 ff.
ὅρκος, ξενικός 130
ὅρκος, Ῥαδαμάνθυος 125, 127, 128₉₉
ὅρκος, σοφιστικός 142
ὅσιος 71

Πάντα and πέντε 31₁₈
papyri and Talmud 3
Paschal lamb 79₉₇, 191
Pharaoh, the reason for his
  punishment 39 ff.
physical exercises 92 ff.
pillars, the world standing on 107 ff.
πιστός 75, 76
prayer of the Athenians 36
prayers for rain 31 ff.
πρεσβεία 22₄₀
Procopius 2
prophets, born after seven
  months of pregnancy 22
proselytes 68 ff.
προστάτης 64
proverbs, Arabic 160₁₁₂
proverbs, Aramaic see Index I
proverbs, Greek 34₁₂, 38, 38₅₁, 38₅₁ₐ,
  124₇₄, 143, 144₂, 145, 148, 148₁₇,
  151, 152, 154–160₁₁₂
proverbs, Hebrew see Index I
proverbs, Latin 145, 152, 153, 154,
  155₁₀₆
proverbs, Samaritan 160₁₁₃
πυρὸς καθαρός etc. 5

ROME, called Babylon 46₉₃
Rome, markets of 145₆
Rome, treaty with 180

SEMI-PROSELYTES 68 ff., 77 ff.
Semi-proselytes various
  groups of 81 ff.
sermons adapted to the
  public 161–162
Severus, Septimius 11
Shema, read in Greek 30
Simeon (b. Abba, R.) 22 ff.
Socrates 40₅₇, 125, 126
superstitions in Palestine 110 ff.
swearing in vain 115₂
Syria 10, 11, 192
Syriac language not recommended
  by R. Juda the Patriarch 21
Syriac original of Bardesan's
  book 63₂₂₅, 99₃₀

TANTURA 140₁₈₆
Ten Tribes 83₁₁₄
theatre 32 ff.
θεοσεβεῖς 77, 79
Tiberias 36, 171
traditions, various in different
  texts 43₇₆, 95₆
translations, Greek 47 ff.
translations, homophones
  preferred 48
Trap 45
Trypho 87 ff.

VAIN mention of His name 35 ff.
Vetus Latina 17₁₅, 56
virtues 71 ff.

WEASEL, bad omen 98₁₉
women's rags 102

YEMENITE Rabbinica, preserved
  uncensored traditions 189₃₀

Date Due

OCT 23 '46			
Dec 17 '46			
May 5 '5~~2~~			
Jan 20 '53			
~~4 APR 1970~~			